ALSO BY JASPER WHITE

Jasper White's Cooking from New England

LOBSTER AT HOME

JASPER WHITE

Photographs by Thibault Jeanson
Illustrations by Glenn Wolff

SCRIBNER

SCRIBNER
1230 Avenue of the Americas
New York, NY 10020

Text copyright © 1998 by Jasper White

Photographs copyright © 1998 by Thibault Jeanson

Illustrations copyright © 1998 by Glenn Wolff

Designed by Margery Cantor
Set in Myriad Multiple Master

Manufactured in the United States of America

3   5   7   9   10   8   6   4

Library of Congress Cataloging-in-Publication Data
White, Jasper.
Lobster at home / Jasper White ; photographs by Thibault Jeanson ;
illustrations by Glenn Wolff.
p.   cm.
Includes index.
1. Cookery (Lobsters)   I. Title.
TX754.L63W48   1998
641.6'95—dc21   98-10238
CIP

ISBN 0-684-80077-2

For my daughters,
Mariel and Hayley

Acknowledgments

I WOULD LIKE to express my deepest gratitude and love to all my family, friends and associates, especially:

- Nancy White, my wife, business partner and true love for more than twenty years.
- Jasper Paul (J.P.), Mariel and Hayley White, my kids, who have eaten almost every dish in this book and who always bring out the best in me.
- Michael, Matt, Julie and Jamie White, my siblings.
- Mary Morgan, my mother, who cooked my first lobster (first everything).
- Jasper White, my father, who taught me where food comes from, and his wife, Natalie.
- Trevor and Muriel Thom, my in-laws, who have the greatest spot in New England for a lobster bake.
- Ida White and Josephine Donoghue, my grandmothers, with special remembrance.
- Maria Guarnaschelli, my editor, who put her magic touch on every line. Her wisdom, creativity and immense talent made writing this book an enriching and exhilarating experience.
- Doe Coover, my agent, my advisor and my partner in many great Chinatown lunches.
- Glenn Wolff, illustrator and calligrapher, who draws with precision, beauty and humor.
- Thibault Jeanson, for his sumptuous photography.
- Roscoe Betsil for his meticulous food styling.
- Kate Niedzwiecki, Beth Wareham, Roz Lippel, Erich Hobbing, M. C. Hald and all the talented people at Scribner.
- Julia Child, who has been a mentor and a treasured friend over the last two decades and who loves Pan-Roasted Lobster.
- Lydia Shire, my best friend and favorite cook, and her husband, Uriel Pineda.
- Roger and George Berkowitz, who have sold more cooked lobsters than anyone I know, for their friendship and support in recent years.
- Jeff Dugan, Melanie Coiro, Nam Van Tran, Debbie Riley, Vincent Maxson, Stan Frankenthaler, Paul O'Connell, Mark Cupolo, Jay Weinstein, Guy Koppe, Patty Queen, Rick Robin-

son, Bob Del Bove, Dean Paris, Jose Faria, Juan Paiz, Juan Henríquez, Carlos Alfaro and all the crew at Jasper's, who, over the years, cooked and served many of the dishes in this book.

- John Stevens, Rusty Court and Phil Willey, Maine lobstermen who have given me a glimpse into their special world. And to all the lobstermen and -women of New England, New Brunswick and the Canadian Maritimes, who provide pleasure to so many.
- Kim Marden, Steve Connolly, Billy Conti, Arthur Kloack and Rod Mitchell, seafood wholesalers, who have kindly shared their knowledge of this tricky business.
- Jim Peterson, Alan Davidson, A. J. McClane, Arie de Zanger, Mike Brown, Mark Bittman, Bruce Ballenger and John Thorne, whose books provided excellent reference.
- Rene Pasnon, Luigi Marenzi, Yves Lansac, Alphonse Thomas, Bob Redmond and Joe Ribas, my mentors, my chefs. Their passion and knowledge have been the foundation of my own.
- Joël Robuchon, Wolfgang Puck, Larry Forgione, Nina Simonds, Douglas Rodriguez, Daniel Boulud, Stephan Pyles, Gerald Clare, Bob Kinkead, Emeril Lagasse, Johanne Killeen, George Germon, Mark Miller, Alain Senderens, C. K. Sau, Anne Rosenzweig, Rick Bayless and Ed Brown, who have contributed or inspired special recipes in this text.
- Todd English, Jimmy Burke, Chris Schlesinger, Moncef Meddeb, Gordon Hamersley, Bob Levey, Rick Katz, Jacques Pepin, Susan Regis, Jody Adams, Michael Schlow, Chris Douglas, Steve Johnson, Tony Ambrose, Michela Larson, Natalie Jacobson, Doc Willoughby, Sally Sampson, Sheryl Julien, Christopher Kimball, Corby Kummer, Allison Arnett, Rebecca Alsid and all my friends in the culinary community of New England who have contributed to the great tastes of this region, not the least of which is lobster.

This book was conceived with the help of Rene Becker. I extend my thanks to him for his ideas and his inspiration.

Contents

Introduction

I HAVE ALWAYS loved lobster. The memory of my first experience of biting into the lush white meat has been lost amid other memories of growing up in the sun and salty air of the Jersey Shore, but the taste of lobster is intricately bound to my childhood. Every summer we ate freshly caught lobsters, steamed in my mother's big black kettle, then dipped in bowls of melted butter and popped, dripping, into our mouths. My brothers, sister and I learned to rip open the body and pick out every shred of meat. My mother sighed at the mess, but to us it was delicious summer fun.

Food was always an important ritual in my family. Within the context of suburban American cooking in the 1950s, you could say we were somewhat eccentric. I remember so vividly eating woodcock for my father's birthday; blowfish tails for Mother's Day; shad roe to celebrate the beginning of spring; mussels, blue crabs, Jersey corn and Jersey tomatoes on the Fourth of July. There were so many feasts in our family that we had to be creative to find a special occasion to merit one.

After high school I found myself so intrigued by the complex nature of flavors I decided to become a chef. I enrolled in the Culinary Institute of America in Hyde Park, New York. There I was introduced to the great French classics: Lobster Américaine and Lobster Thermidor. Suddenly, the food I had eaten growing up became part of a larger world of possibilities. After graduation, I spent a few years "cooking around" in restaurants in New York, Florida, California, Washington and Montana. Wherever I went, my knowledge increased, but I yearned for the tastes I grew up with. While cooking in San Francisco, I met my life's companion, Nancy. In 1978 we moved back east to Rhode Island to be close to her family. Shortly after starting a job at the Biltmore Hotel in Providence, Rhode Island, I was offered a better position with the same company at the Copley Plaza Hotel in Boston. As chef of the Café Plaza, the hotel's formal dining room, I soon learned what it meant to cook in Boston: It meant cooking lobsters, and lots of them! At last I had returned to the food of my childhood.

Five years later, in 1983, I opened my own restaurant, Jasper's. It served local fish and shellfish. Lobster was the most popular item on the menu. I cooked it in every way imaginable; many of the recipes in this book were created there. During the twelve years that Jasper's was in business, I learned how the seasons affect lobsters. I learned about methods of lobster fishing and what factors go into the changing market prices. I learned that good cooking means understanding the food you prepare; no fact or idea about lobster is unrelated to its cooking. And I learned that knowledge makes your food taste better.

This book is the result of what I've learned so far about lobster. Too often we reserve it for eating in a restaurant or pass over it in the market in favor of what we think of as more easily prepared food. In this book I hope to show you how easy and rewarding it can be to cook lobster at home.

LOBSTER AT HOME

CHAPTER 1

The Lobster Primer

WITH ITS BRILLIANT contrasts in color, amazing versatility and excellent nutritional value, it is little wonder that lobster is one of the most glamorous ingredients in gastronomy. Unlike other great delicacies, such as truffles, caviar or foie gras, however, lobster is both affordable and approachable. It is not an everyday food, but most working people can afford to buy it every now and then, especially if they prepare it themselves at home.

The creatures we Americans call lobsters, those that we boil or steam and dip in butter, are *Homarus americanus,* better known as American lobsters or Maine lobsters. Distinguished by their large, powerful claws, they are but one of many varieties of lobster. A similar lobster known as the European lobster (*Homarus vulgaris* or *Homarus gamarus,* depending on the classification) is found in the cold waters off Ireland, England, Scotland, Brittany, Germany and Norway. Although it tastes just as good and has a similar anatomy, it is caught in relatively small quantities and is rarely exported. American lobster is what is sold in most fish markets across the United States. Even in Europe the majority of lobsters in fish markets are American lobsters that have been imported from Canada and the United States. There are simply not enough European lobsters to satisfy the demand in Europe.

Several species of crustaceans are mistakenly called lobster. These clawless creatures, found in the waters of the Caribbean, Mediterranean, Africa, Australia and even Scandinavia, do not belong to the genus *Homarus.* Rock lobsters, also called spiny lobsters *(Palinurus vulgaris),* are probably the most famous of these impostors. In Europe they are called *langouste.* As far as I am concerned, because of the superior taste and availability of American lobster, there is no competition between the different species—American and European lobsters are in a class by themselves. The recipes in this book are tailored to American and European lobsters because the unique structure of their bodies—their large claws—does not allow them to be used interchangeably with rock lobster. However, in recipes where cooked lobster meat is given by weight, you may substitute cooked rock lobster meat.

The Maine Lobster Promotional Council has trademarked the slogan "Maine lobster, the ultimate white meat," an observation that is both brilliant and true. Along with its fragrance, flavor and texture, which in themselves would be enough to earn lobster this title, lobster meat is also extremely healthful. A 3.5-ounce portion, about the amount of meat in a 1-pound lobster, has only 98 calories and only 72 milligrams of cholesterol, less than is found in the same amount of skinless chicken. Lobster is also high in Omega-3 acids, which are known to help reduce cholesterol levels.

In 1995 the total catch of *Homarus americanus* in New England and Canada exceeded 65 thousand tons. In Maine alone the catch was about 38 million pounds; the lobster is hardly a rarity, certainly not an endangered species. In colonial times it was so abundant it was considered a poor man's dinner. Jumbo lobsters, considered unfit to eat, were most often used as fertilizer. It was not until 1896, when Fannie Merritt Farmer published *The Boston Cooking School Cookbook,* introducing such great dishes as bisque, Newburg and à la Américaine, that lobster began to be thought of as a delicacy. Her cookbook, which became the bible for homemakers across America, offered many innovative recipes for lobster. The popularity of lobster increased steadily during the early part of this century. It became the preferred dish of sophisticated New Yorkers seeking to emulate the Europeans, who had long known the elegance of lobster. In the 1950s, the efficiency of over-the-road and air shipping made live lobster a national and international commodity. Its price, now reflective of the world market, rose drastically, even in New England, elevating its status as a local food. The cost advantage of living there is now minimal, and many older Yankees still prefer Maine shrimp, haddock or halibut over lobster.

LOBSTER FISHING

Along the coast of Maine and farther up in Canada, lobstering is a common denominator that binds the community together. Almost everyone is either in the lobster business or related to someone who is. While popular lore depicting lobstermen and their families as proudly independent people living near the water's edge and abiding by their own laws might be somewhat of an exaggeration, lobstermen do guard their culture passionately. At sea they live by their ingenuity and instinct, not only to earn a living but to survive on the often fierce Atlantic Ocean. On shore, they look out for one another and view strangers with suspicion.

The actual process of trapping lobsters is simple. The lobster pot, or trap, consists of an entrance and two "rooms," separated by hand netting. The lobster enters the first room, the "parlor," and passes into the next room, the "kitchen," where the bait sits. Once there, it is unable to turn around to leave. Lobstermen have been using this same design for more than a hundred years. Today, steel and wire traps are replacing the traditional wooden traps. Pots are either rectangular or semicircular. Rectangular ones are used in Massachusetts and farther south where lobsters are fished in sandy areas. The flat sides keep the traps from rolling around. Semicircular traps are most common along the rocky coast of Maine and Canada, where rolling rarely occurs. The bait varies; herring, sardines, menhaden (pogies), mackerel, alewife and fish heads and frames (backbones) from redfish, flounder and other species are all used. Even crabs are set out in areas where they are plentiful. Lobsters love to eat crabs. The lobster pots are lowered to a depth of 10 to 250 feet along inshore areas, up to ten miles off the coast. Far offshore, lobster pots may be dropped as deep as 1,500 feet. They are strung on lines—pot-warp—with one or more pots on each line, sometimes as many as fifty pots to a line. The line attaches to a buoy, which clearly denotes the rightful owner. Buoy colors are registered and are not allowed to be duplicated within a designated region. Lobstermen have a way of dealing with their buoys and territories; messing with buoys or traps is worse than stealing a horse from a cowboy!

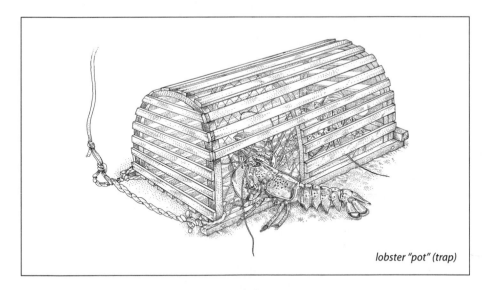

lobster "pot" (trap)

If you have ever been fishing, you know the basic setup: hook, line, rod and reel. You probably also know that this is only the starting point, that the variations are endless. The same is true of lobstering: pot, bait, line and buoy; after that, lobstering is determined by the lobsterman. Some traps have the entrance on the right side, some on the left. Some have two entrances and two parlors. Bait varies. Depths and locations vary. Some lobstermen move their pots frequently, others never change location. Each lobsterman has his own style, and his income is a direct reflection of that style.

Lobster boats tend to be as similar as their gear. Most are a variation of the Jonesport lobster boat, a sturdy, deep-hulled fishing vessel with an open deck. The boat is equipped with a hydraulic winch used to haul the heavy pots. Though they may not appear so because of their weather-beaten exteriors, lobster boats are almost always very well maintained.

Jonesport lobster boat

BUYING LOBSTERS

Selecting the Place

There is no surer way to make an enemy in a New England coastal town than to set your own lobster pot. Lobstering is a trade that is proudly passed from parent to child. Waters that have been harvested by the same family for generations are considered personal property, and while it is fine to boat in these waters, the moment you drop a lobster pot into them, you have broken an unwritten law. The safest and most honorable way to get hold of lobsters if you are not from a lobstering family is to purchase them.

The best place to buy lobsters is straight from the boat. They are always freshly caught, and since they have never really been taken out of their natural habitat, they carry the taste of the sea with them. If you cannot find a boat, seek out a lobster co-op or company. They deal primarily in lobsters and are always located near a harbor, river or bay where they pump natural salt water into their storage tanks. Many companies even use biological filters to improve the purity of the water, thereby improving the quality of the lobsters kept alive in their tanks.

WHY BUY CRABS FROM A LOBSTER COMPANY?

Rock crab, better known as Maine crab, is a species native to the cold waters of Canada and New England, north of Cape Cod. A close relative of the Northwest Dungeness crab, it has a similar sweetness and lots of red coloration in the meat. Because they inhabit the same waters as lobsters and have similar feeding habits, they are caught on a regular basis in lobster pots. Traditionally, rock crabs are steamed and their meat is picked out mostly by women who are usually related to lobstermen and whose fee is half the meat that the crab yields. They then sell the meat privately, often putting up a small sign near their home. Because the catch is small, rock crabs are rarely sold outside of New England. Lobster companies usually offer whole live crabs or cooked meat. Both are wonderful tasting.

WHY BUY STEAMERS FROM A LOBSTER COMPANY?

Steamers, also known as soft-shell clams or "pisser" clams (because they spray out of their long siphons), are one of New England's greatest treats. Steamers are raked at low tide from sand or mud flats along tidal rivers and bays. In Maine, clamming is a small business that depends on the lobster industry as its main channel of distribution. Tanks that store lobsters are perfect for storing clams. Not only do they keep steamers alive and fresh, but they enable the clams to maintain their salinity while at the same time purging them of mud and sand. Maine steamers are justly famous for their small to medium size, their salty-sweet flavor and their pristine quality. Although more expensive than their Chesapeake counterparts, they are well worth the extra price.

Lobster Cooperatives

A lobster co-op is a business owned by a group of lobster fishermen working together to purchase bait, fuel and other supplies in quantities large enough to ensure a savings. More important, the co-ops serve as a place to store and market their catch directly to consumers at the highest price. A few co-ops even run clam shacks (restaurants) that greatly add to their profitability. A co-op can also function as a bank, advancing fuel or bait in lieu of future lobsters to a member who is behind on his profits.

Lobster Companies

There are literally hundreds of lobster companies up and down the North Atlantic coast that buy, store and sell lobsters. Some keep inventories as high as 100,000 pounds. They all buy directly from boats, and most focus primarily on selling live lobsters to seafood markets, restaurants and dealers located inland or out of state. Almost all operate their own retail market. Lobster companies play an important role in the lobstering community, often providing services to lobstermen similar to those provided by cooperatives. The largest enterprises, which are mostly Canadian, concentrate their efforts on supplying Europe and Asia with both live and processed (frozen and canned) lobsters. They also supply live lobsters to the American market, especially in late winter and early spring, when prices are at their highest. Buying lobsters from the retail markets of small to medium-size lobster companies is often the best way to avoid the price increases of a food chain and to ensure lobster of excellent quality. In addition to lobster, most companies sell rock crabs and steamer clams. Many companies also offer mail order.

Mail Order

The craving for fresh, succulent lobster can strike at any time, anywhere—even far from the New England coast. Luckily, ordering by mail, if done correctly, is a surprisingly reliable way to buy fresh lobster. If the idea of ordering your own lobster by mail seems risky, remember that the lobsters in your local markets were shipped from New England anyway, so why not purchase lobsters that are shipped especially to you?

As a general rule, lobsters do not like to travel. They can survive only in salt water, and once taken from their tanks, their days are numbered. Kept under optimum conditions—moist and cold—strong lobsters will live three to five days out of water; weak lobsters sometimes die within twenty-four hours. The pressurized atmosphere of a jet flying at high altitudes increases their mortality rate greatly. Weak lobsters, especially soft-shell lobsters, have less than a 50 percent chance of surviving the airfreight ordeal. However, while shipping lobsters is risky, it is also the main business of many lobster companies, and they have come up with some techniques that increase the likelihood of the healthy arrival of fresh lobsters. Most select the highest-quality hard-shell lobsters for shipping so that the buyer ends up with lobsters that are equal to the best found in New England.

When ordering lobsters, remember the following rules:

1. ORDER FROM COMPANIES THAT SELL PRIMARILY LOBSTER. Companies that purchase directly from lobster boats will have the best lobsters at the best prices.

2. ASK FOR LARGER, HARD-SHELL LOBSTERS. Smaller lobsters, such as chickens, and soft lobsters have a higher mortality rate than larger lobsters. Selects (1½- to 2½-pound lobsters) are a good bet. Be specific about the size of the lobster you want when ordering.

3. ORDER THE LOBSTERS TO ARRIVE ON THE DAY YOU WANT TO COOK THEM. If you are nervous, the day before will probably be okay, but be sure to check the lobsters for liveliness and follow the guidelines on page 14 for storing them.

There are many reliable operations that routinely ship lobsters by airfreight. A list of mail-order sources that I have used with great satisfaction begins on page 229. For a complete listing of companies, write to Maine Lobster Promotional Council, 382 Harlow Street, Bangor, Maine 04401, or call (207) 947-2966.

Fish and Seafood Markets

Good seafood markets are few and far between. Even in the Boston area, a veritable seafood mecca, I have often been disappointed with the lobsters I have found. The seafood business is one of the most challenging food businesses, selling the most highly perishable of products. Because freshness is the single most important factor in determining the quality of seafood, a good store must find creative ways to sell its seafood while still fresh and must at all times maintain strict temperature control. The busier a market is, the more easily it is able to adhere to high standards. Often the liveliness of the market itself will be the best clue to the quality of the lobsters it sells.

The difference between lobsters sold at seafood markets and those sold by lobster companies has less to do with price than with the way lobsters are stored. Lobster companies, always located on the water, pump fresh saline bay or river water into and through large holding tanks, storing the lobsters in water similar or identical to the water they matured in. Seafood markets store lobsters in tanks filled with artificially salinated and oxidized water. In this environment lobsters weaken and become dormant, losing the integrity of their natural flavor. When buying from a seafood market, make sure it is a busy one that turns its inventory of lobsters frequently.

Airports

If you have ever flown through the Northeast, you have probably seen small vendors with lobsters for sale in the airport terminals. In general, they tend to sell lobsters of good over-all quality but at higher prices than those of markets or companies. Before you purchase lobsters from these vendors, take a good look at the tank to check for overcrowding and liveliness, and be very specific in your ordering—hard-shell selects transport most successfully.

Supermarkets

It is no accident that I have saved supermarkets for last, because, with very few exceptions, they should be your last choice for buying lobster. The markets are often so large that they are unable to focus on the details of maintaining a fresh and fast-moving seafood program. When purchasing a lobster from a supermarket, pay special attention to the condition of the tank in which the lobsters are stored. Is it overcrowded? Is the water murky? Is there an obvious presence of algae in the water? Are there any dead lobsters in the tank? Do the lobsters flap their tails or swing their claws when taken out of the water? If your answer is yes to any but the last question, I recommend taking a stroll over to the meat counter and saving lobster for another day.

SELECTING LOBSTERS

All lobsters are not identical. Their sex, the time of year in which they are caught and the way in which they are stored influence their quality. When choosing a lobster, it is impor-tant to keep these factors in mind. Lobsters are available year-round, even in winter when commercial lobster fishing is almost at a standstill. In the United States there is no com-mercial lobstering season. Lobstermen can set their traps anytime they wish. The lobster supply is managed by limiting the size of the lobster, with severe penalties for those who do not abide by the regulations. In Canada, although no size-limit regulations are in effect, each lobster region is closely monitored, with specific legal seasons for lobstering. Ameri-can lobstermen provide a live food resource that changes throughout the year. Canadian lobstermen, working in an industry that, more than the American industry, tends to be commercially owned, provide live hard-shell lobsters that are more consistent. The Cana-dian lobstering season is limited to a six-month maximum, staggered and broken up to avoid the molting and mating season. Canada focuses its efforts on supplying hard-shell lobsters for markets where lobsters are sold live and reserves the remaining catch for pro-cessing (canning and freezing).

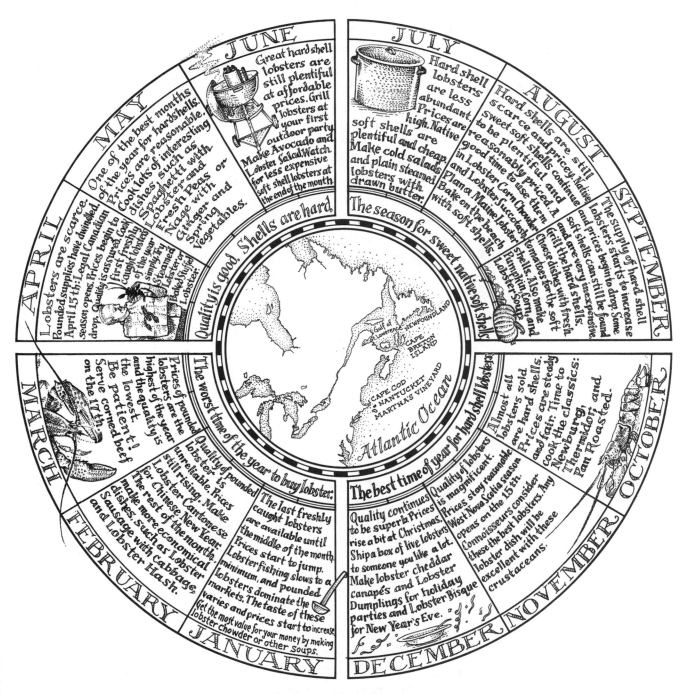

JUNE Great hard shell lobsters are still plentiful at affordable prices. Grill lobsters at your first outdoor party. Make Avocado and Lobster Salad. Watch for less expensive soft shell lobsters at the end of the month.

JULY Hard shell lobsters are less abundant. Prices are high. Native soft shells are plentiful and cheap. Make cold salads and plain steamed lobsters with drawn butter.

AUGUST Hard shells are still scarce and pricey. Native sweet soft shells continue to be plentiful and reasonably priced. A good time to use them in Lobster Corn Chowder, and Lobster Succotash. Plan a Maine Lobster Bake on the beach with soft shells.

SEPTEMBER The supply of hard shell lobsters starts to increase and prices begin to drop. Some soft shells can still be found and are very inexpensive. Choose dishes with fresh, grill the hard shells. Also make tomatoes for the soft Pumpkin Corn, and Lobster Soup.

MAY One of the best months of the year for hardshells. Prices are reasonable. Cook lots of interesting dishes such as Spaghetti with Lobster and Fresh Peas or Nage with Ginger and Spring Vegetables.

APRIL Lobsters are scarce. Pounded supplies have dwindled. Legal Canadian season opens. Prices begin to drop. Quality is assured. Cook first freshly caught lobster of the year. Fry Steamed Lobster or Baked Stuffed Lobster.

OCTOBER Almost all lobsters sold are hard shells. Prices are steady and fair. Time to cook the classics: Newburg, Thermidor, and Pan Roasted.

MARCH Prices of pounded lobsters are the highest of the year and the quality is the lowest. Be patient! Serve corned beef on the 17th.

FEBRUARY Quality of pounded lobster is unreliable. Prices still rising. Make Lobster Cantonese for Chinese New Year. The rest of the month, make more economical dishes such as Lobster Sausage with Cabbage, and Lobster Hash.

JANUARY The last freshly caught lobsters are available until the middle of the month. Prices start to jump. Lobster fishing slows to a minimum, and pounded lobsters dominate the markets. The taste of these varies and prices start to increase. Get the most value for your money by making Lobster chowder or other soups.

DECEMBER Quality continues to be superb. Prices rise a bit at Christmas. Ship a box of live lobsters to someone you like a lot. Make lobster cheddar canapés and Lobster Dumplings for holiday parties and Lobster Bisque for New Year's Eve.

NOVEMBER Quality of lobsters is magnificent. Prices stay reasonable. West Nova Scotia season opens on the 15th. Connoisseurs consider these the best lobsters. Any lobster dish will be excellent with these crustaceans.

Quality is good. Shells are hard.

The season for sweet native soft shells.

The worst time of the year to buy lobster.

The best time of year for hard shell lobsters.

Gulf of St. Lawrence NEWFOUNDLAND
CAPE BRETON ISLAND
CAPE COD
NANTUCKET
MARTHA'S VINEYARD
Atlantic Ocean

THE LOBSTER YEAR

When one talks about seasons for a lobster, one is referring to the lobster's reaction to different water temperatures. Lobsters thrive only in cold waters that range in temperature from above freezing to 70 degrees Fahrenheit. The waters of northeastern Canada and New England reach the low 30s in late January and the high 60s in August. Although lobsters live as far south as North Carolina, they are found only in the cold waters of the deep offshore canyons. The quality of the lobster meat changes significantly through their seasons.

Mid- to Late Spring (Late April, May and June)

In the cold winter months, lobsters are fairly dormant, moving and feeding very little. When the waters start to warm up in mid-April, lobsters begin to feed more actively and the local lobstering season in New England begins. As the waters become warmer and the lobsters feed more and more aggressively, the lobster catch increases substantially. Lobster prices, at their highest in winter, fall slightly but remain quite high until mid-May. On May 15, Canada opens the first of its fisheries and the lobstering season goes into full swing. The supply increases, and prices throughout Canada and the States drop quickly. Spring lobsters are hard-shelled and fairly meaty at reasonable prices. They are extremely versatile, suitable to any cooking technique. Late spring is an excellent time for buying and cooking lobsters.

Summer (July, August and September)

The supply of lobsters continues to increase as the waters warm. July is the beginning of the molting season, when lobsters shed their shell to grow a new one. Although there is no scientific explanation for what triggers the molting process, there is some speculation about a "molting gland" that responds to water temperatures. Lobsters of legal size (over 1 pound) molt approximately once a year, gaining about 14 percent in length with each molt. The newly molted, newly legal lobsters account for most of the summer's inshore catch. This explains the abundance of soft- and new-shell chicken (1-pound) lobsters in the summer. These lobsters are very sweet and tasty but often do not survive when shipped or stored. They are wonderful when steamed or boiled, and their meat is perfect for lobster salad, but because of their high water content they are unsuitable for grilling, pan-roasting or baking. During the summer months it is important to be very choosy when buying lobsters.

Autumn (October, November and December)

In early autumn, when the water is still warm, soft-shell lobsters remain a common item on the market. As the season progresses, hard-shell lobsters become easier to find. The molting seasons ends when the waters begin to drop in temperature. By late October the quality and supply of lobsters—as well as oysters, scallops, crabs and other shellfish—is first-rate. The finest lobsters of the year emerge from the sea from November to mid-January. On November 15 the season for "West Novies" (lobsters from Digby Bay, Nova Scotia) opens. These beauties are considered by many, including myself, to be the finest of *Homarus americanus.* What timing: The most splendid lobsters of the year, perfect for any recipe, coincide with Thanksgiving, Hanukkah, Christmas and New Year's!

Winter (January, February and March)

In normal years, when the winter weather is no harsher than usual, New England and Canadian lobstermen work well into the month of January. But by the end of January, Canada's legal season ends and most New England lobstermen turn to less severe ways of making a living. During the winter months they mend traps, repair and service boats and prepare for the next season. At this time of year only the poorest and most desperate fishermen attempt to catch lobster. Their catch is always small. Most of the lobsters sold in fish markets from February to mid-April come from Canadian lobster pounds, holding tanks where lobsters are stored. These lobsters are hard-shelled but past their peak, often bland and almost always expensive. Soups are a good choice for late winter because they can make lobster affordable as well as satisfying.

Lobster Sizes

People often debate the quality of the meat from different-size lobsters, often claiming the smaller the lobster, the sweeter its meat. As long as I have cooked them, I have found no difference in the taste up to 5 pounds—they are all delicious! The largest lobster I have ever seen on the market was 22 pounds. That was eighteen years ago. I recently saw a 24-pound lobster at the New England Aquarium, but these giants are becoming scarce. The largest lobster I ever cooked was a 9-pounder. I bought it when I was chef at the Bostonian Hotel, and I can still remember the expression on the faces of my staff as they gaped at its claws. The walking legs resembled Alaskan king crab legs, flaky and tender to the bite. The rest of the lobster was good but not great tasting, much tougher and less fragrant than the more common smaller lobsters. In the past ten years I have avoided lobsters over 5 pounds. I find it unsavory to cook the giants and feel that extremely large lobsters should be protected in the same manner that small ones are.

   Chicken lobsters, the smallest and most abundant allowable lobsters in the United States, must be at least 3¼ inches, measured from behind the eye socket to the end of the carapace (body). In order to be legal for sale, it must weigh in at a little over 1 pound. It is probably seven or eight years old, and in the process of reaching this age it will have molted about twenty-five times, beating odds of a thousand to one for survival. It will probably be caught before summer ends. Chicken lobsters are usually simply called *chickens,* or, in an odd but common abbreviation, *chix.*

Select lobsters weigh between 1½ and 2½ pounds. They are always the most expensive lobsters and are in great demand by restaurants. Because of their large size range, selects are most often ordered by weight. When ordering selects it is best to be as specific as possible, while still leaving a ¼-pound range to ensure that you get the best lobsters; for example, specify six each, 1¾- to 2-pound select hard-shell lobsters.

Jumbo lobsters weigh 2½ pounds and up. They are no longer common and are often expensive. The amount of meat found in a jumbo lobster is more than I like to eat at one meal, and I prefer to cook selects or chickens. When ordering jumbos, order in ½-pound increments.

Lobster culls are lobsters with only one mature claw. Sometimes they have lost a claw in a fight, sometimes it has been broken off because of improper handling and sometimes one of the claws is still in the process of regenerating. Culls are usually available in all sizes and are often priced well. They are excellent for cooking off and using in dishes that call for the meat out of the shell.

LOBSTER SIZES

Shorts	under legal size (never purchase this size)
Chickens	about 1 pound
Quarters	about 1¼ pounds
Halves	about 1½ pounds
Selects	1½ to 2½ pounds (order in ¼-pound increments)
Jumbos	2½ pounds and up (order in ½-pound increments)
Culls	various sizes

Male and Female Lobsters

Although there is no noticeable difference in the meat of male and female lobsters, occasionally a recipe calls for roe, the eggs found in the carcass of the female lobster. Because of this, it is important to be able to distinguish between male and female lobsters. Lobster roe, also called coral, is green-black when raw and orange-red when cooked. It has a mild, pleasing flavor and a dry, crumbly texture, and it is best when broken up into small pieces. To determine the sex of a lobster, turn it on its back and look at the abdomen. You will see five pairs of small fins called swimmerets. On the female the top pair, closest to the carcass, are soft and feathery. On the male they are hard and thin.

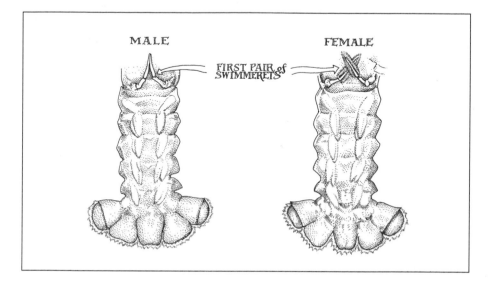

Choose a Lively Lobster

In addition to checking the lobster for general appearance, hardness of shell, length of an-tennae and weight (in relation to size), I also look for a lively disposition. A freshly caught, healthy lobster should swing its claws at you like a prizefighter. When you pick it up, its claws should extend straight out and its tail should flap vigorously. Watch out for drooping claws—they mean the lobster is weak and will probably die soon.

Once you have gotten what appears to be a healthy lobster home, there is still a chance that it might die. If you are planning to store it overnight, check it every six to eight hours. If it appears dead or is weak and not responding to your touch, cook it immediately. While not great for eating alone, it can still be used in soups and salads. But be careful: If the meat is not firm when you remove it from the shell, do not eat it, because the lobster was proba-bly dead too long for it to be safely eaten.

Handling a Lobster

Lobsters are almost always placed in a bag when you buy them. Never stick your hand in without looking first. I learned this lesson the hard way and have a scar to show for it. Tear the bag open before handling a lobster. Let the lobster fall gently onto the counter, then pick it up by placing your thumb and forefinger over the carapace, behind the large claws. In this position the lobster's crusher, or pincer, claw cannot reach you.

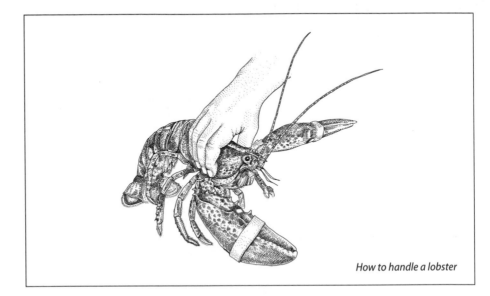

How to handle a lobster

Purchasing Cooked Lobster Meat

Occasionally a recipe calls for lobster meat by weight. In this case you have two options: Buy enough live lobsters to supply the desired amount of meat or buy cooked meat from a vendor. Vendors often offer good prices on cooked meat because it is a way for them to utilize sleepers (dormant and weak lobsters), culls or any other lobster they want to move out. If the price is right, this option can be an excellent way to save time. A quick way to tell whether lobster meat is being sold at a fair price is to multiply the price of chickens or culls by five. If a live chicken lobster costs $4.00 per pound and the price for a pound of cooked meat is under $20.00, you have found a good deal. If you are preparing a recipe that calls for lobster meat and cannot find lobster meat at a fair price, remember to buy live lobsters for price, not size. Stay away from the selects; it would be foolish to spend the extra money when you will just be picking the meat out anyway.

TRANSPORTING AND STORING LOBSTERS

It is always best to buy lobsters the day you plan to cook them. Once they are removed from the tank, whether naturally or artificially salinated, their days are numbered. Most will die within two to three days. A lobster, once dead for an extended period, will cook into an inedible mush. When lobsters are stored together, they tend to nibble on one another, and if a rubber band holding a claw shut comes loose, will hurt each other. Any puncture to the lobster's shell causes loss of a clear, gelatinous liquid, the lobster's blood, which is not only vital to the life of the lobster but necessary for full-flavored meat.

The two most essential conditions for successfully storing lobster are moisture and temperature. Lobsters should be kept moist but never wet. Tap water or any non-salt water will kill a lobster quickly, which is why it should never be stored on ice. The ideal way to store a lobster out of the tank is to wrap it gently in a damp sheet of newspaper, keeping it both moist and separated from the other lobsters. Lobsters should be stored at the coldest possible temperature above freezing available in the refrigerator. Cold temperatures slow their metabolism and increase their longevity; 35 degrees Fahrenheit is ideal. In home refrigerators, which usually have an average temperature of about 40 degrees, the best place for them is in the coldest spot, on the bottom shelf toward the back. Never store live lobsters in your freezer.

APPROXIMATE YIELDS OF COOKED MEAT PER POUND OF LIVE LOBSTER*

TYPE OF LOBSTER	MEAT FROM CLAWS, KNUCKLES AND TAIL	ALL MEAT, INCLUDING CARCASS AND WALKING LEGS
Hard-shell chicken (1 pound)	3 to 3¼ ounces**	3½ to 3¾ ounces
Soft-shell chicken (1 pound)	2½ to 2¾ ounces	3 to 3¼ ounces
Hard-shell select (1½ to 2½ pounds)	3¼ to 3½ ounces	3¾ to 4 ounces
Soft-shell select (1½ to 2½ pounds)	2¾ to 3 ounces	3¼ to 3½ ounces
Jumbos (2½ pounds and up)	3½ to 4 ounces	4 to 4½ ounces
Small culls (1 to 2½ pounds)	2¾ to 3 ounces	3¼ to 3½ ounces
Jumbo culls (2½ pounds and up)	3 to 3¼ ounces	3¾ to 4 ounces

*Use this chart as a guideline, not as a guarantee. Soft-shell lobsters vary widely and can yield lesser amounts than shown. Culls vary depending on the size of the one good claw.
**Ounces refers to ounces per pound.

YIELDS

As a rule, the amount of meat you get from a lobster ranges between 20 and 25 percent. In other words, a 1-pound live lobster yields 3¼ to 4 ounces of meat. This varies, of course, according to the type of lobster you use and the extent to which you pick it. Larger lobsters yield more meat per pound, but the higher price of larger lobsters almost always offsets this difference. Culls and soft-shell lobsters often yield a lower percentage of meat, so before buying them, make sure they are being sold at a substantially lower price.

THE RULES

I have been told by my family that I can be somewhat overzealous when talking about lobster. For those of you who just want the facts, I have condensed into a few short rules the process of picking out the perfect lobster and handling it with care. Follow these rules for the foundations of a mouth-watering meal.

1. BUY LOBSTERS THE DAY YOU COOK THEM, AND TRANSPORT AND STORE THEM CAREFULLY. Make seafood shopping your last stop. If possible, have a cooler ready to store the lobsters in for the trip home. Refrigerate immediately upon returning. Keep lobsters moist but never on ice. If you cannot avoid extended storage, wrap lobsters in a damp sheet of newspaper. Do not store more than thirty-six hours.

2. LOCATE THE BEST SOURCE FOR THE MOST RECENTLY CAUGHT LOBSTERS. If you live near the coast of eastern Canada or New England, find a lobsterman or lobster company to supply you with local lobsters. Otherwise, choose the best seafood market in your area. If you do not live in lobster territory, consider purchasing by mail order as a viable option.

3. DETERMINE THE RIGHT SIZE OF LOBSTER FOR YOU. But remember to be flexible at the market. It is better to buy the best lobsters than to be stubborn about the size you want.

4. CHOOSE A HEALTHY, LIVELY, FRESHLY CAUGHT LOBSTER. Look at the length of the antennae. If they are short or show signs of algal growth, the lobster has probably been stored in a pound for a long time and may taste bland. Hold the lobster up. If its claws droop, do not buy it. If the lobster shows a frisky disposition by flapping its tail and swinging its claws, buy it.

5. ALWAYS BUY THE HARDEST-SHELLED LOBSTERS YOU CAN FIND. Give a gentle squeeze to the carapace. Shake the lobster gently. If it "rattles," it may be extremely soft. Check for comparative weight. If the lobster feels heavy compared to a similar-size lobster, it is meaty—an extremely desirable quality.

6. NEVER STICK YOUR HAND INTO A BAG OF LOBSTERS. It is dangerous. Cuts and stabs from lobsters can produce bad infections. A large lobster can crush or rip open your hand or fingers.

7. BE ENVIRONMENTALLY RESPONSIBLE. Never buy shorts (lobsters under 1 pound), an action that is both illegal and immoral. Avoid canned or frozen meat imported from Canada, where the regulations against using baby lobsters are much less stringent than in our country. Avoid jumbo lobsters over 5 pounds—let us keep them as breeding stock. If you want a female lobster for a certain dish, check the sex but do not be greedy. If half your lobsters are female, you will have more than enough roe to go around.

LOBSTER ANATOMY: As It Pertains to Culinary Matters

Lobster Parts

The biggest problem with explaining the anatomy of a lobster is the lingo, a motley mix of scientific terminology and regional slang. Many of its body parts have more than one name, adding to the confusion. For example, the *head sac,* or stomach, located behind the lobster's mouth, is also called the *sand sac* or *grain sac.* The *carapace,* and the body parts it protects, is called the *carcass* by most cookbook authors but the *body* by most New Englanders. To make things easier for us all, the figure of the split lobster on page 18 lists the name I use when I refer to different parts of the lobster. In most cases, I have chosen the term that I feel is most easily understood by a national audience. My apologies in advance to all the Yankees who must read about making their chowder from lobster carcasses rather than bodies.

Blood

The clear liquid found throughout the lobster is its *blood.* It cooks into a white substance resembling egg white. It is quite delicious and when available should always be whisked into pan sauces.

Carcass

The *carcass* is the lobster with the knuckles, claws and tail removed. It is covered by a single piece of protective shell called the *carapace.* The carcass houses plenty of good meat between the gills and the walking legs, as well as the tomalley and roe in females. Carcasses, called *bodies* in New England, are used mainly for soups and sauces. They can be stored in the freezer for up to six weeks.

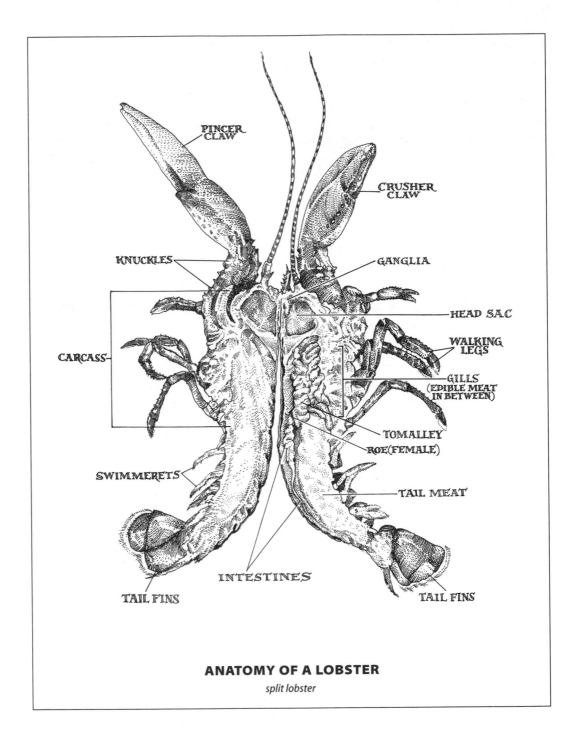

ANATOMY OF A LOBSTER

split lobster

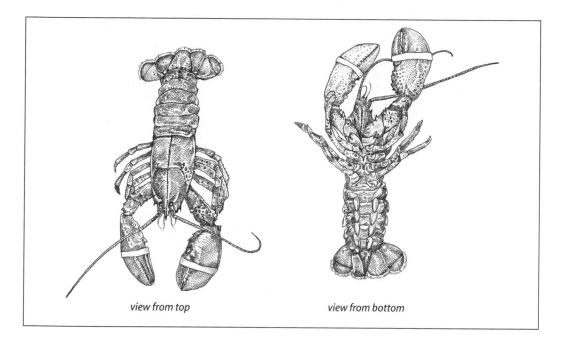

view from top   *view from bottom*

Claws

The larger of the two claws is called the *crusher claw*. The lobster uses it to crush or crack open its food, such as oysters and sea urchins. The smaller claw, called the *pincer,* is also sometimes called the *cutter claw*. The lobster uses it to tear and hold food. The claws can be found randomly on either the right or the left side. Studies have shown that whichever claw the lobster uses most frequently will develop into the crusher. These two claws can grow to enormous sizes and are full of very tender, sweet meat.

Eyes and Face

The eyes are little more than an ornament for the lobster, which uses chemoreception (smell) to navigate its world. For our purposes, they help to locate other parts of the lobster's cluttered face. The sharp, pointy spike that sticks out between the eyes is called the *rostrum.* On both sides of the rostrum are *antennules,* which serve as sensory devices for the lobster. Next to the antennules are *maxillipeds,* short appendages that assist the lobster in shoving food into its mouth. The *antennae* are very long and are used as feelers to explore the environment. Short antennae are a sign that the lobster has been in captivity for an extended period (because they are nibbled at by other lobsters). Marine biologists have observed that lobsters rub their antennae together as a form of foreplay before mating.

Ganglia

The small, opaque clumps of nerve tissue found behind the rostrum (between the eyes) are called the *ganglia*. They serve as the lobster's "brain" and are usually removed with the head sac because of their close proximity to it. Hence, when asked to remove the head sac, you should remove the ganglia as well.

Gills

Behind the walking legs are twenty pairs of *gills,* which oxygenate the lobster's blood. In between the gills are clumps of extremely tasty body meat.

Head sac

Also called the *grain sac* or *sand sac,* the *head sac* is a sort of stomach with teeth. It contains several small parts that efficiently grind the lobster's food. Its inside is gritty and inedible.

Intestine

This long, thin tube, which is the lobster's digestive tract, begins near the tomalley and extends all the way through the tail to the holes in the *telson* (the center tail fin) where the lobster excretes. If the lobster has been feeding recently, the intestine will appear dark. If the intestine is clear, the lobster has recently purged its digestive tract. I always remove the intestine before serving.

Knuckles

The two joints that connect the large claws to the carcass are called the *knuckles* or the *arms.* They are full of meat—absolutely the tastiest morsels in the lobster.

Roe

Also called *coral,* these tiny black eggs turn bright orange-red when cooked and add little bursts of flavor and texture to sauces and soups. The roe is located near the tomalley and into the upper part of the tail, where it is released through two openings near the second pair of swimmerets. It is illegal to take a female lobster that is "berried" (showing eggs on the outside of her abdomen). When this happened at my restaurant, we would take the lobster to the pier (about three hundred yards away) and release it into the harbor.

Swimmerets

There are five pairs of appendages underneath the tail of the lobster. Although used by the male in mating and by the female for holding her eggs prior to their release, *swimmerets* help the lobster mainly with movement. There is no edible meat inside the swimmerets; for our purposes, they are useful for determining the sex of a lobster. On the female, the pair of swimmerets closest to the walking legs are soft and feathery; on the male, they are thin and hard.

Tail

The six jointed sections at the rear of the lobster hold the single biggest piece of meat in the lobster. It is succulent and delicious, but I find most of the other meat to be tenderer and even a bit sweeter. The tail fins, called *telson* (center) and *uropods* (outer), contain small morsels of tasty meat. The telson is slightly wider on the female, as is the underside of the tail, called the *abdomen*.

Tomalley

This soft greenish mass functions as a liver. Lobster lovers cherish its rich flavor, spreading it on toast, simmering it in lobster dishes or whipping it into pan sauces. *Warning:* If the lobster is caught in contaminated waters, especially in waters containing PCPs, the impurities will often have settled in the tomalley. Be aware of this fact and avoid lobster "specials" where the price seems too good to be true. These are often a way of getting rid of lobsters taken from illegal waters.

Walking legs

The lobster has four pairs of legs attached to the carcass, which it uses primarily for walking. The front two pairs have small claws used for feeding. The *walking legs* contain tender little strips of meat that can be removed by a combination of squeezing and sucking or by using a small rolling pin to push the meat out (page 37).

CHAPTER 2

Basic Cooking Techniques

LOBSTER IS ONE of those uniquely satisfying meals to prepare; its hard shell and seemingly endless crevices reward one's hard work with fragrant morsels of tender meat. What most people do not realize is that learning a few basic skills in the art of preparing and eating lobster makes the process of finding the rich nuggets of meat easy and a highly sensual experience. This chapter outlines these techniques, taking you step by step through killing, cooking and eating lobsters.

KITCHEN EQUIPMENT FOR COOKING LOBSTERS

You will probably find most of this equipment already in your kitchen. There are, however, a few specialty items that I have found invaluable.

Charcoal grill

When you are choosing a grill for lobsters, the biggest consideration is size. A lobster that has been split for grilling takes up almost 1 square foot. Most types of grills will work, including gas grills with covers. Lobsters are best grilled directly over the hot coals, with a shallow cover. At home I grill on a large Weber grill using pie tins or small roasting pans to cover the lobsters.

Chimney

I always heat the coals for the grill with a chimney, a funnel-like device available at many hardware stores that allows you to heat coals without using lighter fluid.

chimney

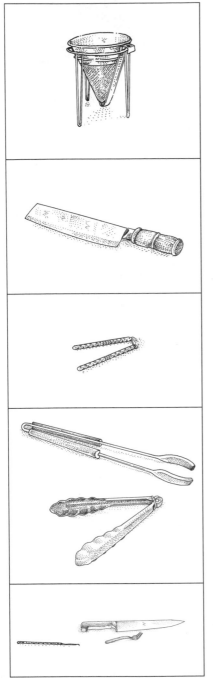

China cap

Also known as a *chinois,* this cone-shaped strainer is invaluable for straining lobster stocks, broth and soups. Commercial china caps are large enough to cover the entire surface of a pot or bowl, preventing pieces of shells or other objects from falling into the strained liquid. Because they are so sturdy, it is easy to pass liquids through the small holes by pushing down with a ladle. Restaurant-supply stores are the best place to buy china caps.

Chinese cleaver

There is absolutely no better knife for cutting up lobsters than a medium-weight Chinese cleaver. Its sleek design and weight make the task of killing the lobster a swift one, benefiting both the cook and the lobster. It also greatly reduces the risk of accidents, which can happen when struggling with the hard shell of a lobster.

Lobster cracker

The same thing as a nutcracker, this is an indispensable utensil for cracking open the claws and knuckles of a whole lobster at the table. In the kitchen, knives and shears can perform these tasks more efficiently, but for presentation and ease in eating, nothing beats a lobster cracker.

Long and short tongs

Tongs are invaluable when cooking lobster. Long tongs prevent burns when pulling lobsters out of a boiling or steaming pot of water. Short tongs are helpful for turning pieces of lobster during searing and for putting hot lobster on plates.

Picks and oyster forks

A three-pronged oyster fork, more useful than the single-pronged pick, is perfect for picking out the little pieces of lobster meat that are hard to get at with your fingers.

Rolling pin

The easiest way to remove the meat from the walking legs is to break them off and, starting from the little claw (only the front four have claws), press down and roll over them with a rolling pin. The meat will pop out in one piece. Although at the table this meat is usually extracted through sucking and squeezing, using a rolling pin in the kitchen will save enormous amounts of time.

Sauté pans

These pans are necessary for searing lobster pieces cut up in the shell in hot oil or butter. Because the process of searing requires a very steady high heat, I recommend using a heavy stainless-steel pan; it will become hotter and stay hotter than a lighter one. It is a good idea to have three sizes: a 9-inch pan to cook one lobster; a 12-inch pan to cook two lobsters; and a 14-inch pan to cook three lobsters. Cooking more than three lobsters requires an extra pan.

Small pots

You will need a 10- or 12-quart pot for making soup, stock and broth. A small 3- or 4-cup pot is necessary for melting butter and preparing butter sauces, and a 2- or 3-quart pot is perfect for more elaborate sauces such as Fra Diavolo and Mornay. Copper is great because its ability to conduct heat allows you to set your burner at a lower temperature, thus preventing scorching. If copper is out of your price range, any heavy pot, such as aluminum-covered stainless steel, will do a fine job. When all is said and done, it is what you put in the pot that really counts.

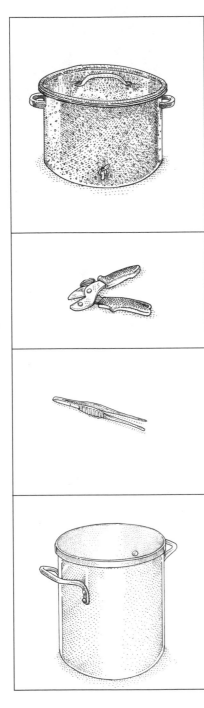

Steamer

A tall, narrow cooking pot can easily be converted into a steamer by placing a vegetable steam rack or even an upside-down colander in the bottom and securing the top with a tight-fitting lid. You can use a few inches of rockweed (seaweed) as a "rack" for your lobsters. Another wonderful piece of equipment is the venerable three-piece black steamer with a spigot at the bottom, originally intended for steaming clams (it even says STEAMERS on the side). It has been around for as long as I can remember and is sold in New England hardware stores, seafood markets and cookware stores. It is 14 inches wide and 20 inches tall and has ample space to steam four chicken lobsters.

Straight-edged garden shears

It is occasionally necessary to cut through the lobster shell to remove the delicious meat from the claws or the knuckles in one piece. Thin, lightweight straight-edged garden shears, much stronger than culinary scissors, are perfect for the job.

Surgical tweezers

This tool serves only one purpose when cooking lobster: removing the intestinal tract from the tail. Although it is easier to remove the tract with a knife, this can be messy, and the only way to retain beautiful presentation is by using these specialty tweezers. They are also called *Kelly clamps,* and you can find them at uniform stores, medical-supply stores and specialty-tool stores.

Tall, narrow cooking pot

This is the most important piece of equipment for boiling lobsters. Because most home ranges have small burners, a tall, narrow pot that holds 4 to 6 gallons water is ideal. It will hold four select or six chicken lobsters without hanging off the burner, thus ensuring a steady boil throughout. It is also wonderful as a steamer because it can hold more lobsters above the water line than a standard-size stockpot. Although aluminum pots are okay, they tend to buckle over time. Look for thick, heavy stainless steel—it will conduct heat evenly and allow for a quicker return to the boil.

BOILING AND PARBOILING LOBSTERS

Boiling is such a popular method that many people do not realize there are other ways to cook lobsters. In fact, whenever I mentioned this book to friends outside the food profession, they looked at me strangely and said, "It must be a small book. What else do you need to know about lobsters besides how to boil them?" As you can see by glancing through these pages, there are many ways to prepare lobsters, but boiling and parboiling are still of the utmost importance.

Lobster should be boiled in fresh ocean or tidal water. To my way of thinking, the ultimate achievement when preparing seafood is to deliver the fish—whether oysters, clams, bass, tuna or lobsters—tasting clean and distinctive and, most important, tasting of the ocean. It is the briny-sweet taste of the sea, where all life began, that is so intensely satisfying and sensually stimulating. Boiling a lobster in the clean ocean water it came from produces this flavor experience better than any other cooking method. When ocean water is not available, heavily salted fresh tap or spring water is fine, but it never fully captures the flavor of the sea. Because of this, when no ocean water is available, I usually recommend steaming, a method that produces a pure lobster flavor with little danger of toughening due to overcooking.

That said, why recommend boiling at all? Boiling is an essential method for partially cooking food. Water boils at a steady temperature and comes into direct contact with the food, while the intensity with which steam cooks food varies. In addition, boiling is easier and more accurate to time than steaming. Many lobster dishes, such as soups, pastas and sautés, depend on partially cooked lobster meat that is reheated in the final cooking, resulting in meat that is cooked just right rather than overcooked. Boiling also cooks the lobster fast and hard, from the outside in. The intense direct heat cooks the outer red part of the meat first; this causes it to shrink away from the shell, making it easier to remove. Last, boiling is the easiest method of cooking lobster and thus is great for the first-time lobster cook. Follow my charts, and you are guaranteed success!

The process of boiling, in ocean or homemade salt water, is the same whether the intention is to fully or partially cook a lobster. The three key elements are the pot, the salinity of the water and the water temperature.

The Pot

It is important to choose a pot large enough to stir the lobsters. Do not overcrowd the pot. Allow 3 quarts of water per 1½ to 2 pounds of lobster, taking into account that the pot should be filled no more than three-quarters full. This equates to roughly 1 gallon of space for each select-size lobster; in other words, a 4-gallon pot containing 3 gallons of water is ideal for cooking six 1-pound (chicken) lobsters, four 1½- to 2-pound (select) lobsters or two

2½- to 3-pound (jumbo) lobsters. Plan accordingly, bearing in mind that most home ranges will have trouble boiling water in a pot larger than 4 or 5 gallons. Use more than one pot if needed. If you are uncertain, err on the side of too much room or too much water in the pot.

Salt

If using ocean water, no added salt is necessary. If using fresh water, add ¼ cup of salt for each gallon of water. The water should taste distinctly salty. If any rockweed is available, throw it in. Like putting a little oil in pasta water, it may not be necessary, but it does not hurt and does make some people (like me) feel better.

Temperature

In order to achieve accurate timing, it is crucial to bring the water to a rolling boil before adding the lobsters. In general, most cookbooks (including my own first book) suggest timing lobsters from the moment the water returns to a boil. After numerous tests, however, I have become convinced that it is actually more accurate to time lobsters from the moment they are put in the water, not from the moment the water reaches a boil again. My logic is that since stoves, depending on their power, can vary in the time they take to bring a pot of lobsters back to a boil, and since the difference between boiling and not boiling can be a matter of only a few degrees, the total amount of time in the hot water is more important and is a more accurate measure than the amount of time after the boil.

A great trick before serving a boiled lobster is to punch a small hole in the spot right between the cooked lobster's eyes, using the heel of your cleaver or the tip of a small knife. Lean the lobster with its head down so that the liquids drain from the carcass. This creates less mess when the lobster is opened, and it also allows the tomalley to stay firm.

"Boiling" Jumbo Lobsters

People often complain that jumbo lobsters are not as tender as smaller ones. I think this is because they are often cooked too fast. As with poultry and meat, where it is common knowledge that the larger the roast, the lower the cooking temperature, so it is with seafood. Place jumbo lobsters into boiling water to start. The water temperature will drop instantly. The heat should then be lowered, allowing the lobsters to "poach." The result will be a slower, more evenly cooked lobster with excellent texture. The chart below takes this slower cooking into consideration for lobsters that weigh 2½ pounds or more. For smaller lobsters, leave the heat at its maximum.

The boiling procedure is simple: Bring the salted water to a rolling boil. Pick up the lobsters one at a time and, holding the lobster with your hand wrapped around its carapace, drop it in the pot. Leave the pot uncovered while the lobsters cook. Time according to the chart below. Stir the lobsters once, halfway through the cooking. Use a pair of long tongs to remove the lobsters when they are ready. Before removing all the lobsters from the pot, remove one and break it in half where the carapace meets the tail. The tail meat should be creamy white with no translucency, and the roe, if there is any, should be bright red. If not, let the lobsters cook a little longer. Serve with drawn butter (page 33) or allow them to cool at room temperature. If the meat is to be removed, do it before refrigerating.

BOILING CHART FOR FULLY COOKED LOBSTER

This chart is based on the lobster-to-water ratio recommended on page 27. If you use more water per lobster than recommended, shorten the cooking time by one minute. Conversely, if you crowd the pot, using less water per lobster, add at least one minute to the cooking time per extra lobster.

1 pound	8 minutes
1¼ pounds	9 to 10 minutes
1½ pounds	11 to 12 minutes
1¾ pounds	12 to 13 minutes
2 pounds	15 minutes
2½ pounds	20 minutes
3 pounds	25 minutes
5 pounds	35 to 40 minutes

BOILING CHART FOR PARTIALLY COOKED LOBSTER ———————————

This chart is based on the same lobster-to-water ratio recommended for fully cooked lobsters on page 27. Because it is crucial that the lobsters be in contact with water as close to boiling as possible, and because this is such a quick procedure, there is no reason to crowd the pot. If you need to, parboil lobsters in more than one batch. Just be sure that the water returns to a rolling boil before you cook the second batch. Lobsters weighing more than 3 pounds are not suitable for parboiling because the meat does not cook properly during the second cooking. If you are using soft-shells, deduct at least one minute from the cooking time. Allow lobsters to cool at room temperature. Remove the meat while still slightly warm—it is easiest that way. Keep refrigerated until ready to use.

1 pound	3½ minutes
1¼ pounds	4 minutes
1½ pounds	4½ minutes
1¾ pounds	5 minutes
2 pounds	5½ minutes
2½ pounds	6½ to 7 minutes
3 pounds	7½ to 8 minutes

A FEW WORDS ABOUT SALT

Salt plays two important roles in cooking lobster: boiling and seasoning. For boiling (or parboiling), always use ¼ cup of kosher or sea salt per gallon of water. This may seem excessive, but the idea is to maintain the natural saltiness of the lobster. If you use less, the lobster will actually be less salty than it is naturally.

Salt for seasoning should be used much more sparingly. Salt accentuates the natural sweetness of the lobster, but often the lobster contributes enough salt of its own. The salinity of bays and rivers can vary widely. Commercial tanks where lobsters are stored have far less salinity than their natural environment. Some lobsters need additional salt, while others are enhanced by just a pinch. When a recipe calls for lemon or other flavorings, always add them before the salt—you will find that you use less salt. I love the taste of sea salt and think there is a certain amount of poetic justice in using it to season lobsters.

STEAMING LOBSTERS

Steaming lobsters has several advantages over boiling. Steaming cooks lobsters more slowly than boiling, producing meat that is tenderer, especially with larger lobsters. Steaming is more forgiving than boiling, making overcooking less of a risk and allowing for the inevitable lag time between cooking and serving. It is also safer and cleaner than boiling because there is no spillover or gallons of near-boiling water to dispose of. Last and most important, steam does not penetrate the way water can and therefore preserves the true flavor of the lobster.

There are several methods for steaming lobster: on the grill wrapped in foil, in the oven and even in the microwave (page 32). The most common method, however, is to steam the lobsters in a pot on the stove. Any pot can be transformed into a steamer, although the ideal pot for steaming is the same as for boiling: tall and somewhat narrow but large enough to allow the steam to circulate around the lobsters. The lobsters must be suspended far enough above the water so that when they release liquid during steaming, they do not end up sitting in it. If you do not own the venerable black steamer described on page 26, there are several ways to improvise a rack. A colander placed upside down works well. Rockweed, when available, makes a great "rack" and adds the smell of the ocean to the steamer. Simply place 8 to 10 inches of rockweed on the bottom of the pot with just enough water to get things started (½ inch).

The ratio of lobsters to the pot is similar to that for boiling. A 4- to 5-gallon pot is ideal for steaming a total of 6 to 8 pounds of lobster. That means the pot will comfortably hold six 1-pound (chicken) lobsters, four 1½- to 2-pound (select) lobsters or two 2½- to 3-pound (jumbo) lobsters. Plan accordingly. Use more than one pot if necessary. If the lobsters do not fit comfortably in the pot and if you cannot see the bottom of the pot, it is overcrowded.

The procedure for steaming is simple: Fill the steamer pot with 1 inch of salt water, either ocean water or fresh water with salt added. Set up the steaming rack inside the pot. Turn the heat to high and cover the steamer. The water will boil quickly. When it does, place the lobsters in the pot and cover tightly. Use the chart on page 32 to time the lobsters. Rearrange the lobsters halfway through the steaming. Be careful when removing the lid—the steam is very hot. Using long tongs, move the lobsters around. Work quickly and cover the pot again as soon as possible. When the lobsters have cooked for the recommended time, remove one and break it open where the carapace meets the tail. The tail meat should be creamy white with no translucency, and the roe, if there is any, should be bright red. If not, allow the lobsters to steam for a few minutes more. When they are ready, turn off the steamer and serve as soon as possible.

STEAMING CHART FOR LOBSTER

Time the lobsters from the moment they are added to the pot. Times are based on the lobster-to-pot ratio recommended on page 31. Cover the steamer tightly immediately after adding the lobsters.

1 pound	10 minutes
1¼ pounds	12 minutes
1½ pounds	14 minutes
1¾ pounds	16 minutes
2 pounds	18 minutes
2½ pounds	22 minutes
3 pounds	25 to 30 minutes
5 pounds	40 to 45 minutes

STEAMING LOBSTER IN A MICROWAVE

There are several good reasons to steam lobster in a microwave oven. The combination of direct cooking from the microwaves and steaming produces an evenly cooked, tender lobster. Using this technique is slightly faster than steaming on the stovetop in a pot. And best of all, there is no pot to be cleaned and no hot water to dispose of. The biggest drawback is that you can cook only one lobster at a time, but if you want to cook up a couple of lobsters for salad or another cold preparation, that is no problem.

Because of my wariness of microwave ovens, I had to turn to others for help to come up with a steaming technique that is suited to them. Julia Child suggested to my editor, Maria Guarnaschelli, that I try Roger Berkowitz's method of microwaving lobster. As CEO of Legal Sea Foods, a chain of restaurants and markets known for their consistently high-quality fish and shellfish, he is very savvy when it comes to seafood. He sent me a video he had made for PBS about lobster bakes that included a demonstration of his microwave method. Here is how Roger does it:

To steam lobster in a microwave, you will need a 1-gallon plastic zippered freezer bag. Cut a lemon in half. Spear one lemon half on the head of the lobster (the rostrum will stick right in the lemon). The lemon flavors the steam and at the same time covers the rostrum, thus preventing it from ripping a hole in the bag. Carefully place the lobster in the freezer bag, add a few pieces of rockweed, seal the bag and place on a plate in the microwave. Cook at the highest setting. The water sacs in the rockweed will burst and release steam, like a miniature lobster bake. If no rockweed is available, add ¼ cup of water instead. Follow the chart on page 33 for recommended cooking times.

DRAWN BUTTER

Lobster and butter are like cheese and wine . . . they love each other, they belong together. Although there are many great lobster dishes without butter, there is no denying the perfection of the combination.

Drawn butter is simply melted butter. For some unfathomable reason, many clam shacks and restaurants serve clarified butter (the skimmed clear yellow fat of the butter) as drawn butter. They do not realize that the milk solids which are skimmed from clarified butter are what make drawn butter so tasty. As far as I am concerned, the best butter for dipping is unsalted butter seasoned with lemon, salt and pepper. Simply put the butter in a pot near a warm area of the stove and whisk it now and then so that it emulsifies (blends into a creamy liquid where all components are suspended) slightly as it melts. Or put the pot directly on the heat and bring to a boil, stirring often. This is not a sauce, so if it separates after heating, do not worry. By adding your own salt you can determine the exact flavor of the drawn butter. The lemon, while not traditional, adds a freshness to the butter that can't be beat. I use about a quarter of a lemon for every stick of butter. Figure on using about 2 tablespoons butter per lobster. A great addition to drawn butter is a big spoonful of lobster tomalley. I adore the flavor of tomalley I get with every bite!

MICROWAVE STEAMING CHART FOR LOBSTER ———————————

For lobsters over 2 pounds, you will need a 2-gallon freezer bag. Since every microwave oven is a little different, you may need to adjust your cooking times accordingly.

1 pound	6 minutes
1¼ pounds	7 minutes
1½ pounds	8 minutes
1¾ pounds	9 minutes

A Final Comment on Boiled and Steamed Lobsters

While the flavor and texture of perfectly cooked lobster is difficult to describe, it is instantly recognizable when it meets your tongue, embodying the essence of the salty ocean air and the richness and warmth of the summer sun on your skin. It is a sensual experience that, once tried, is never forgotten. Unlike other fish and shellfish, where care must be taken not to cook a moment longer than necessary, lobster meat is most succulent when allowed to cook one to two minutes past the point when it first appears to be done. If not allowed to cook past this point, the meat will be rubbery. A word of caution is necessary, however: Like other seafood, lobster can toughen from overcooking and eventually turn to mush if not rescued from the heat. Because of this, perfect timing is essential. Even if your instincts tell you it is time to remove the lobster from the pot, trust me on the times given in the recipes—they are the result of years of careful observation.

KILLING AND CUTTING UP LIVE LOBSTERS

Many of the recipes in this book require you to split a live lobster. It is a technique that allows you to kill a lobster instantly. Any twitching you may notice after the fact is the result of postmortem muscle spasms and does not mean the lobster is still alive.

Here's how to split a live lobster in half for grilling, baking, broiling or pan-frying (refer to diagrams on page 35):

1. With the front of the lobster facing you, place the front tip of the knife or cleaver in the center of the lobster, near where the carapace meets the tail (diagram 1). Line up the knife and check to see that the lobster's claws are not in the path of the knife. In one forceful and swift motion, split the front half of the lobster. Turn the lobster around and repeat this same motion, splitting the tail (diagram 2). The lobster is now dead and cut in half.

2. Using your fingers, pull the head sac out of both halves (diagram 3). Find the intestine, which will probably be in one of the halves; it is rare to be so precise as to split the intestine. Remove the intestine with your fingers or with surgical tweezers (diagram 4).

3. Use the back side of the knife or cleaver to tap the claws until their shells crack.

Here's how to quarter a live lobster, a technique that leaves you with six somewhat uniform pieces, perfect for pan-roasting, wok-searing and pan-frying (refer to diagrams on page 35):

1. Follow step one above.

2. Follow step two above.

3. With a knife, cleaver or shears, remove the claws and knuckles by cutting the thin section where the knuckle meets the carcass (diagram 5). Use the back side of a knife or cleaver to tap the claws until their shells crack.

4. Line your knife up where the tail and the carcass meet. With the tip of the front of your knife on the cutting board, "quarter" the lobster by coming down in one swift, forceful motion (diagram 6).

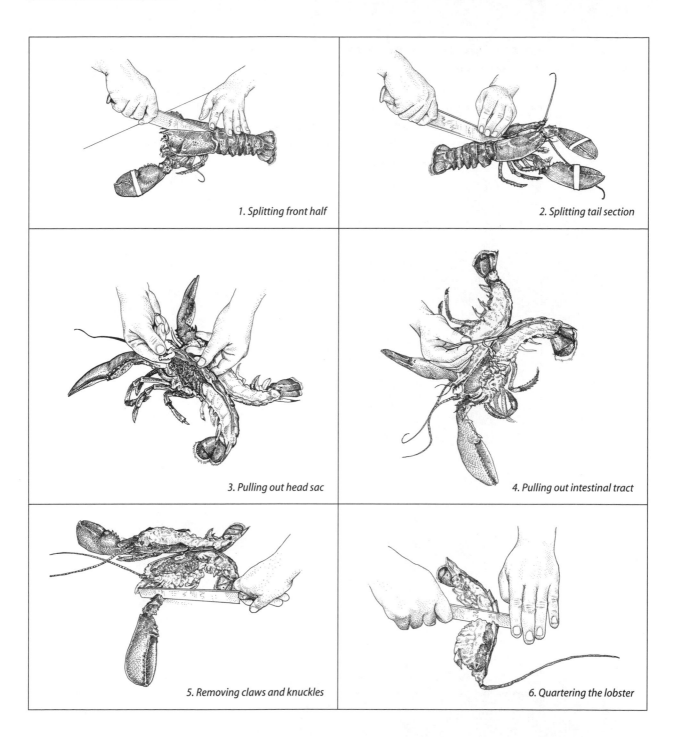

1. Splitting front half

2. Splitting tail section

3. Pulling out head sac

4. Pulling out intestinal tract

5. Removing claws and knuckles

6. Quartering the lobster

REMOVING MEAT FROM A COOKED LOBSTER

If a recipe calls for fully cooked meat, the lobster can be either steamed or boiled. If the recipe calls for partially cooked meat, the lobster is parboiled. Extracting the meat is the same in both cases but can be slightly trickier with partially cooked lobsters, especially when removing the meat from the claws and the carcass. I often deal with this difficulty by simply saving the carcass to make soup. However, if you have no intention of making soup, by all means pick the meat from the carcass. Your hard work will be rewarded with delicious morsels. If you find roe, finely chop it and add it to the meat. The tomalley, unfortunately, is not suited to many cold dishes and, depending on the recipe, should be thrown out or saved to make Tomalley Toasts (page 88).

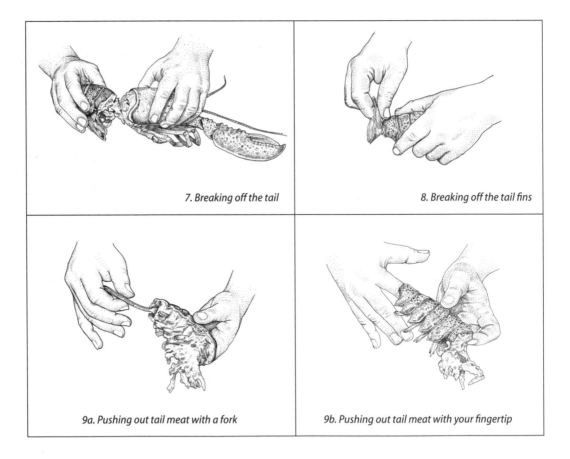

7. Breaking off the tail

8. Breaking off the tail fins

9a. Pushing out tail meat with a fork

9b. Pushing out tail meat with your fingertip

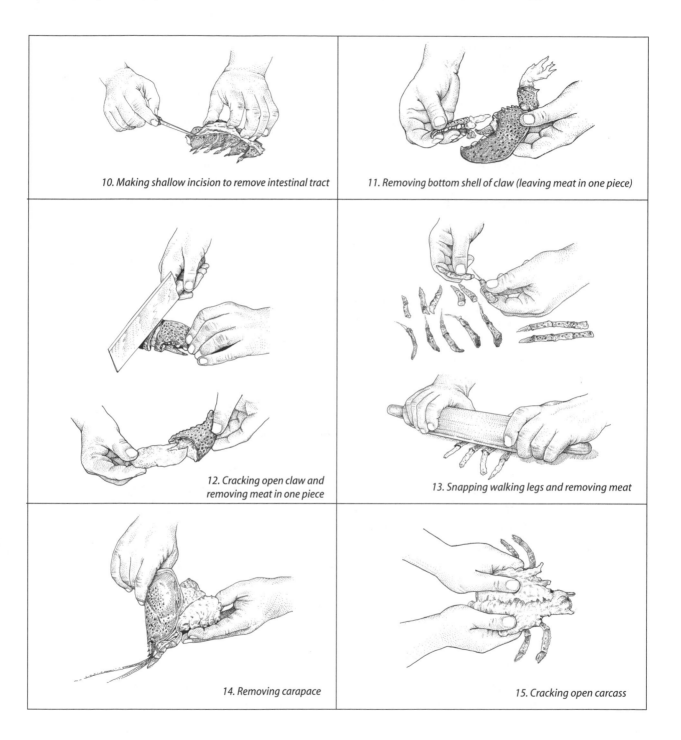

10. Making shallow incision to remove intestinal tract

11. Removing bottom shell of claw (leaving meat in one piece)

12. Cracking open claw and removing meat in one piece

13. Snapping walking legs and removing meat

14. Removing carapace

15. Cracking open carcass

Here's how to remove the meat (refer to diagrams on pages 36 and 37):

1. Hold the carcass in one hand and the tail in the other. With a simple twist, break the two pieces apart; they will separate easily (diagram 7). Grab the tail fins and pull them up toward the top of the tail; they will rip right off (diagram 8). The meat in the telson will remain attached to the tail. The tiny clumps of meat in the uropods can be removed by squeezing.

2. Using either a small fork or your fingertip, push the tail meat from the rear, near the telson, toward the front (diagrams 9a and 9b). Extract the intestine using a technique dependent on what you will do with the meat. If you are planning on dicing or chopping the tail meat, split the tail in half lengthwise and pull the intestine out with your fingers. If you are going to slice the tail meat, make a shallow incision along the top of the tail and remove the intestine with your fingers (diagram 10). For very fancy slices, use surgical tweezers to pull the intestine out, leaving the tail intact. If the intestine does not come out cleanly, go ahead and slice the tail, using the tweezers to pull the intestine from the individual pieces.

3. Separate the knuckles from the carcass by either twisting them off with your hands or cutting them away with shears. Separate the knuckles from the claws. Remove the knuckle meat by tapping the shells until they crack or by cutting the shells open with shears. Remove the claw meat in one piece by grabbing its smaller lower section and moving it from side to side until you feel it snap. Pull it away from the shell (diagram 11). If the meat gets stuck in the claw, tap the smaller half on your work surface until the meat inside comes out. Then use the back of your knife to tap around the center of the claw until the shell cracks. Break open the claw, and the meat is sure to come right out (diagram 12). If you are lucky enough to have a lobster that is very full of meat, you may have some trouble removing it from the shell. When this happens, slip a paring knife between the meat and the shell to loosen it. There is thin cartilage located in the center of the claw. Because it is difficult to remove without tearing the claw meat, do not bother to try to remove it if the recipe calls for the claw to be left intact. If you are going to dice the meat, remove this inedible cartilage.

4. Using your hands, snap off the eight walking legs. Snap each leg in half, breaking them at the joint. Push a small rolling pin over them, starting at the tip (diagram 13). The meat will fly out!

5. If you'd like to pick the meat from the carcass, remove the carapace by lifting it from the back where it met the tail (diagram 14). It will come right off. Hold the remaining carcass with both hands and crack it open (diagram 15). With a little effort it will split in half lengthwise. Now break these pieces again; you will see small chunks of meat between the gills and cartilage. Be careful to pick only the meat, because the gills and cartilage are inedible.

HOW TO EAT A WHOLE LOBSTER (Like a Yankee, not a Tourist!)

For most New Englanders, including myself, eating whole steamed or boiled lobsters is really a summer ritual, done at a picnic table outdoors or at a "lobster shack" at the beach. It's casual, it's outdoors and the native lobsters are usually soft-shelled in summer, making them easier to eat. I do not recommend serving whole lobsters when your guests are even slightly dressed up. As far as I am concerned, lobster bibs do little more than provide the lobster juices a funnel straight to your lap.

The process of eating a lobster in the rough is very similar to the process described in Removing Meat from a Cooked Lobster (page 36). The only difference is in your utensils. You will be equipped with crackers and can use them to crush the claws and the knuckles. Presentation is not important, so do not worry about tearing the claw meat—it's going straight from the shell into the butter and then into your mouth. Follow the same steps, but remember that the order in which you eat the different parts is important. Eat the tail, claws and knuckles first so that you can eat the greatest amount of lobster at the hottest temperature. I love cold lobster—but not dipped in drawn butter! And don't forget: Eating lobster is, above all, a sensual experience. Savor the juices, the cracking shell and the texture of the sweet, tender meat dipped in melted butter as it meets your tongue.

GRILLING LOBSTERS

Once you have tasted grilled lobster, you will crave the salt-water smokiness and pronounced fragrance this method imparts. Nothing can elevate a casual outdoor meal to an exciting event like the sight and smell of whole lobsters on the grill, their shells turning brilliant red and then crisply lined black and the air smelling like a bonfire made of driftwood. Your guests will love grilled lobster for another reason—it is not wet and messy like boiled lobster. The dry heat of the grill makes the lobster shells brittle and easy to crack.

The one minor obstacle to grilling lobster is space. You must reserve 1 square foot of grilling space per select-size lobster. Most home grills can hold only two or three selects at a time. Luckily, grilling parties are easygoing affairs, and your guests will be happy to have the food come in waves. If you serve half a lobster per person, you can cook twelve portions—two batches—in about twenty minutes. Having a second grill for bass, quail, steak or sausage is another option. A mixed grill is not only fun but cuts down on the expense of the meal.

The perfect grilling lobsters are 1½- to 2-pound hard-shell selects. Smaller lobsters cook too quickly to receive the full effect of the charred and smoked flavors. Larger lobsters become too charred and smoky because of the extended time on the grill. Soft-shells cook too quickly to absorb the flavors of this technique, burn easily and release so much liquid that they weaken the fire.

Ideally, the grill should be fired by wood charcoal. Briquettes are okay, but the taste they impart does not compare to the smoky flavor of wood charcoal. In any case, you need a "chimney" (page 23) to get the fire going quickly and evenly without imparting the flavor of lighter fluid to the smoke. To use a chimney, simply put the charcoal in the upper portion and put two sheets of newspaper in the bottom. Place the chimney inside the grill (for safety reasons) and light the paper. In about twenty minutes you will have a container of red-hot coals that you will pour into the grill and spread. The coals will be ready to use for most foods, but for lobster it is best to let them burn down for ten to fifteen minutes longer.

A gas-fired grill, which uses pumice bricks, can also be used successfully, but again, the flavor of the smoke is not as pronounced as when using real wood. If you do use a gas- or propane-fired grill, make sure you have plenty of fuel. Lobsters need to be grilled quickly and without interruption.

To grill a lobster, split the lobster (page 34) and remove the head sac and intestine. To prevent the loss of all juices, crack the claws in the center of the side that will not be exposed directly to the hot coals and brush the claws with oil. Brush the carapace and the shell of the tail, as well as the exposed meat, with butter or oil. Place the lobster, shell side down, directly over medium-hot coals and cover the claws and carcass with a pie tin or shallow roasting pan. Lift the covering once or twice during the cooking and quickly baste with butter or oil. Do not turn the lobster over during the cooking process because you will lose the tomalley and the juices. The lobster will be ready to eat in a few minutes. For a 1½-pound lobster, I recommend a cooking time of eight to ten minutes, but it is merely a recommendation. Grilling is an art that relies on the cook's confidence to determine when the cooking is complete. After eight minutes, take your tongs and pry around to get a glimpse of the tail meat where it enters the carcass. If it is cooked through, it will be creamy white. The tomalley should be hot and should even bubble slightly. The roe, if there is any, should be a bright orange-red.

A note on covering the lobster: It is important to cover the lobster as it cooks in order to speed up the cooking process and ensure even cooking throughout. Because the claws and carcass require a longer cooking time than the tail, it is especially important that they be covered. A pie plate or shallow roasting pan effectively holds in the heat. Aluminum foil will not hold in the heat, and the cover that comes with the grill is not useful here, for it creates too much smoke and lengthens the cooking time.

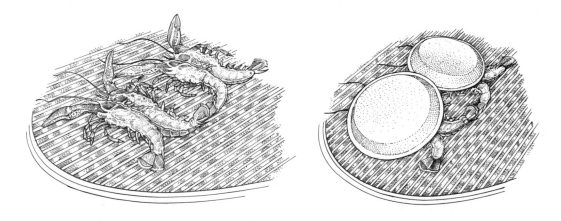

A note on using butter or oil: Brushing the lobster with oil or butter serves two purposes: It enhances the charring of the shell, and it flavors and moistens the meat. With this in mind, flavored butters and oils are often tasty. Try flavoring the butter with different ingredients, such as shallots, garlic, lemon zest, herbs, chiles or spices. Extra butter or sauce with grilled lobster gilds the lily. A squirt of lemon is all you really need.

Grilled Lobster with Garlic Oil

BASIC GRILLING RECIPE

This is a precise version of the grilling technique for lobster. The bread crumbs in this recipe are not intended to look or taste like "stuffing." Their purpose is to hold the oil, parsley and seasoning in a firm mix with the tomalley.

   Equipment: You will need a medium Chinese cleaver or large chef's knife, a small mixing bowl, a charcoal grill, a chimney, a wire brush, a cover (pie plate, shallow roasting pan or double-thick aluminum foil), a large spatula and a pastry brush.

2 live 1½-pound hard-shell lobsters	kosher or sea salt
4 tablespoons fresh white bread crumbs	freshly ground black pepper
1 tablespoon chopped fresh parsley	½ lemon, cut into 4 wedges
3 tablespoons Garlic-Flavored Olive Oil (page 44), plus extra for basting	

1. Prepare the charcoal fire, preferably with real wood charcoal. Fill the upper portion of the chimney with the charcoal and put 2 sheets of newspaper in the bottom part. Place the chimney inside the grill (for safety reasons) and light the paper. In about 20 minutes the charcoal should be red-hot. Dump the coals into the grill and spread them evenly. Let the coals burn down to a medium heat; this will take another 10 to 15 minutes. Place the grilling rack over the coals while they are burning and brush it clean with a wire brush (a hot rack is much easier to clean). You are now ready to begin grilling. If you are using a propane or gas-fired grill, preheat it at a medium setting for about 15 minutes, then clean the rack with a wire brush. Do not oil the rack as you would if you were cooking steaks or chops; there is no chance of the lobster sticking to the grill.

2. With a cleaver or chef's knife, split each lobster in half lengthwise (page 34). Remove the head sac and intestine. Crack the claws in the center on the side that will not be exposed directly to the hot coals.

3. Remove the tomalley and the roe if present and place in a small bowl. Break it into small pieces with a fork. Add the bread crumbs, parsley and 3 tablespoons of the garlic oil. Sprinkle with a little salt (about ¼ teaspoon) and some freshly ground pepper. Mix gently.

4. Using a pastry brush, brush the shells of the lobsters with some of the extra basting oil. Lift the lobster halves up and brush the undersides. This prevents the loss of the lobster's juices. Also brush any exposed meat.

5. Spread the tomalley mixture evenly throughout the cavities from where the tail enters the carcass to the tip of the head so that it will cook evenly. Season the lobster very lightly with salt and pepper. (Even though they are dead, they will twitch—don't freak out!)

6. Check that the fire is at medium heat and that the coals are spread evenly. Place the lobsters, shell side down, directly over the coals. Cover each lobster loosely with a pie plate, roasting pan or aluminum foil. Do not worry if the tail is not completely covered—it is the carcass and claws that really need the extra heat this provides. Cook for 8 to 10 minutes. *Do not turn the lobster over.* Baste the lobster two or three times during grilling with the oil. Check for doneness by gently prying around where the tail meat enters the carcass. If it is cooked through, the meat will be a creamy white and the tomalley mixture will be bubbly hot.

7. Remove from the grill and put on a platter or individual plates. Brush one last time with the garlic oil and serve immediately with the lemon wedges in a small bowl.

Serving Suggestions: Grilling parties are a fun and delicious way to enjoy lobster without stretching your budget too far. A menu might include several salads (always one with ripe tomatoes), other grilling food such as steak or sausage and some fresh fruit, including melon, a superb finish to an outdoor summer meal. While the above recipe is for two lobsters, which will fit comfortably on almost any home grill, it can be multiplied to suit your party. Just be sure to leave enough grilling space and time. And remember, if people do not seem to pay as much attention to your salads and other grilling meats, it is only natural, for nothing rivals the smoky, briny taste of grilled lobster.

Makes 2 whole grilled lobsters or 4 halves

Garlic-Flavored Olive Oil

Because this oil is intended for cooking, I use a refined olive oil, not extra-virgin. It is light in color, is simply labeled "olive oil" with no further description and is relatively inexpensive. More expensive types are not suited to grilling because they burn at a lower temperature. Since I love the taste of garlic and use this oil all the time for everyday cooking, I make a whole bottle at a time, but you may halve or quarter this recipe if you like. This recipe has a pronounced garlic flavor. After you make it once, you may wish to adjust it to your own taste.

1 small head or ½ large head garlic	1 bottle (750 milliliters) refined olive oil

1. Break open the head of garlic and separate the cloves, but do not peel them. Smash each clove with the flat side of a knife or cleaver. Combine the garlic with ½ cup of the olive oil in a small pan and slowly warm the oil over low heat for 15 to 20 minutes. Do not let the garlic pick up any color. When the oil is hot to the touch, remove it from the heat.

2. Saving the bottle for later, pour the remaining oil into a glass bowl and stir in the hot garlic and oil. Cover with plastic wrap and let steep for 2 days, stirring a couple of times each day.

3. Line a funnel with cheesecloth and strain the oil into the original bottle. Cover tightly. Empty wine bottles also make good containers. Label the bottle clearly and store in a dark place. Do not refrigerate. The garlic oil will keep well for up to 3 months.

PAN-ROASTING LOBSTERS

"Pan-roasting" is a term first coined in the early 1980s. Young American chefs like me needed a word to describe the type of restaurant dishes that started in a pan on top of the stove, made a very short visit to the oven and then often ended up back on top of the stove to be finished. These dishes were both sautéed and roasted. At a time when menu descriptions were becoming elaborately specific, a new term was needed. "Pan-roasted" has since become something of a catchall phrase.

I first offered Pan-Roasted Lobster with Chervil and Chives at Jasper's in 1984. During the twelve years that we served it, it was the most popular item on the menu. Many of my regular customers, including Julia Child, ordered it every time they came in. The idea for quartering lobster came from watching my friend C. K. Sau, chef at the Chinese restaurant next door, prepare his famous Lobster with Ginger and Scallions (page 184). I loved the idea of lobster served in the shell in a way that presented no difficulty in eating it, and I admired the perfect texture and speed with which my friend cooked it. I wanted to create a dish using this technique.

Remembering a recipe from the great French chef Fernand Point that combined lobster with Cognac, chervil, chives and butter—of course—I set out to combine the Chinese technique with these seductive flavors. I discovered that without a commercial wok, a short time in a very hot oven was needed to cook the lobster properly. After many tests I changed the Cognac to bourbon, and instead of a hot oven I began using the salamander (broiler) for the short roasting period. The dish had reached perfection. The cooks who left me took the technique with them, adding their own unique flavorings, and after many years I realized that pan-roasting had become a popular, almost standard, lobster-cooking technique. It thus makes sense to present the dish here to illustrate the basic pan-roasting technique.

Before you decide to prepare pan-roasted lobster, consider the number of guests, your kitchen and your time. The dish cooks quickly, but you will need about twenty minutes to cut up the lobsters and organize your ingredients. For two select lobsters, you will need a 12-inch sauté pan or two 9-inch sauté pans. If your home range can handle two large sauté pans, you can easily double this recipe, but even a trained professional would have trouble pan-roasting more than four lobsters at a time. Save this preparation for an intimate gathering of two to four people whom you are comfortable spending time with in your kitchen.

Hard-shell 1½- to 2-pound selects are perfect for pan-roasting—both for the length of their cooking time and for the portions they yield. Smaller lobsters cook too quickly, and larger lobsters take extra time during the roasting process and yield awkward-size portions. Soft-shell lobsters release too much liquid to make searing and roasting possible. I prefer to use a broiler for the "roasting" part of this recipe, but a very hot oven also works quite well.

Jasper's Pan-Roasted Lobster with Chervil & Chives

The bourbon in this recipe adds a sweetness that mingles potently with the sweetness of the lobster. An excellent Cognac or brandy can be substituted for similar results. Fresh chervil imparts a hint of anise flavor to the lobster; if unavailable, fresh parsley mixed with a small amount of fresh tarragon (½ teaspoon) will give a taste almost as good.

Equipment: You will need a medium Chinese cleaver or large chef's knife, a heavy ovenproof 12-inch sauté pan and tongs.

2 live 1¾-pound hard-shell lobsters	6 tablespoons unsalted butter, cut into small pieces and chilled
2 tablespoons peanut oil	1 tablespoon finely chopped chervil
2 shallots (1½ ounces), finely diced	1 tablespoon finely chopped fresh chives
¼ cup bourbon or Cognac	kosher or sea salt
2 or 3 tablespoons dry white wine	freshly ground black pepper

1. Preheat the broiler or preheat the oven as hot as possible (500° to 550°F). Position the oven rack in the upper third of the oven. You may need to shorten the cooking time slightly if the broiler rack is close to the heat.

2. Quarter the lobsters (page 34), removing the tomalley and the roe if present. Place the pieces of lobster, shell side down, on a plate.

3. Place the tomalley and roe in a small bowl. With a fork, break them into small pieces. Cover.

4. Place a heavy 12-inch sauté pan over the highest heat possible. Allow the pan to heat for 3 to 5 minutes until it becomes extremely hot. Add the oil and heat until it forms a film on the surface of the pan. Slide the lobster pieces, shell side down, into the hot oil. Using tongs, move the pieces in order to evenly sear all the shells. Because the lobster pieces are not flat, you will need to hold them with the tongs and press the shells into the hot oil to accomplish this. The claws need to be seared on only one side. When the shells have all turned bright red, which should take no more than 2 minutes, turn the pieces over. The oil will also have taken on a beautiful red tinge. Add the tomalley and roe to the pan.

5. Place the pan in the oven. If using the broiler, cook for 2 minutes. If using the oven, cook for 3 minutes. The shells should be slightly browned, even a bit charred in places.

6. Remove the pan from the oven and return it to the stove at maximum heat. Turn off the oven and put your plates in to warm. This will take only a minute. *Warning:* The handle of the pan will be red-hot and will stay hot until the dish is complete. To avoid burns, wear oven mitts from now until the dish is complete.

7. Add the shallots to the fat in the pan and stir. Add the bourbon and ignite. Shake the pan until the flames die down. Add the wine and let the liquid in the pan reduce until the pan is almost dry. Turn the heat to low.

8. Quickly remove the pieces of lobster and place, shell side down, on warm plates. I like to "reconstruct" the lobster so that it looks similar to a split lobster. Arrange the claws so that they lean into the center of the lobster.

9. Return the pan to the heat and add the butter, chervil and chives. Swirl or stir the butter in the pan to create a creamy sauce with the pan juices. Season to taste with salt and pepper. Use very little salt, if any, because the lobster adds its own salt. Spoon the sauce over the lobster pieces (see photograph insert following page 50) and serve at once.

Serves 2 as a generous main course or 4 as a light meal or first course

COOK'S NOTE: *In my restaurant I used to serve the claw and knuckle meat out of the shell to make it easier for my guests to eat lobster in a more formal atmosphere. I do not bother with this extra step when I serve lobster at home, but if you would like to, here's how to do it: Have a small pot of boiling salted water ready and waiting. Also have ready a bowl of ice water large enough to hold the claws. Quarter the lobsters as indicated in step 1, but do not crack the claws. Instead, submerge the claws in the boiling water. Cook for exactly 3 minutes. Using tongs, remove the claws from the boiling water and place in the ice water. Crack the claws and knuckles and remove the meat (diagrams 11 and 12, page 37). Proceed with searing the lobster pieces (step 3), omitting the claws and knuckles. Add the meat from the claws and knuckles to the pan at the same time you add the tomalley, right before it goes into the oven. Follow the rest of the recipe as instructed. When presenting the dish, arrange the meat from the claws and knuckles in the cavity of the carcass.*

Pan-Roasted Lobster with Garlic, Lemon & Olive Oil

I love the simple, light flavors of this dish and would be hard-pressed to choose between it and its buttery cousin. The beautiful aromatic taste of garlic is ruined when used to excess. Choose fresh, firm garlic and be cautious with it. You will need two kinds of olive oil for this dish: a clear refined oil for the initial searing and a green, fruity extra-virgin oil for finishing.

2 live 1¾-pound hard-shell lobsters
2 tablespoons olive oil
3 or 4 cloves garlic, peeled and chopped
¼ cup dry white wine
juice of ½ lemon

2 tablespoons extra-virgin olive oil (green)
2 tablespoons chopped fresh parsley
kosher or sea salt
freshly ground black pepper

Preheat the broiler or preheat the oven as hot as possible (500° to 550°F). Position the oven rack in the upper third of the oven. You may need to shorten the cooking time slightly if the broiler rack is close to the heat.

Prepare Jasper's Pan-Roasted Lobster with Chervil and Chives (page 46) through step 5, substituting olive oil for the peanut oil in the initial searing. The pan has now been taken out of the oven or broiler and is back on the stove at maximum heat.

Add the garlic to the fat in the pan and stir until it begins to brown lightly. Add the white wine and lemon juice. Let the liquid in the pan reduce until the pan is almost dry. Turn the heat to low.

Quickly remove the pieces of lobster and place, shell side down, on warm plates. Reconstruct the lobster so that it looks similar to a split lobster (see photograph insert following page 50). Arrange the claws so that they lean into the center of the lobster.

Return the pan to the stove and add the extra-virgin olive oil and parsley. Swirl or stir to combine with the pan juices. Season to taste with salt and pepper if needed. Remember: Lobster adds its own salt, and lemon brightens the flavor. Spoon the mixture over the lobster pieces and serve immediately.

Pan-Roasted Lobster with Saffron

Sear the lobster in 2 tablespoons olive oil. When the lobster is roasted and put back on the stove, add ¼ cup Savory Lobster Broth (page 54) or Quick Lobster Stock (page 57) and a pinch (¼ teaspoon) crumbled saffron threads.

Let the liquid in the pan reduce until the pan is almost dry. Remove the pieces of lobster and place them, shell side down, on warmed plates. Add 2 tablespoons unsalted butter or extra-virgin olive oil to the pan. Season lightly with salt and pepper and spoon the sauce over the lobster pieces.

Pan-Roasted Lobster with Fresh Tomato & Mint or Basil

Score 2 ripe medium tomatoes (about 12 ounces) with a paring knife. Drop into boiling water for about 30 seconds until the skins loosen. Cool the tomatoes in ice water and peel them. Quarter the tomatoes. Cut out the juicy center and place in a strainer. Push the "guts" through the strainer; you should get ¼ cup fresh tomato juice. Cut the tomato flesh into ½-inch dice. Sear the lobster in 2 tablespoons olive oil. When the lobster is roasted and put back on the stove, add the diced tomatoes, juice and 2 tablespoons chopped fresh mint or basil leaves. Simmer for 2 minutes. Quickly remove the pieces of lobster and place, shell side down, on warmed plates. When the sauce has thickened, finish with 2 tablespoons unsalted butter or extra-virgin olive oil. Season lightly with salt and pepper and spoon over the lobster pieces.

Pan-Roasted Lobster with Ginger, Scallions & Butter

The idea for this variation came from my friend Bic Ng, who tells me that many Chinese like butter with the classic ginger and scallion combination for lobster.

Sear the lobster in 2 tablespoons peanut oil. When the lobster is roasted and put back on the stove, add 2 teaspoons finely chopped fresh ginger and 3 thinly sliced scallions to the pan. Stir. Add ¼ cup Chinese cooking wine or sake. Mix well and cook for a few minutes until the pan is almost dry. Quickly remove the pieces of lobster from the pan and place them, shell side down, on warmed plates. Add 2 tablespoons unsalted butter to the pan. Season lightly with salt and pepper and spoon the sauce over the lobster.

Pan-Roasted Lobster with Citrus

Sear the lobster in 2 tablespoons olive oil. When the lobster is roasted and put back on the stove, add ½ thinly sliced sweet or red onion (3 ounces), 1 teaspoon very thinly sliced or grated lemon zest and 1 teaspoon very thinly sliced or grated orange zest. Stir and let cook for 1 minute. Add the juices of 1 large orange and ½ lemon (should equal about ⅓ cup) and 1 teaspoon chili oil. Let the liquid reduce until the pan is almost dry. Quickly remove the pieces of lobster from the pan and place them, shell side down, on warmed plates. Add 2 tablespoons unsalted butter to the pan. Season lightly with salt and pepper and spoon the sauce over the lobster. (Chili oil is sold in Asian markets and specialty-food shops.)

Pan-Roasted Lobster with Herbs & Garlic

Finely chop a mixture of fresh herbs, such as parsley, chives, savory, chervil, tarragon and thyme. Go easy on the tarragon and thyme—they are potent. You will need a total of ¼ cup. Sear the lobster in 2 tablespoons clarified butter or peanut oil. When the lobster is roasted and put back on the stove, add 1 teaspoon chopped garlic and stir. Add ¼ cup dry white wine and the fresh herbs. Cook until the pan is almost dry. Quickly remove the pieces of lobster from the pan and place them, shell side down, on warmed plates. Add 2 tablespoons unsalted butter to the pan. Season lightly with salt and pepper and spoon the sauce over the lobster.

Pan-Roasted Lobster with Roasted Pepper Puree

Roast 1 small red bell pepper over a gas flame until charred on all sides. Place in a paper bag for a few minutes, then peel and seed. Puree it in a blender or food processor; you should get about ½ cup. Sear the lobster in 2 tablespoons olive oil. When the lobster is roasted and put back on the stove, add 2 tablespoons dry white wine, 2 tablespoons chopped fresh parsley and the roasted pepper puree. Simmer the lobster in this mixture for a minute. Quickly remove the pieces of lobster from the pan and place, shell side down, on warmed plates. Add 2 tablespoons unsalted butter to the pan. Season lightly with salt and pepper and spoon the sauce over the lobster.

Removing Steamed Lobster (page 31)

Steamed Lobster (page 31), family style

Jasper's Pan-Roasted Lobster with Chervil & Chives (page 46)

Lobster & Corn Chowder (page 74) with common crackers (page 75)

Lobster Pizza (page 90)

Avocado & Lobster Salad with Toasted Almonds (page 143)

Lobster Potpie (page 164)

Lobster Pad Thai (page 204)

CHAPTER 3

Soups, Broths, Chowders & a Bisque

LOBSTER IN ITS liquid form . . . nothing stirs the soul and satisfies the spirit like an aromatic bowl of lobster soup, warm like the sun and briny like the sea. It's as if the liquid goes straight to your heart. Lobster soups have unique and deeply intense flavors that emerge after long, slow cooking, usually of the carcasses and shells. Soups seldom have lobster meat in them except as a garnish, and so they are the most economical way to serve this wonderfully versatile creature. Because of the cool climate in New England, soups and chowders are always well received. In many cases, soups like minestrone, stew and chowder are served as the main dish, not just as starters. A big pot of soup with some crusty bread or buttery crackers is a great way to feed family and friends. You can prepare it ahead of time so that you can savor the homey, nurturing flavors with your guests.

After you have been bombarded with pages of possibilities, I hope you will understand how simple it is to turn a great broth or stock into a great soup. After you try a few of these ideas and have become a skilled soup cook, you need only glance at the ingredient list. Use what you have available on any given day, substituting different ingredients freely, to create delicious and satisfying soups. Have fun!

Traditional Lobster Stew

The British have a wonderful expression for what we Americans call comfort food. They call their most traditional dishes nursery food. To many New Englanders, especially those from Down East Maine, lobster stew, probably the most popular dish in lobster land, goes a step beyond nursery food—it is mother's milk! *Down Easterners rarely partake in the tourist ritual of "ripping and dipping" whole lobsters. For many of them, lobster is something you sell, not something you eat. But when they do sit down to eat lobster at home, stew is what they want.*

Lobster stew, the only recipe in this chapter that uses lobster meat instead of carcasses for its flavor, is a deceptively simple soup. Keep a very close watch when making it, cooking it ever so gently and adding each ingredient at exactly the right moment. The sitting time is crucial: When the recipe calls for you to remove the stew from the heat and let it sit, take heed! The stew is best when made with a few female lobsters. The tiny bits of roe lend an exquisitely subtle flavor and also look stunning floating in the soup. Always use the best butter and freshest *whole* milk you can find; 2 percent or less will curdle, and the few extra calories is a small price to pay for the heavenly flavor of a traditional stew.

4 live 1-pound chicken lobsters, or equivalent weight of other lobsters	freshly ground black pepper
4 tablespoons unsalted butter	5 cups whole milk
1 teaspoon Hungarian paprika	kosher or sea salt
	snipped chives to finish

1. Parboil the lobsters, following the instructions on page 30. Using tongs, remove the lobsters to a pan or platter and let cool to room temperature. When cool enough to handle, remove the meat from the tails, knuckles and claws, reserving any liquid from the lobsters. Cut the meat into ¾-inch chunks. Remove the roe from the female lobsters, coarsely chop it and add it to the lobster meat. You may also pick the meat from the carcasses and the walking legs; otherwise, wrap and freeze them for later use.

2. About 1 hour before you wish to serve the stew, drain the chunks of lobster so that they are somewhat dry, reserving the juice. Over medium heat, warm a 10- or 12-inch skillet or sauté pan with 2- to 3-inch sides (you want lots of surface area). Melt the butter in the pan. When it is gently bubbling, add the lobster meat with the roe and sizzle gently for about 1 minute. Using tongs, turn the pieces over and cook for 1 minute more. The butter will now have a red color. Sprinkle with the paprika and grind a little fresh pepper over as well. Reduce the heat to low. Stir and cook for 1 minute more.

3. Pour the milk over the lobster and add any lobster juice. Let it heat up slowly for 5 to 6 minutes until the stew is hot but not quite boiling. *Do not boil!* Remove from the heat and let sit for a minimum of 30 minutes. The sitting time is crucial, for it allows the flavors to expand and the stew to transform itself from good to great. If the stew must sit for longer than 1 hour, cover and refrigerate it to retard the growth of bacteria.

4. When ready to serve, return the stew to low heat. Taste and season again with pepper and a little salt if needed. When the stew is very hot but not boiling, ladle it into warmed cups or bowls and sprinkle with chives. The lobster stew will be a pale pink color, with rosy chunks of lobster and little red dots of butter and roe. Serve at once. Keep it simple: Buttered and toasted common crackers (page 75) are great, as are warm biscuits or good country bread.

Makes about 7 cups; serves 8 as a starter or 4 as a main course

Savory Lobster Broth
A RECIPE OF MAJOR IMPORTANCE

The exquisite flavor and fragrant aroma of this broth comes from roasting lobster carcasses and simmering them with caramelized vegetables, wine, tomatoes, herbs and spices. The flavor is slightly reminiscent of the classic French fish soup soupe de poissons *but has a more pronounced lobster taste and is not as thick. Powerful on the first sip, it gradually softens with lingering layers of complex flavors. Like raw oysters, this broth enlivens the palate and gives you a surge of energy. It serves as the base for many other dishes made with fish and shellfish, such as Lobster and Cod Braised with Leeks and Mushrooms in a Savory Broth (page 179); it can make a quick sauce for pasta, such as Lobster Ravioli (page 116); and it is the foundation for more serious sauces such as Lobster Thermidor (page 172).*

For the home cook, this broth takes more time than effort. Like other stocks and broths, once you put it together, it is simply a matter of being at home while it cooks. This recipe makes approximately 5 quarts; you may halve the recipe if desired, but it will reduce faster and yield a little less broth.

This recipe can be made with the carcasses from lobsters weighing 1 to 3 pounds. Carcasses from larger lobsters will take longer to cook in order to extract their full flavor, but the flavors will be the same whatever the size you use.

Equipment: You will need a medium Chinese cleaver or large chef's knife, a large stockpot (at least 12 quarts), a roasting pan or baking sheet and a china cap or strainer.

8 small or 4 to 6 medium lobster carcasses, 2½ to 3 pounds total

2 tablespoons plus ¼ cup olive oil (not extra-virgin)

8 to 10 cloves garlic, sliced

3 or 4 medium onions (1½ pounds), coarsely chopped

3 or 4 medium carrots (8 ounces), peeled and coarsely chopped

1 small bulb fennel (8 ounces), coarsely chopped (*optional;* not available in early summer)

5 quarts water, plus a little more for deglazing

1 bottle (750 milliliters) dry white wine

3 or 4 ribs celery (8 ounces), coarsely chopped

1 can (28 ounces) good-quality Italian plum tomatoes

2 tablespoons whole black peppercorns

1 teaspoon Spanish saffron threads

½ to 1 teaspoon dried red pepper flakes

2 bay leaves

4 sprigs fresh thyme

6 sprigs fresh tarragon

kosher or sea salt

freshly ground black pepper

1. Preheat the oven to 400°F.

2. With a cleaver or chef's knife, split the lobster carcasses in half lengthwise and remove the head sacs and half of the tomalley. If using the carcasses of large lobsters, split them again to quarter them. Place the carcasses, shell side up, in a large roasting pan or on a baking sheet and drizzle 2 tablespoons olive oil over all. Place in the oven and roast for about 45 minutes, turning the pieces over halfway through the roasting. The roasted carcasses will be brittle and slightly browned (even a little charred) and will release a heavy, sweet smell.

3. Pour the remaining ¼ cup olive oil in a 12-inch sauté pan over medium heat. Add the garlic, onions, carrots and fennel to the pan and cook without stirring for 5 minutes. Then stir every 3 or 4 minutes to prevent sticking for about 20 minutes until the vegetables are well browned. Place in the stockpot. Deglaze the pan with a little water and add to the pot as well.

4. Combine the 5 quarts water and the wine in the pot with the browned vegetables. Add the celery. Break the tomatoes into pieces using your hands or a fork and add to the pot. Bring to a boil, then reduce the heat for a steady simmer.

5. Add the roasted lobster carcasses to the pot. Deglaze the roasting pan with a little water, scraping the little browned bits from the bottom of the pan. Add to the pot.

6. Skim the foam from the top of the broth if necessary and add the peppercorns, saffron threads, red pepper, bay leaves, thyme and tarragon. Lobster broth should not simmer as slowly as chicken stock. Look for a steady bubbling but not a rolling boil. It takes this more aggressive simmer to extract the full flavor of the broth. Simmer for 1½ to 2 hours, stirring occasionally. After 1 hour, lightly salt the broth and begin periodic tastings at intervals of 10 minutes. It should taste rich and savory with a distinct flavor of lobster and subtle underlying flavors of the other ingredients.

7. Strain the broth and season to taste with salt and pepper. Use a ladle to remove some of the oil that settles on top, but do not remove all of it because it has great flavor and character. Cover and chill the broth until needed. Refrigerated, it will keep well for 2 to 3 days. It can be frozen for up to 4 weeks.

Makes 5 quarts

ABOUT LOBSTER STOCK

With the exception of Traditional Lobster Stew (page 52), every recipe in this chapter calls for a slow simmering of lobster carcasses in water and other liquids with vegetables, herbs and spices. Although the stocks and broths will differ, they should always be kept at a steady simmer, never at a boil. After the stock cooks for an hour, I add a small amount of salt and take the first of many tastes. It is important to taste frequently—once every ten minutes after the initial hour of cooking. If at any point you do not notice an improvement (stronger flavor), then it is time to remove the stock from the heat. If at any point you begin to notice a slight bitterness, then it is time to remove the stock from the heat. And if you detect a darkening of the color after the initial hour of cooking, remove the stock from the heat. Overcooking can be as damaging as undercooking.

Making lobster stock is not a precise process. There are several variables. The first is cooking temperature. Higher heat causes the liquid to reduce faster, resulting in less stock. The second is ingredients. Some release a lot of liquid and others absorb a great deal, adding to the puzzle. And third, there is the pot. Tall, narrow pots yield a greater amount of stock than wide pots. As long as you are aware of these variables, you can make the stock as strong and as tasty as you'd like. And one last word of advice: If you come up short, just add water.

ABOUT DOUBLING RECIPES

To double any soup recipe in this book, double all the ingredients *except* the water. Because larger batches take more time to reduce, too much water at the beginning will result in a weak-tasting stock. What could be worse after taking all the time to make it? Here is my foolproof formula for doubling: Start with slightly less liquid than the amount called for in each recipe. For example, if the stock recipe calls for 8 cups water, add only 7 cups for each recipe to double it—that is, 14 cups in total. Watch the process closely by tasting along the way and adding a little more water during the cooking if you think the stock needs it. It is better to have less of a very strong stock, because you can always add water to it, than more of a weak stock.

Quick Lobster Stock

This stock is the "made easy" version of Savory Lobster Broth and can be used as a substitute for the broth in many recipes in this book. Unlike the Savory Lobster Broth, this stock is made in one easy step. Though it lacks the intensity and deep complex flavors of the broth, it is nonetheless very tasty and quite useful in many preparations. White wine and saffron are both optional in this recipe. For more savory preparations like risotto, you may wish to add them. For simpler dishes like potpie or succotash, they are not necessary.

5 medium lobster carcasses, 2 pounds total

1 can (14.5 ounces) good-quality Italian plum tomatoes with their juice

1 cup dry white wine or water

2 medium onions (6 to 8 ounces), cut into ½-inch dice

2 ribs celery (2 to 3 ounces), cut into ½-inch dice

2 small carrots, (2 ounces) peeled and thinly sliced

5 cloves garlic, crushed

¼ teaspoon fennel seeds

¼ teaspoon dried red pepper flakes

1 teaspoon whole black peppercorns

4 sprigs fresh thyme, or ½ teaspoon dried thyme

½ teaspoon saffron (optional)

kosher or sea salt

1. With a medium Chinese cleaver or large chef's knife, split the lobster carcasses in half lengthwise and remove the head sacs and half of the tomalley. (Freeze the excess tomalley for future use or discard.) Place the carcasses in an 8- to 10-quart stockpot and cover with 3 quarts water. Bring to a boil, then reduce the heat for a steady simmer, not a rolling boil. Using a ladle, skim any white foam from the top.

2. Add the tomatoes, wine, onions, celery, carrots, garlic, fennel, red pepper, peppercorns, thyme and saffron. Continue to simmer for 1 hour, then lightly salt the stock and taste for a rich lobster flavor. If it seems light, cook it for up to 20 minutes more.

3. Strain the stock, then cover and chill as quickly as possible. If you are not going to use it all, it will keep well for 2 to 3 days in the refrigerator. It can be frozen for up to 4 weeks.

Makes 2 quarts

IDEAS FOR VARIOUS SOUPS MADE FROM LOBSTER BROTH

Once you have made a batch of Savory Lobster Broth, you possess the basis for a variety of soups. It is magical how easily lobster broth can be turned into one of our treasured favorites, such as noodle soup, vegetable and rice and minestrone, adding an elegant dimension to familiar flavors. Many of the classic French garnishes for consommé, such as celestine (julienne crêpes), brunoise (finely diced vegetables) and *vert pré* (tapioca, peas and green beans), blend splendidly with this broth. Asian ingredients, such as rice noodles, dried mushrooms, bok choy, bean sprouts and Chinese cabbage, can also be added to create wonderfully intriguing soups. The flavor of lobster broth is equally splendid when used as the predominant flavor or when it plays a lesser role to other full-flavored ingredients.

The following ingredients are recommended for Savory Lobster Broth. The recipes that accompany these recommendations are intended to serve as a guideline for creating your own uniquely delicious soups, using my broth as a base. Any of these soups may be enhanced with a garnish of diced lobster meat, but it is optional. The soup will be so good without the garnish that you will not even miss it.

VEGETABLES

You can make vegetable soup year-round with vegetables that reflect the season. In spring use peas, asparagus, fava beans, scallions, spinach, fiddlehead ferns and more. In summer use tomatoes, corn, peppers, green beans, carrots, summer squash, new potatoes and too many others to list. In autumn try leeks, shell beans, pumpkins, celery root, fennel, Swiss chard and other greens. And in winter, cabbage, onions, stored roots and squash are great. Leafy green vegetables, such as spinach and Swiss chard, are best when blanched separately in boiling salted water, then cooled, drained and chopped before adding to the broth toward the end of the cooking process. Starches such as pasta, dried beans and rice are great additions to vegetable soups as well.

Lobster Broth with Vegetables

2 tablespoons unsalted butter or olive oil
1½ cups diced (½ inch) mixed vegetables
3 cups Savory Lobster Broth (page 54)
½ cup coarsely chopped cooked greens, such as spinach or Swiss chard

1 lemon wedge
kosher or sea salt
freshly ground black pepper

1. In a medium saucepan (2 to 3 quarts), combine the butter and diced vegetables. Over medium heat, gently sauté the vegetables for 6 to 8 minutes until softened but not browned.

2. Add the lobster broth and bring it to a slow simmer. Simmer for 10 minutes. Add the cooked greens and simmer for 2 minutes. Squeeze the juice from the lemon wedge into the soup and season to taste with salt and pepper. Serve in warmed soup cups.

Serves 4

VARIATION

Increase the diced vegetables to 2 cups and omit the cooked greens.

Mushrooms

For lovers of mushrooms, a simple but extremely potent autumn soup can be made by sautéing any type of mushroom briefly, then simmering with lobster broth. Leeks, shallots and various onions and scallions in small quantities are all perfect companions to mushrooms served in broth. They should also be sautéed before being added to the soup (with the exception of scallions, which should be added directly to the broth in the last minute of cooking). The character of the soup will vary according to the variety or mixture of mushrooms used. Mild-flavored cultivated mushrooms will highlight a strong lobster flavor. Chanterelles or other deep-flavored mushrooms will dominate the flavors.

Cultivated mushrooms

Button type, shiitake and pleurottes (oyster mushrooms) are the ones I use most often. I avoid cremini, Roman, trumpets and other dark mushrooms because they tend to turn the broth an unpleasant grayish color.

Wild mushrooms

Chanterelles are my favorite. Avoid the similar-looking *pied de mouton* (lamb's foot) because the fuzzy underside of the cap tends to come loose in the soup, giving it a swampy appearance. Other delicious wild mushrooms are cèpes (porcini), morels, matsutaki and hen-of-the-woods. Every once in a while, Benjamin Maleson (my wild-mushroom man) will bring in a few lobster mushrooms, a thick, white tree-type mushroom with a brilliant red-orange cap. It is always great to pair them with lobster, not only for the play on words but for the mushrooms' wonderful contrast of flavor and color. Experts recommend that wild mushrooms be cooked for at least fifteen minutes.

Lobster Broth with Mushrooms

2 tablespoons unsalted butter	3 cups Savory Lobster Broth (page 54)
¼ cup finely diced shallots, leek or onion	1 tablespoon chopped Italian parsley
6 ounces fresh mushrooms, one type or mixed, thinly sliced	kosher or sea salt
	freshly ground black pepper

1. In a medium saucepan (2 to 3 quarts), combine the butter and shallots and sauté over medium heat for 1 minute. Add the mushrooms and continue to sauté until the mushrooms are softened, about 5 minutes.

2. Add the lobster broth and bring it to a slow simmer. Simmer for 10 minutes (15 minutes if using wild mushrooms). Add the parsley and season to taste with salt and pepper. Serve in warmed soup cups.

Serves 4

Truffles

Truffles and lobster have long been intimately paired in both classic and contemporary French cooking. The thought of lobster broth served with elegantly thin slices of white or black truffle and lobster meat brings heaven to mind. A less expensive way to enjoy this combination is to drizzle a little white truffle oil into the hot broth.

Lobster Broth with Truffles & Lobster

1 live 1-pound chicken lobster

3½ cups Savory Lobster Broth (page 54)

2 tablespoons unsalted butter

1 ounce fresh truffle (white or black), peeled and thinly sliced

kosher or sea salt

freshly ground black pepper

1 tablespoon finely minced fresh chives

1. Parboil the lobster (page 30). Let cool to room temperature. Remove the meat from the tail, knuckles and claws and cut into thin slices. Save the carcass for another use.

2. In a small pot, heat the lobster broth until hot but not boiling. In a medium saucepan (2 to 3 quarts), combine the butter and truffle and sauté over very low heat for 2 minutes. Add the lobster and sauté for 2 minutes. Be careful not to break the truffle slices. Pour the hot broth over the truffle and lobster and simmer for 1 minute more. Season to taste with salt and pepper and sprinkle with the minced chives. Serve in warmed soup cups.

Serves 4

Seafood

The most appropriate seafood garnish for lobster broth is, of course, freshly cooked lobster meat. The briny-sweet flavor of the meat, used in small quantities or large, in small dice or big chunks, contrasts with and complements the intense flavor of the broth. Add it to any of the variations for delicious results, but do not go overboard—the broth speaks for itself. Lobster broth makes an excellent steaming liquid for shellfish. The broth lets the bivalves add just enough fullness of flavor to the "new" broth that cannot be achieved by the bivalves on their own. Try serving a heaping bowl of steamed shellfish, such as clams, scallops (in their shell) or mussels, in lobster broth with large slices of crunchy garlic toast. It's a knockout! Only oysters are not taken to a new level by this broth.

Lobster Broth with Clams & Mussels

2 tablespoons olive oil

½ medium carrot (2 ounces), peeled and cut into thin 1-inch julienne

1 small leek (white and light green parts only), cut into thin 1-inch julienne

2½ cups Savory Lobster Broth (page 54)

12 littleneck clams, scrubbed and rinsed

1 pound medium mussels (about 16), de-bearded, scrubbed and rinsed

freshly ground black pepper

1 tablespoon chopped Italian parsley

1. Place a 12-inch sauté pan or straight-sided skillet over medium heat. Add the olive oil and carrot and sauté for 1 minute. Add the leek and sauté for 2 to 3 minutes until the leek begins to soften.

2. Add the lobster broth, clams and mussels. Turn the heat to high and bring to a boil. As soon as the broth boils, place the lid over the pan, lower the heat to medium and let the shellfish cook for 5 minutes. After 5 minutes, the mussels and clams should open. If not, cook for 1 to 2 minutes more.

3. Remove the pan from the heat and, using tongs, divide the clams and mussels equally among 4 soup plates or bowls (3 clams and 4 mussels each). Return the broth to the heat and season with black pepper. Salt will not be needed. Stir in the parsley and ladle the hot broth over the shellfish. Serve at once.

Serves 4

Rice and Other Grains

River rice, converted rice, basmati rice, brown rice and wild rice all work well as a garnish in soup. The starchier rices, Italian (Arborio) and Asian (rose and Chinese), are not as suitable because they tend to thicken the soup as it sits. In most cases, rice is best used in small quantities, about ½ cup cooked rice for every 2 cups broth, and with other vegetables. The following recipe demonstrates a balance of rice and vegetables that is both tasty and filling. Couscous, barley and tapioca are all suitable in small quantities as soup garnish. Tapioca has a special affinity for soup. Not only is it an unexpected surprise but its texture and neutral flavor work beautifully with the intense broth. Fully cook all rice and other grains, using the method appropriate for that grain, before adding it to the lobster broth.

Lobster Broth with Vegetables & Rice

½ cup converted rice

1¼ cups water

1½ tablespoons unsalted butter

½ medium carrot (2 ounces), peeled and finely diced

½ small leek (white and light green parts only), finely diced

2 ounces fresh shiitake mushrooms, stems removed and finely diced

3 cups Savory Lobster Broth (page 54)

2 ounces cooked lobster meat, finely diced (optional)

1 tablespoon chopped Italian parsley

kosher or sea salt

freshly ground black pepper

1. In a small saucepan (4 cups), combine the rice and water. Bring to a boil, then lower the heat so that the rice simmers. Cover and cook for 20 minutes. Remove from the heat and let cool without stirring. Drain if any liquid remains.

2. In a medium saucepan (2 to 3 quarts), heat the butter. Add the carrot, leek and mushrooms and sauté over medium heat for about 5 minutes until the vegetables are softened but not browned. Add the lobster broth and turn up the heat. Simmer the soup for 5 minutes. Add the cooked rice and simmer for 5 minutes more. Stir in the lobster meat and parsley, and season with salt and pepper. Divide the soup evenly among 4 bowls and serve at once.

Serves 4

Pasta

Soups made with pasta are found in abundance in both Eastern and Western cooking, and no wonder: Noodles and other pastas take on a life of their own when served in broth. Always cook pasta in boiling salted water and drain well. Cook the pasta al dente—firm to the bite. The time will vary according to shape and size. Add to the soup toward the end of cooking. In some instances, such as the recipe that follows, the noodles are placed directly in the bowl and the broth is ladled over them. Figure on 6 to 8 ounces dried pasta for 4 cups broth. When using fresh pasta, use about 12 ounces pasta for every 4 cups broth.

For soup, I prefer the very thin fresh Chinese egg noodles from Hoy Toy Noodle Company in Boston's Chinatown. More readily available and also excellent is angel-hair pasta, or capellini. Believe it or not, I find the Prince brand best for this soup. It is a little thicker and keeps its texture better than the imported *capelli d'angelo*.

Lobster Broth with Angel-Hair Pasta

2½ cups Savory Lobster Broth (page 54)

2 ripe medium to large plum tomatoes (5 ounces), peeled, seeded and finely diced, or ½ cup good-quality canned tomatoes, finely chopped

6 ounces angel-hair or other pasta

4 scallions, thinly sliced

2 ounces cooked lobster meat, finely diced (optional)

kosher or sea salt

freshly ground black pepper

4 heaping tablespoons grated Parmigiano-Reggiano cheese

1. Heat the lobster broth and diced tomatoes in a small saucepan (4 cups) over low heat until hot.

2. Meanwhile, bring a 4-quart pot of salted water to a rolling boil. Add the pasta to the boiling water. Angel-hair will take 2 to 4 minutes, depending on the brand. One minute before the pasta is ready, add the scallions and lobster meat to the broth. Season lightly with salt and generously with pepper.

3. Drain the pasta very well and divide evenly among 4 warmed soup plates. Using tongs, try to lift the noodles so that they form a little stack in the middle of the bowl. Ladle the hot broth around the noodles and sprinkle with the cheese. Serve at once.

Serves 4

Lobster Minestrone

I created this recipe for the wedding of my sous-chef, Melanie Coiro. I wanted to pay homage to her Italian ancestry with a lobster soup. Lobster minestrone is a festive main course with bowls of freshly grated Parmigiano-Reggiano and crusty Italian bread passed at the table. It also makes a dazzling starter, provided the portions are small and the rest of the menu is light. Save this dish for those times when you need a hearty all-in-one main course for a houseful of family or friends.

The vegetables need not be cut uniformly but should be fairly close in size so that they cook evenly. The style of the dice should be *paysanne.* Prepare all ingredients before starting the soup. The actual cooking time is under one hour.

8 ounces dried cannellini, white lima or other large white beans

3 ounces meaty salt pork (such as Smithfield or Gwaltney) or pancetta, cut into ¼-inch dice

3 tablespoons good-quality olive oil

5 cloves garlic, chopped

1½ to 2 medium onions (12 ounces), cut into ½- to ¾-inch dice

2 to 3 carrots (6 ounces), peeled and cut into ½- to ¾-inch dice

2 to 3 ribs celery (4 ounces), cut into ½- to ¾-inch dice

2 quarts Savory Lobster Broth (page 54) or Quick Lobster Stock (page 57)

1 large Maine or other all-purpose potato (8 ounces), peeled and cut into ½- to ¾-inch dice

¼ head Savoy cabbage (6 ounces), shredded

1 small zucchini (4 ounces), cut into ½- to ¾-inch dice

10 ounces ripe plum tomatoes, peeled, seeded and cut into ½- to ¾-inch dice, or substitute good-quality canned plum tomatoes

8 basil leaves, chopped

½ bunch green Swiss chard or spinach (4 ounces), stems removed, leaves blanched and coarsely chopped

8 ounces cooked lobster meat, cut into ½- to ¾-inch dice

kosher or sea salt

freshly ground black pepper

grated Parmigiano-Reggiano cheese

crusty Italian bread

1. Soak the beans in water overnight. If this is not possible, go ahead and use them as they are (dry). Simmer the beans in unsalted water until very tender but not falling apart, then drain. Reserve half of the best unbroken beans and mash the remaining beans or pass through a food mill.

2. In a large heavy soup pot (8 quarts), fry the salt pork in the olive oil over medium heat for about 5 minutes until crisp and light brown. Add the garlic and stir well for about

30 seconds until it begins to pick up a golden color. Add the onions, carrots and celery and cook, stirring often, for 6 to 8 minutes until the vegetables are tender.

3. Add the lobster broth, bean puree, potato and Savoy cabbage. Stir until the bean puree is dissolved. Bring the mixture to a boil. Lower the heat and simmer for 8 to 10 minutes until the potatoes begin to soften.

4. Add the zucchini, tomatoes, basil and cooked whole beans. Simmer for 10 minutes more. Remove from the heat.

5. When ready to serve, heat the soup to a near boil. Stir in the Swiss chard and lobster and simmer for 5 minutes. Season to taste with salt and pepper. Serve in large soup plates or bowls. Sprinkle lightly with grated cheese and serve extra grated cheese in small bowls. Good Italian bread is needed to complete this one-pot meal.

Makes about 6 quarts; serves 10 to 12 as a main course

COOK'S NOTE: *Minestrone traditionally uses dried white cannellini beans, but I prefer A-1 dried white limas from Maine. These big, creamy beans are available throughout New England. Another difference here is that my minestrone gets most of its flavor from the lobster broth, so the recipe does not include a lot of herbs, spices or seasoning. Exact amounts of ingredients are not crucial for this hearty, peasant-style soup, but stick fairly close to my guidelines. A bit of extra celery, carrot or Swiss chard will not change its character, but be frugal with the cabbage—too much can overpower the soup. Other ingredients such as green beans (4 ounces cooked and diced) or pasta (6 ounces cooked macaroni or tube-shaped pasta) may also be added.*

CHOWDERS

The origin of chowder, a thick stew that evokes the salty air of New England more than any other dish, is obscured by a haze of conflicting stories and a lack of sound historical data. The name most certainly derives from one of three French words: *chaudière,* a forged kettle brought to the New World by French fishermen and trappers; *chaudron,* the French word for cauldron; or *faire la chaudière,* a fish soup from Brittany. The *faire la chaudière,* regrettably no longer in existence, was a community undertaking in which fishermen from an entire village contributed to the pot and took home a portion of the finished soup. Imagine what a wonderful affair it must have been! Despite the French origin of the name, there are no records of chowders being part of French or even English cuisine, and they most certainly evolved on fishing vessels and in the coastal villages of New England and Canada.

The oldest chowder recipe on record was published by *The Boston Evening Post* on September 23, 1751. It was a dish layered with salt pork, fish and crackers. The liquid used in early chowder recipes was water and occasionally cider or red wine. Potatoes found their way into chowders in the early 1800s, and milk was added in the late 1800s. The earliest chowders were made with fresh, smoked or dried fish. Cod, haddock and bass were preferred. Clam chowder and "farmhouse" chowders, made with corn, parsnips, eggs or even chickens, were later adaptations. There is no true or classic chowder. It is a dish that continues to evolve, a fact that I find comforting, since I have taken my share of liberties with it. In fact, thickened clam chowder, which is now thought of as the standard, was created by Howard Johnson's restaurant chain in the 1940s and bears little resemblance to the dish from which it evolved. What distinguishes a chowder for me is not so much the specific ingredients used, but how they are presented. Chowder is a one-pot meal, more like a stew than a soup. The best chowders are briny-sweet, chunky and hearty, tasting like the sea. If you make chowder with this in mind, you will be halfway there. Success is guaranteed.

Chowder is the sum of its ingredients, with every flavor playing an equal part. When all the ingredients are top-notch, the flavor is exquisite. I have been making chowders for years, refining a technique I first learned in 1978 from Chef Bob Redmond at the Copley Plaza in Boston. I have a passion for this dish and since learning Bob's technique have made it almost daily with every kind of seafood, in batches for four to four hundred. I adore creamy New England–style chowders but also love the Rhode Island (Portuguese) style, made with tomatoes, and the unusual Bermudian Chowder, in which fish is simmered for hours in beef broth with tomatoes, vegetables and spices, then finished with dark rum and "sherry peppers."

A dinner of chowder should start with raw shellfish or another light appetizer, such as marinated vegetables, and a green salad. Follow with the chowder in large shallow soup plates with chunks of vegetables and lobster sticking up out of the broth. This charming presentation is accomplished by first using a slotted spoon to remove lobster and vegetables from the chowder and mounding them in the center of the soup plate, then ladling the broth around. New Englanders usually eat toasted common crackers (page 75) with their chowder. Warm homemade Cream Biscuits (page 166) are also wonderful. So are cornmeal-based Sweet Corn Fritters (page 76). Another terrific side dish is Tomalley Toasts (page 88). Finish the meal with fresh fruit or melon in the summer and a fruit-based dessert the rest of the year.

SALT PORK VERSUS SMOKED BACON

Salt pork was an important staple for all Americans from colonial times through the early years of this century, and it is considered one of the ingredients that makes a chowder authentic. These days, however, it is almost impossible to find good-quality salt pork. The two brands I recommend are Smithfield and Gwaltney, available at most quality butcher shops. Because salt pork is so hard to find, there is a chance when you do find it that it may be old and not very good. Look for clear white fat and pink streaks of meat. Any yellow or brown discoloration is a sign of age and should be avoided. If you live near an Italian market, pancetta is an excellent substitute. A good country-style smoked slab bacon, such as Harrington's, is a more than adequate substitute and to my taste is superior to salt pork for lobster chowder. I love the way the smoky bacon and sweet lobster flavors combine.

Salt pork and bacon are best handled differently in chowders. When using salt pork, remove the cracklings (diced pork) from the pan once they are browned, leaving the fat to flavor the chowder. When the chowder is finished, reheat the cracklings and sprinkle on top. When using bacon, discard most of the fat after the diced bacon is browned but leave the bacon in the pot to simmer. This results in a deeper, milder smokiness that does not overpower the other chowder ingredients.

New England–Style Lobster Chowder

This traditional chowder is made with lobster, pork (salt pork or bacon), onions and potatoes but differs from New England church-supper-type recipes in that it is not made with milk. I learned long ago from Chef Bob Redmond at the Copley Plaza Hotel in Boston that the very best New England–style chowders are made with strong stock and cream, which give an intensity of flavor and a smoothness in texture that cannot be achieved with milk. This is the new "traditional" chowder, more closely resembling the chowder made with the fattier fresh farm milk of the past. Unlike milk-based chowder, stock-and-cream-based chowder almost never separates (curdles).

Although I am certainly no slave to tradition, I have never strayed from the idea of chowder as a one-pot meal, a stew, thick from its ingredients and not from a roux or other starches. The only starch here comes from the potatoes during cooking and the crumbled crackers that Yankees add to it at the table.

2 live 1-pound chicken lobsters	1 teaspoon Hungarian paprika
4 sprigs fresh thyme	1 pound Maine or other all-purpose pota-
1 teaspoon whole black peppercorns	toes, peeled and cut into ¾-inch dice
2 bay leaves	1 cup heavy cream
4 ounces slab country bacon	freshly ground black pepper
kosher or sea salt	about 2 tablespoons chopped fresh chives
2 tablespoons unsalted butter	and/or parsley for garnish
2 medium onions (10 ounces), cut into ¾-inch dice	

1. Parboil the lobsters (page 30). Let stand until cool enough to handle. Remove the meat from the tails, knuckles and claws. Cut into large (¾- to 1-inch) pieces, cover and refrigerate. Split the carcasses in half and discard the head sacs. Remove the roe if there is any, chop it and add it to the lobster meat. Leave about half of the tomalley in the body to flavor the stock. Reserve the rest for Tomalley Toasts (page 88) or discard. (Too much tomalley will make the broth bitter.) Place the shells and carcasses in a 6- to 8-quart pot and cover with 2 quarts water. Bring to a boil.

2. Meanwhile, pick the leaves off the thyme and add just the stems to the stock. Also add the peppercorns and bay leaves. Trim the rind from the bacon and add the rind to the stock. Cut the bacon into ½-inch dice. Turn down the heat and simmer for 1 hour. Lightly salt the stock and taste for strength. Simmer for up to 30 minutes more if needed. Strain the stock. You should have 3 to 4 cups.

3. Fry the bacon in a heavy 4-quart soup pot over medium heat until crisp and browned and most of the fat has been rendered. This will take about 8 minutes. Pour off all but 1 tablespoon fat, leaving the bacon in the pot. Add the butter, onions and thyme leaves. Cook over medium heat for 8 to 10 minutes until the onions are tender but not browned. Stir in the paprika. Add the potatoes and enough stock to cover them (about 3½ cups; add a little water if you do not have enough stock). Turn up the heat and boil for 15 to 20 minutes until the potatoes are tender. This hard cooking will break up some of the potatoes so that their starch is released and the chowder becomes slightly thickened. Remove the pot from the heat.

4. Add the lobster meat and heavy cream. Season with salt (very little will be needed) and pepper. Let the chowder sit off the heat for 30 minutes to 1 hour. If you let it sit longer than 1 hour, cover and refrigerate it. You can make this a day in advance if desired.

5. Reheat the chowder, check the seasoning and divide evenly among 4 large soup plates. Sprinkle with chives and serve at once.

Serves 4 as a main course or 8 to 10 as a starter

VARIATION

While this recipe calls for bacon, the same amount of salt pork (without the rind) may be substituted. Leave the fat in the pot and reduce the amount of butter by half.

Rhode Island (Portuguese-Style) Lobster Chowder

New Englanders, with their long-standing inferiority complex about New York (which probably stems from the Yankees–Red Sox rivalry), hate to concede that Manhattan has a chowder of its own. In New England, chowders made with tomato and no milk are referred to as Rhode Island or Portuguese style, never Manhattan. I believe this style of chowder originated in Rhode Island, but I do not begrudge New Yorkers their own chowder. Clams from the Harlem River were abundant in the 1800s. It is quite probable that Manhattan clam chowder descended from zuppa di vongole, a clam soup served in New York fish houses run by Neapolitans. However, Portuguese settlers who arrived in New England in the late 1700s did prepare a chowder with tomatoes and fish that was pickled, a preserving method popular with Portuguese fishermen. The rivalry is fun and the history interesting, but it does not mean much when you are hungry. Manhattan, Rhode Island or Portuguese, tomato-based chowders taste great.

This red chowder grew out of my experience at the Parker House in Boston. Chef Joe Ribas (Papa) always sat at the head of the large table set up in the kitchen for lunch. The menu there was distinctly Portuguese: fish-head stew, *caldo verde* (kale soup), *porco alentejana* (pork with clams) and a chowder similar to this one. Although I have taken the liberty of using lobster instead of the traditional clams or hake, I do use chorizo, a dry, garlicky, spicy Portuguese sausage. (See page 230 for mail-order information.) Portuguese linguica or Cajun andouille make fine substitutes. Like other chowders, this is best as a main course, served with crusty bread or toasted common crackers.

2 live 1-pound chicken lobsters

4 to 6 cloves garlic, about ½ head, finely chopped

1½ medium onions (10 ounces), cut into ½- to ¾-inch dice

2 medium ribs celery (4 ounces), strings removed, cut into ½- to ¾-inch dice

1 medium green bell pepper (4 ounces), cut into ½- to ¾-inch dice

3 cups Italian plum tomatoes with their juice

kosher or sea salt

2 tablespoons olive oil

2 bay leaves

4 whole allspice, crushed

¼ to ½ teaspoon dried red pepper flakes (optional)

2 medium Maine or other all-purpose potatoes (12 ounces), peeled and cut into ¾- to 1-inch dice

6 ounces chorizo, casing removed, sliced ¼ inch thick

4 sprigs cilantro, finely chopped with stems

freshly ground black pepper

4 sprigs Italian parsley, leaves picked and coarsely chopped

1. Parboil the lobsters (page 30). When the lobsters are cool enough to handle, remove the meat from the tails, knuckles and claws. Cut into large (¾- to 1-inch) pieces, cover and refrigerate. Split the carcasses in half and discard the head sacs. Remove the roe if there is any, chop it and add it to the lobster meat. Leave about half of the tomalley in the body to flavor the stock. Reserve the rest for Tomalley Toasts (page 88) or discard. (Too much tomalley will make the broth bitter.) Place the shells and carcasses in a 6- to 8-quart pot and cover with 2 quarts water. Bring to a boil.

2. Place all scraps from the chopped garlic, onions, celery and bell pepper in the stock.

3. Remove the tomatoes from their juice. Halve each one over the can so as not to lose any juice. Cut each tomato into ¾-inch dice. Add the juice to the pot with the lobster shells. Simmer the stock for 1 hour. Lightly salt the stock and taste for flavor. Taste again in 10 minutes. If it has not improved (become stronger), turn off the heat. If it is still improving, simmer for another 10 to 20 minutes. Strain the stock; you should have 4 cups. If not, add water to make a total of 4 cups.

4. Heat the olive oil with the bay leaves in a heavy 4-quart soup pot over medium heat until the bay leaves turn brown. Add the allspice, red pepper and garlic. Cook for 30 seconds to 1 minute until the garlic is golden brown. Add the onions, celery and bell pepper and cook for 8 to 10 minutes until the vegetables are tender but not browned. As soon as they start to pick up color, add the 4 cups stock.

5. Add the potatoes and tomatoes together and simmer for 15 minutes. Add the chorizo and simmer for 10 minutes more. Remove the pot from the heat and stir in the lobster meat and cilantro. Let the chowder sit off the heat for 30 minutes to 1 hour. If you let it sit longer than 1 hour, cover and refrigerate it. Season with pepper, and salt if needed (it probably will not need much salt because of the sausage). You can make this a day in advance if desired.

6. When ready to serve, heat it through quickly, stir in the parsley and serve in warmed cups or bowls with bread or common crackers (page 75) on the side.

Serves 4 as a main course or 8 to 10 as a first course

Lobster & Corn Chowder

This recipe, one of my signature dishes, has been featured on magazine covers and in many newspapers. I think its enormous appeal lies in that, for locals and visitors alike, it epitomizes summer in New England when, up and down the coast, summer lobsters and sweet corn are abundant. It is not chowder. It is a Martha's Vineyard, Boothbay Harbor, Point Judith, Glouces- ter and Block Island vacation in a bowl.

For this recipe I prefer yellow or bicolor varieties of corn, such as Earlivee, Sugar Buns, Tuxedo, Butter and Sugar, Clockwork, Pilot and Double Gem—all are varieties that thrive in New England. They hold up well to the long cooking that this recipe requires and make the soup more colorful. If you cannot find these varieties, do not worry; as long as you use sweet local corn, the chowder will be a success.

ingredients for 1 batch New England– Style Lobster Chowder (page 70)	2 large or 3 small ears fresh sweet corn

1. Follow the recipe for New England–Style Lobster Chowder, making the following two adjustments: Husk the corn and wipe away any silk. Cut the kernels from the cobs; you should have 1½ cups. Chop the cobs into 3 or 4 pieces. Add to the stock in step 2 and let simmer with the lobster shells the entire time.

2. Add the corn kernels at the same time you add the potatoes in step 3.

COMMON CRACKERS

Common crackers are a yeast-risen, flaky, round cracker, little known outside of New England. They taste similar to pilot biscuits or saltines (in other words, a little bland) but soak up the flavors of chowder wonderfully and are absolutely traditional. Common crackers have been sold commercially for nearly three hundred years. Because of this, almost no one knows how to make them at home. I tried to make them once, years ago, but for all the trouble it took, they were, frankly, not very good. New Englanders can find common crackers in most specialty stores and seafood markets; I have even seen them in supermarkets. If you live outside of New England, order common crackers by mail. I order mine from my friend Bob at the Vermont Country Store (page 230). Otherwise, serve homemade biscuits, fritters, oyster crackers, pilot crackers or saltines.

TO PREPARE COMMON CRACKERS FOR CHOWDER

Preheat the oven to 350°F. Use a paring knife to split the crackers in half. They will split easily; some may already have split by themselves. Spread each cracker half lightly with softened unsalted butter and line them up on a cookie or baking sheet. Bake for 10 to 12 minutes until the crackers are golden brown. Serve warm.

Sweet Corn Fritters

These crisp golden fritters, made with fresh sweet corn and cornmeal, are a perfect side dish for chowder. They are also great with boiled, steamed or grilled lobster and are delicious all by themselves as an appetizer or snack. Use any variety of sweet corn, although the yellow and bi-color varieties will make the fritters more colorful.

It will take about twenty minutes to fry the entire batch, so have a heated oven (200°F) ready to keep them warm. You can make great fritters with yellow cornmeal, but for authentic New England flavor, use real jonnycake meal (see page 230 for mail-order information), a stone-ground meal made from White Flint Indian corn.

Equipment: You will need a heavy saucepan 8 to 10 inches in diameter and 6 inches deep and a frying thermometer. If you have a FryDaddy or other deep fryer, here is your chance to use it. Form the fritters with an ordinary table or soup spoon or, best of all, a small ice-cream scoop. A wire mesh or slotted spoon is perfect for removing the fritters from the fat.

2 large or 3 small ears fresh sweet corn, husked	1 teaspoon kosher or sea salt
1 small red bell pepper (4 ounces), very finely diced	½ teaspoon freshly ground black pepper
	¼ teaspoon cayenne pepper
3 tablespoons unsalted butter	5 scallions (green and white parts), thinly sliced
1½ cups all-purpose flour	3 large eggs, beaten
½ cup jonnycake meal or yellow cornmeal	1 cup milk
1 tablespoon baking powder	corn oil for frying

1. Bring a pot (4 quarts or more) of lightly salted water to a boil. Wipe away any corn silk sticking to the ears of corn. Drop the ears in the water and cook until the corn is tender, 1 to 5 minutes, depending on the corn. Generally, the younger and fresher the corn, the quicker it will cook. I always take a little nibble to test for doneness. Use tongs to remove the corn and let cool to room temperature. With a knife, cut the kernels from the cob. With the back of the knife, scrape out any milky remains and add to the kernels. You should have 1½ cups.

2. Combine the bell pepper and butter in a small skillet over low heat and simmer for about 5 minutes until tender. Remove from the heat. This may seem like a lot of butter for the pepper, but the butter will also serve as the fat in the batter.

3. In a large mixing bowl, stir together the flour, jonnycake meal, baking powder, salt, pepper and cayenne. Add the corn, bell pepper and butter, scallions, eggs and milk. Mix thoroughly but do not overmix, or the fritters will be too chewy. Cover and chill the batter for at least 1 hour and up to 6 hours.

4. Before you fry, check the consistency of the batter; it should be thick enough to hold its shape on a spoon. It will be thicker than most batters (such as muffin batter) and have a gritty texture. The batter can be thickened by sprinkling in more flour, or it can be thinned with a few drops of milk. Heat 3 inches oil to 350°F in a deep, heavy saucepan. Use one spoon to scoop out some batter and another to free the batter from the spoon. If you are using an ice-cream scoop, squeeze the handle to release the fritter. Drop 1 fritter into the hot oil and fry, turning it with tongs or a spoon so that it cooks evenly, for about 2 minutes until it is deep golden brown. Remove it with a mesh or slotted spoon, give it a little shake over the pot of oil to drain and place it on a plate lined with paper towels to absorb the excess oil. Check the size; it should be about the size of a golf ball, no larger. Taste this test fritter and adjust the seasoning and consistency if necessary. Salt plays an important role in cornmeal-based breads, enhancing the flavor of the corn and the cornmeal.

5. Drop 5 or 6 fritters into the pot. There should be enough space for them to move freely. Cook 2 to 3 minutes until golden brown, turning frequently so that they cook evenly. Remove, drain and place on a plate lined with paper towels. Keep them in a warm oven while you continue to fry. Bring the oil back to 350°F between batches. Serve as soon as possible.

Makes 2 dozen small fritters

VARIATIONS
These fritters are even better with a little ham or bacon. Add 2 to 3 ounces cooked ham, finely diced, or 3 ounces bacon, fried crisp and finely chopped. You can also substitute the rendered bacon fat (3 tablespoons) for the butter. This recipe can be halved, but beware: Even when it is just my wife and three kids, half a batch leaves us wanting more!

New England September Soup of Pumpkin, Sweet Corn & Lobster

Autumn is a bountiful time in New England. Because of New England's long, fierce winters, summer crops start later there than in other parts of the country. Tomatoes and peppers ripen well into October, and sweet corn abounds through September. This late harvest creates a window of four to six weeks when summer and autumn crops coincide, an occurrence unique to this part of the world. Because of the cool fall weather, a late-August planting of spring vegetables such as spinach and peas usually does well. Autumn is also the prime time for savoring hard-shell lobsters as well as oysters and other shellfish. The great migratory fish, such as bluefin tuna and swordfish, are in New England coastal waters in the fall. All of these elements combine to give New England one of the most sumptuous autumn harvests in the United States.

It is not surprising, then, that over the years I have created a small repertoire of "September dishes." They all feature combinations of the local ingredients that coincide during this brief period. Rhode Island peppers, sugar pumpkins and sweet corn; sweet peas and spinach from my garden; Nantucket pheasant or Canadian goose with Vermont chanterelles; Martha's Vineyard swordfish with fennel and ripe tomatoes; autumn raspberries, quince and Gravenstein apples . . . to name a few. This soup, made with sweet corn, pumpkin and lobsters, is one of these special dishes. It is sweet, full-flavored and hearty—perfect for a chilly night.

This recipe, which makes about 2 quarts of soup, will keep for two or three days if you have leftovers. If you want to halve the recipe, you may need to add a little extra liquid (lobster stock or water), because the smaller batch tends to cook down faster.

The success of this soup hinges on the fresh pumpkin. Use only small sugar pumpkins or one of the similar hybrids. Avoid ornamental pumpkins, which, though resembling sugar pumpkins, lack their tender flesh and rich flavor. Look for small "cooking" pumpkins of 2 to 4 pounds that have a rich orange-brown color. The skin should be thin and peel easily with a paring knife. The flesh should have a rich color and should be relatively tender, even in its raw state. If you cannot find a pumpkin like the one I have described, substitute ripe butternut, golden acorn or another autumn squash. This recipe calls for a 2-pound sugar pumpkin, which yields about 1⅓ pounds of peeled and seeded flesh. Keep this weight in mind when substituting squash or using a slightly larger sugar pumpkin.

This recipe calls for 2 cups chicken stock or broth. I like the way it deepens the flavor, but you can still make a great soup without it by simply substituting water. I call for lobster carcasses rather than whole lobsters because a richly flavored stock is a necessity when competing with the powerful tastes of pumpkin and corn. The amount of diced lobster meat in the garnish is really up to you.

4 to 5 small or 3 to 4 medium lobster
carcasses (about 1½ pounds)

2 cups chicken stock or broth or water

2 quarts water

3 large ears sweet corn, preferably one of
the yellow or bicolor varieties, husked

4 sprigs fresh thyme

1 bay leaf

1 teaspoon whole black peppercorns

kosher or sea salt

1 small sugar pumpkin (about 2 pounds)

1 tablespoon unsalted butter

2 medium onions (12 ounces), thinly
sliced

⅛ teaspoon freshly grated or ground
nutmeg

⅓ to ½ cup heavy cream, or ¾ cup milk

freshly ground black pepper

pinch of cayenne pepper, or drop of
Tabasco sauce

4 to 6 ounces cooked lobster meat, finely
diced

a few sprigs chervil or parsley, leaves
picked and coarsely chopped

1. Using a medium Chinese cleaver or large chef's knife, split the lobster carcasses in half. Remove the head sacs and half of the tomalley. Reserve the other half for another use (freeze for use in Tomalley Toasts, page 88) or discard it. Place the carcasses in a medium stock- or soup pot (6 quarts is enough) and cover with the chicken stock and water. Bring to a boil, skim the foam from the surface and lower the heat to a simmer.

2. Cut the kernels off the corn. You should have 2½ to 3 cups. Break the cobs in half and add them to the stock.

3. Add the thyme, bay leaf and peppercorns. Simmer, partially covered, for 1 hour. Salt lightly, taste and simmer for up to 30 minutes until the stock tastes richly of lobster and corn.

4. Pour the stock through a medium strainer. You should have about 6 cups stock. This can be done a day in advance if you wish.

5. Peel the pumpkin, remove the seeds and stringy center, and cut into slices no wider than ¾ inch.

6. Melt the butter in a heavy soup pot (4 quarts) over medium heat. Add the onions and cook for 8 to 10 minutes until soft and lightly browned. Add the broth, corn kernels, pumpkin and nutmeg. Simmer for about 45 minutes until the pumpkin is very tender. Remove from the heat and puree very smoothly with a hand blender or in several small batches in a food processor. Strain the puree through a medium strainer directly into another pot. Add the cream and reheat the mixture. Season to taste with salt, pepper and cayenne. Just before serving, add the lobster meat. Ladle into warmed cups and sprinkle with a little chervil or parsley. Serve at once.

Serves 8 as a starter

Cambodian-Style Lobster Soup

I first tasted this bright, spicy soup at Elephant Walk in Somerville, Massachusetts, widely ac-claimed as one of the best Cambodian restaurants in America. One of the waiters who worked there was kind enough to tell me the original recipe. Although traditionally made with shrimp and chicken stock, it adapted extremely well to lobster. I like the richness that the chicken stock adds, but it is not absolutely necessary. If not using chicken stock, substitute an equal amount of water. The flavors of ginger, tomatoes, garlic, mint and lime, combined with the mellow un-derlying taste of lobster, are enough to bring this soup to a magical level. Serve in warmed cups as a fiery start to a summer dinner.

The recipe calls for two or three Thai chiles, which can be found in most Asian markets and even in some supermarkets. Because they are about as hot as chiles get, you can safely substitute other types, bearing in mind that Thai chiles are about 1½ inches long and ⅓ inch wide. This soup is mildly hot, like the original version. You may wish to modify it to suit your taste.

After you have made the stock and prepared the vegetables, the soup takes only ten minutes to make. Unlike other soups that benefit from sitting for extended periods, it is best shortly after being completed. Make it as close to the time you wish to serve it as possible.

2 live 1-pound chicken lobsters	4 ounces fresh shiitake mushrooms
1 pound ripe tomatoes	3 to 4 scallions
2 cups chicken stock or water	1 tablespoon peanut oil
7 cups water	1 teaspoon dark sesame oil
10 cloves garlic	1 tablespoon sugar
2 to 3 small Thai chiles	8 sprigs fresh mint, leaves picked
1 thumb-size piece fresh ginger	juice of 2 or 3 limes
kosher or sea salt	freshly ground black pepper

1. Fill a 10- to 12-quart pot about two-thirds full with water. Add enough salt to make the water distinctly salty (¼ cup) and bring to a boil. With your hand on the carapace of the lob-ster, place each one in the pot and cook for exactly 3½ minutes from the time they go in. Using tongs, remove the lobsters to a platter and let cool at room temperature. Keep the water on the heat.

2. Score the tomatoes with an X on the bottom of each one. Drop the tomatoes into the same boiling water you used for the lobsters. After 30 to 45 seconds the skins will blister or shrivel. Remove the tomatoes from the boiling water and submerge in ice water immediately to stop the cooking. Peel the tomatoes and quarter them. Using a paring knife, cut out the center. Discard the hot water and add the tomato "guts" and skins to the pot. Slice the tomatoes in strips about ⅓ inch wide and reserve.

3. Remove the lobster meat from the tails, knuckles and claws. Cut into ⅓- to ½-inch-thick slices, cover and refrigerate. Split the carcasses lengthwise and remove the head sacs and half of the tomalley. Reserve the remaining for Tomalley Toasts (page 88) or discard it. Place the shells and carcasses in the pot with the tomato skins and guts and cover with the chicken stock and the water. Bring to a boil and skim the foam off the top. Turn the heat to low and cook at a steady simmer.

4. Peel the garlic, crush 3 cloves and add to the stock. Slice the remaining garlic very thin and reserve. Split the chiles in half lengthwise and add to the stock. Peel the ginger, cut into very fine julienne strips and reserve. Add the ginger peels to the stock. Simmer the stock for 1 hour. Season it very lightly with salt. Taste; it may need another 15 to 30 minutes to develop full flavor. When it is ready, strain through a fine strainer or china cap. You should have about 6 cups. This can be done as much as a day in advance. If you make the stock ahead, reheat it before starting the soup.

5. Slice the shiitake mushrooms into strips about ¼ inch wide. Slice the scallions, white and green parts, very thinly on a diagonal.

6. Place a medium-size heavy saucepan (2 to 3 quarts is enough) over high heat and add the peanut and sesame oils. Add the sliced garlic and sauté for 30 to 60 seconds until lightly browned. Add the ginger, stir and sauté for 30 seconds. Stir in the mushrooms and sauté for 1 to 2 minutes, stirring often. Add the stock, tomatoes and sugar. Lower the heat and simmer for 5 minutes. Add the lobster meat, scallions, mint and lime juice. Season with salt if needed and pepper. Serve at once.

Serves 6 to 8 as a starter

Gazpacho with Lobster

The classic Andalusian-style gazpacho, a "soup-salad" with a chilled tomato and cucumber base, has become so popular in America that it has inspired hundreds of variations. I was lucky enough to sample what must be one of the best of these variations, Spicy Yellow Gazpacho with Maryland Lump Crab, created by my friend Mark Miller at his restaurant Red Sage in Washington, D.C. It was so extraordinary that it inspired me to make a lobster version of gazpacho. I started with the classic Andalusian-style ingredients and added lobster broth instead of water. After a few minor adjustments I came up with a version that has all the refreshing qualities of gazpacho with the added treat of lobster. When I first made gazpacho with lobster, I had never heard of or tasted it elsewhere. Since then, I have seen it twice. One version using lobster, leeks and cream is published in Larousse Gastronomique. *It is obviously older than my recipe, a humbling reminder that being original is not an easy task.*

My recipe for gazpacho requires chilled lobster broth or stock that can be made a day or two ahead or up to a month in advance if kept frozen. Also remember to let the bread dry out at least one day before. The rest takes minutes. Gazpacho is most appropriate during the hot days of summer when tomatoes are at their best.

I like to serve this in a glass bowl or cup that is placed in a bed of crushed ice in a larger bowl. This is not only visually enticing and suggestive of the refreshing tastes to come but also functional because it keeps the soup cold at all times. You can set up these bowls and ice ahead of time and keep them in the freezer until it is time to serve. If your refrigerator is not absolutely cold, I recommend that you store the soup on ice as well.

⅓ French baguette (3 to 4 ounces)

4 cups Savory Lobster Broth (page 54) or Quick Lobster Stock (page 57), chilled

2½ pounds ripe tomatoes (about 16 plum or 5 regular)

2 medium red or green bell peppers (8 ounces)

1½ pounds cucumbers

3 cloves garlic

2 medium Spanish onions (10 to 12 ounces)

2 sprigs fresh thyme, leaves picked and chopped

2 sprigs fresh basil, leaves picked and chopped

8 sprigs cilantro, chopped with stems

½ cup green extra-virgin olive oil

¼ cup good-quality red wine vinegar

about 2 tablespoons kosher or sea salt

about 2 teaspoons freshly ground black pepper

cayenne pepper or Tabasco or other hot sauce

12 ounces or more cooked fresh lobster meat, diced and chilled

1. The day before you make the soup, trim the crust from the baguette, then cut the bread into cubes and spread the cubes on a baking sheet to dry overnight.

2. The day you want to serve the soup, soak the bread cubes in 2 cups of the lobster broth or stock. Keep the remaining 2 cups refrigerated.

3. Rinse the tomatoes. Make a garnish with 8 ounces of them by quartering them and cutting out the centers. Finely dice the outer walls of the tomatoes, cover and refrigerate. Quarter the remaining tomatoes and combine with the "guts" from the garnishing tomatoes.

4. Remove the seeds from the peppers. Make a garnish with about a third of 1 pepper by finely dicing it. Cover and refrigerate. Coarsely chop the remaining peppers.

5. Peel the cucumbers. Make a garnish with half of 1 cucumber by splitting it lengthwise, scooping out the seeds and finely dicing the flesh. Cover and refrigerate. Cut the remaining cucumber into chunks.

6. Peel the garlic. Peel the onions and coarsely chop. In a large bowl, combine the soaked bread with the tomatoes, peppers, cucumbers, garlic and onions. Add the herbs to the bowl. Add 1 cup lobster broth and combine thoroughly. Puree the mixture in 2 or 3 batches in a food processor or blender. Add the oil and vinegar slowly, alternating them during the processing so that they become emulsified. Strain through a coarse china cap or other strainer. Stir in the tomato, pepper and cucumber for garnish. Season with salt, pepper and cayenne. Adjust the consistency of the soup by adding the remaining lobster broth (up to 1 cup) if necessary. Chill the gazpacho thoroughly. Taste and season again before serving. Serve in chilled soup plates with a generous dollop of freshly diced lobster meat in the center of each bowl.

Makes about 3 quarts; serves 10 to 12 as a starter

Classic Lobster Bisque

Lobster bisque is an elegant special-occasion soup. Bisque, which first appeared in seventeenth-century France, has always been regarded as a soup of high style. Originally, it was a sumptuous puree made with small game birds, such as quail or pigeon. A garnish of crawfish tails was added in the mid-1800s, and by the end of the century, the soup had evolved into crawfish bisque (bisque d'écrevisses), *a creamy thickened puree of shellfish. Soon afterward, bisques made with lobster and shrimp became popular. Intensely flavorful, silky and rich, bisque became the standard by which the best hotels in Europe and America were judged.*

Auguste Escoffier (1846–1935), the celebrated French chef who spent the better part of his extraordinary sixty-two-year career at the helm of the Savoy and Carlton Hotels in London, improved upon the standard bisque by replacing bread with rice or tapioca as a thickener and by adding burnt brandy, white wine and white consommé made with veal as enrichments. My recipe pays homage to his classic bisque but addresses contemporary concerns about fat and ease of preparation. By adding an abundance of pureed fresh vegetables to the soup, I produce a lighter texture than the original. The ⅓ cup cream for 10 cups soup provides a sense of the original richness without the original fat. The small bit of dried red pepper flakes adds a distinctly modern flair to the dish.

The diced lobster meat added as garnish is really optional, but I urge you to be as generous as you can afford. At the end of cooking, the soup should have a reddish brown color with little specks of red (from the roe) and a slightly thickened, smooth texture. It can be made one or two days in advance. Tomalley Toasts (page 88), served on the side, make a wonderful garnish. Serve simply, in beautiful soup cups with a sprinkle of snipped herbs, such as chervil, parsley or chives. Save this bisque for a special occasion, such as New Year's Eve. It is a modern rendition of one of the greatest soups ever created and a salute to the splendor and depth of French cuisine.

2 to 2½ pounds cooked lobster carcasses (5 or 6 carcasses)

4 tablespoons olive oil

6 cloves garlic, coarsely chopped

2 medium or 3 small onions (12 ounces), coarsely chopped

2 or 3 medium carrots (8 ounces), coarsely chopped

2 ribs celery (5 to 6 ounces), coarsely chopped

1 small bulb fennel (8 ounces), coarsely chopped

1 can (28 ounces) Italian plum tomatoes with their juice

2 quarts plus 1 cup water

1½ cups veal, beef or chicken stock or broth

2 cups white wine (acidic young wines are best)

½ teaspoon dried red pepper flakes

2 bay leaves

4 sprigs fresh thyme

4 sprigs fresh tarragon

½ teaspoon Spanish saffron threads

kosher or sea salt

freshly ground black pepper

⅓ cup converted rice (Uncle Ben's)

¼ cup good brandy or Cognac

⅓ cup heavy cream (or a little more if you want to indulge your guests)

4 to 8 ounces cooked lobster meat, finely diced

6 to 8 tablespoons Amontillado or Fino sherry (optional)

1. Preheat the oven to 400°F. With a medium Chinese cleaver or large chef's knife, split the lobster carcasses in half lengthwise and remove the head sacs. Remove the tomalley and the roe if present, cover and refrigerate. Place the split carcasses, shell side up, on a baking sheet or in a roasting pan and drizzle 2 tablespoons of the olive oil over all. Roast in the oven for 35 minutes, turning the shells over halfway through. The shells will become brittle and browned in places and will release a distinct lobster aroma as they roast.

2. Heat a large soup pot (8 to 10 quarts) over medium-high heat and add the remaining 2 tablespoons olive oil. Add the garlic, onions, carrots, celery and fennel and cook, stirring to prevent sticking and scorching, for 10 to 12 minutes until the vegetables are well browned. Break up the tomatoes with a fork or by hand and add to the pot with their juice. Add 2 quarts water, the stock and the wine. Bring to a boil.

3. By now, the lobster carcasses should be ready. Transfer them to the soup pot. Deglaze the roasting pan with 1 cup water and add this to the pot. When the liquid reaches a boil again, skim the foam from the top. Add the red pepper, bay leaves, thyme, tarragon and saffron. Turn the heat to low and simmer steadily, partially covered, for 1½ hours, stirring occasionally. Season lightly with salt and pepper. Taste. Simmer for another 30 minutes. Taste again. The liquid should have a very full, pronounced lobster flavor.

4. Using tongs, remove the lobster carcasses one at a time, shaking off any vegetables or herbs. Drain the carcasses in a colander placed over a bowl or pan. Remove the bay leaves and discard. At this point the soup should be thick with vegetables, like a minestrone, but should have enough liquid to cover them easily. If this is not the case, add water.

5. Stir in the rice. Add the tomalley and roe. Cover the pot and simmer for 30 minutes, stirring occasionally to prevent the rice from sticking to the bottom. The rice should be tender and slightly overcooked. Add the drippings from the lobster carcasses to the pot. The soup is now ready to be pureed.

6. If you own a hand (immersion) blender (a fabulous tool made by both Cuisinart and Braun that is perfect for pureeing soups and sauces), put it in the pot and puree until the soup is very smooth. Otherwise, transfer the soup in small batches to a food processor (fill the bowl not more than halfway) and puree until very smooth. It should take three batches in a standard-size food processor. Strain through a medium china cap or other strainer. If you will not be eating the bisque right away, cover and refrigerate it. The soup can be made up to this point and kept for 1 or even 2 days.

7. When you intend to serve the soup, heat it to a simmer and skim off any foam that comes to the surface. Heat the brandy in a small pan, ignite and let the flames burn off completely. Add it to the pot. Finish by adding the cream and lobster meat. Season to taste with salt and pepper and serve in warmed bowls. Add a little sherry just before bringing the dish to the table if you like. I find it quite nice!

Makes about 10 cups; serves 10 to 12 as a first course

CHAPTER 4

Hot Appetizers & Small Dishes

THIS CHAPTER IS a collection of my favorite "small" lobster dishes, recipes that use moderate amounts of lobster to create enticing hot hors d'oeuvre, appetizers, fish courses and light meals. You will find everything from simple and quick pasta and rice dishes to more complex creations that require a greater amount of time to prepare. Explore them, keeping in mind that some are best suited for special occasions while others are so exquisitely simple that you will want to prepare them meal after meal.

Tomalley Toasts

Tomalley, the digestive organ of the lobster, is the light green mass found in the carcass. It has a soft, rich, exquisite flavor that blends gracefully into the background, disappearing as it adds new complexity to sauces. When tomalley is forced to take center stage, however, it is another story: The green color, seldom favorably associated with seafood, tends to arouse a squeamish reaction even in the most adventurous of dinner guests. So what do you do with lobster tomalley? My advice is to wrap it tightly in plastic wrap and freeze it. It will keep for up to five weeks. When you have saved about half a cup (from eight to ten lobsters, depending on their size), you will be able to transform the mushy green tomalley into crispy golden-edged croutons with a soft buttery tomalley-and-herb center. These make a luscious hot hors d'oeuvre and are great served as a side dish to lobster bisque or chowder.

If using frozen tomalley, take it out of the freezer at least twelve hours before you want to use it. Place it in the refrigerator, covered, and allow it to defrost slowly for minimum damage to the tomalley. The tomalley spread can be made in a food processor or by hand using a small whip and mixing bowl. For safety issues concerning lobster tomalley, see page 21.

½ cup cooked lobster tomalley	1 tablespoon minced fresh chives
1 teaspoon finely minced garlic	kosher or sea salt
4 tablespoons unsalted butter, softened	freshly ground black pepper
1 tablespoon chopped Italian parsley	1 French baguette

1. Place the tomalley in a fine strainer and let drain about 15 minutes. Keep refrigerated until ready to use.

2. In the smallest frying skillet you own, sauté the garlic in 1 tablespoon of the butter over medium heat for about 1 minute, just long enough to soften the garlic. Let cool a bit.

3. In a small mixing bowl or the bowl of a food processor, combine the cooked garlic in butter with the remaining softened butter. Add the parsley and chives. Mix into a paste using a whip or by pulsing in the food processor. Add the tomalley and blend until smooth. Season with salt and pepper.

4. Preheat the broiler. Cut the baguette crosswise into slices about ⅔ inch thick. You should get 20 slices. Put the slices on a baking sheet and broil until golden brown. Turn the slices over and toast the other side. Let the toasts cool. Turn off the broiler and preheat the oven to 400°F.

5. Spread the tomalley mixture evenly over the toasts. Just before serving, bake them for 6 to 8 minutes until the toasts are crisp and light brown and the tomalley mixture has dissolved and is bubbling on top.

Makes about 20 small toasts

COOK'S NOTE: *If you omit the baguette from this recipe, you will have a tomalley-flavored butter that can be used on grilled lobster and, believe it or not, is delicious on grilled steaks. If you want to serve lobster and steak together, this tomalley butter ties the ingredients and makes sense out of a dish (surf and turf) that often falls short. Simply roll the butter in a sheet of parchment or wax paper into a cylinder about 1½ inches thick. Wrap again in plastic wrap and chill. To serve, cut the cylinder into ⅓-inch-thick slices and remove the paper.*

Lobster Pizza

This wickedly good pizza is as thin and crisp as a cracker. Garnished with just enough lobster meat, cheese and tomato, it is never soggy and never falls apart. Serve it at cocktail parties— your friends will adore the treat. If you serve it as a meal, count on one pizza per person. The recipe makes four pizzas and can easily be doubled.

The secret to this pizza is the extremely thin dough, allowing for quick cooking—less than ten minutes—which is essential for keeping the lobster from becoming rubbery. Although the amount of dough may not appear to be enough for four pizzas, it is extremely strong and will roll out very thin without tearing. The trick is to roll the dough twice, with a short rest in between. Do not worry about keeping a perfectly round shape when you are rolling out the dough; irregular shapes are charming and are the authentic mark of a home-made crust. For this pizza I do not use a stone, which would cook the thin dough too quickly; just bake it on a cookie sheet, and it will be perfect.

8 ounces fully cooked lobster meat, or 2½ pounds live lobsters

1 batch Dough for Seafood Pizza (page 92), divided into 4 balls

2 medium or 3 small ripe tomatoes (12 to 14 ounces), thinly sliced

10 to 12 fresh basil leaves, thinly sliced (chiffonade)

8 ounces soft mozzarella cheese for melting, grated

1½ to 2 ounces Parmigiano-Reggiano cheese, grated

all-purpose flour for dusting

yellow cornmeal for sprinkling on the cookie sheets

freshly ground black pepper

3 tablespoons extra-virgin olive oil

1. If you are cooking your own lobster for meat, look for the best deal available; culls or 1-pound chicken lobsters will probably be the most economical. Fully cook the lobsters according to their weight by boiling (page 29) or steaming (page 32). Remove the meat from the claws, knuckles and tails. Reserve the carcasses for soup. Remove the cartilage from the claws and the intestine from the tail. Cut the lobster into thin (½-inch) slices. Cover and refrigerate.

2. Before rolling out the dough, prepare and organize the ingredients that will go on top. Preheat the oven to 450°F.

3. Lightly flour your work surface and roll out each ball to about 6 to 8 inches. Do not worry if they are not perfectly round. After you finish rolling out the 4 balls, roll out the first one to about 11 to 12 inches. The dough will be paper-thin. Do the same with the remaining 3 rounds. Place each pizza crust on a cookie sheet that has been dusted with cornmeal. If using baking sheets with sides, turn them upside down and put the crusts on the backs of the pans. This allows the crusts to slide easily.

4. Divide the toppings evenly among the 4 crusts, placing the sliced tomatoes on first and then the sliced lobster, taking care that each slice of finished pizza will have a bit of tomato and lobster. Sprinkle with the basil and top with the mozzarella and Parmigiano-Reggiano. Season with pepper, then drizzle olive oil over each pizza. Place on the middle racks of the oven and bake for 8 to 10 minutes until the crusts are crisp and brown and the cheese is bubbling. Slide the pizzas onto a cutting board. Using a large cleaver, chef's knife or pizza cutter, make fast, deliberate motions to cut each pie into 6 or 7 wedges for hors d'oeuvre or 4 or 5 wedges for a meal. Serve at once.

Makes four 12-inch pizzas

COOK'S NOTE: *In most home ovens it is best to cook the pizzas two at a time. More will cause the temperature to drop too low, and the pizzas will not cook evenly or quickly enough.*

Dough for Seafood Pizza

2 teaspoons active dry yeast

2 teaspoons sugar

⅔ cup warm water

2 cups bread or all-purpose flour, plus a little extra for kneading and rolling

1 teaspoon olive oil, plus a little more for proofing the dough

1 teaspoon salt

1. Combine the yeast and sugar in a large mixing bowl. Add the warm water and mix well. Let stand for 5 to 10 minutes to allow the yeast to "bloom." A frothy foam will appear when it is ready. Add the flour, 1 teaspoon olive oil and salt. Mix until a dough begins to form.

2. Transfer to a lightly floured work surface and knead for 12 to 15 minutes until a smooth and very strong dough is formed. While kneading, you may adjust the consistency of the dough by adding a little more flour to tighten or a little more water to loosen. The dough should be smooth and elastic but firm. Lightly grease a large mixing bowl with olive oil. Place the dough in the bowl and turn it over so that it is oiled on all sides. Cover loosely with plastic wrap or a lightly dampened towel. Let rise in a warm spot until the dough has doubled in bulk, 45 minutes to 1 hour.

3. Punch the dough down and divide evenly into 4 small balls. Lightly oil the balls, place them several inches apart on a baking sheet and cover as you did before. Let rise again in a warm spot until doubled, 30 to 45 minutes. Punch the dough down again, reshape into balls and wrap each one tightly in plastic wrap. If not using right away, refrigerate until ready to use, up to 6 hours in advance.

Makes four 12-inch crusts

LOBSTER WITH PASTA

One of my family's favorite meals is pasta cooked and tossed with buttery sautéed lobster and fresh vegetables. It is simple to cook, satisfying and delicious. I do not know which makes me happier—the smiles on my children's faces at the sight of this meal or the perfect marriage of flavors and textures that results when these simple ingredients are put together.

The four recipes that follow, one for each season, use a simple formula: two 1-pound chicken lobsters for every 8 ounces dried pasta. The method is the same for all four dishes: Parboil the lobsters and then extract and dice the meat; sauté the lobster meat in oil or butter and add the vegetables. Cook the pasta al dente (firm to the bite) and toss with the lobster and vegetables. The oil or butter has a distinct lobster flavor that coats the pasta, imparting its delicious fragrance to every bite. Once you have tried my recipes a few times to get the hang of things, you can create your own great seasonal combinations by substituting different shapes and types of pasta as well as different vegetables. You will need to adjust the timing of any recipe when you substitute types of pasta. Usually the recommended cooking time on the box is very accurate.

If you double the recipes, remember that you will need a larger pot with more salted water and a larger sauté pan.

Fettuccine with Lobster & Fresh Peas or Asparagus—Spring

Peas love cool climates and are very easy to grow in New England. In late spring they are so plentiful that they are available at almost every market and roadside stand. You can also use fresh asparagus for a slightly more elegant version of this recipe.

2 live 1-pound chicken lobsters	freshly ground black pepper
1 pound fresh garden peas, or 8 ounces fresh asparagus	2 tablespoons unsalted butter
8 ounces dried fettuccine	kosher or sea salt
2 tablespoons olive oil	1 ounce Parmigiano-Reggiano cheese, grated

1. Parboil the lobsters (page 30), drain and let cool at room temperature. Use a cleaver to crack and remove the meat from the claws, knuckles and tails. Remove the cartilage from the claws and the intestine from the tail. Cut the lobster meat into ¾-inch dice. Cover and refrigerate. You have the option of either cracking open and picking the carcass for meat to be added to the diced meat or reserving it to make soup.

2. Shuck the peas; you should have about 1 cup. Blanch them in boiling salted water for about 1 minute until tender. Remove the peas from the boiling water and submerge in ice water immediately to stop the cooking. Drain and reserve. If using asparagus, peel them unless they are small and tender "pencils" and cut on the diagonal into ¾-inch pieces. Blanch in boiling salted water for 1 to 3 minutes until tender. Remove the asparagus from the boiling water and submerge in ice water immediately to stop the cooking. Drain and reserve.

3. Fill a 6- to 8-quart pot with 4 quarts water and add 4 tablespoons salt. Bring to a rolling boil. Before you add the fettuccine, organize the other ingredients. There will be no time to spare once you start cooking the pasta. Heat a large sauté pan (10 inches) over medium heat. Add the fettuccine to the boiling water. It will take 5 to 6 minutes to cook.

4. After the pasta has been cooking for 2 minutes, add the olive oil and diced lobster meat to the sauté pan. It should be sizzling. Grind a little pepper over the lobster. Sauté the lobster for about 2 minutes, turning the pieces with tongs. The oil will turn red. Add the peas or asparagus, lower the heat and sauté for 1 minute more.

5. Drain the pasta in a colander, shaking the colander well so that the pasta is as free of water as possible, and add it to the sauté pan. Add the butter and toss or stir the fettuccine so that it becomes coated with the pan juices. Season lightly with salt and adjust the pepper. Place in a large bowl or divide evenly among warmed bowls. Sprinkle with cheese and serve at once.

Serves 4 as a first course or 2 as a hearty main course

Spaghetti with Lobster, Tomatoes & Capers—Summer

Spaghetti and fresh, ripe tomatoes are a perfect marriage. With basil, capers and lobster, this dish has all the freshness of a summer day. Because summer is the season for soft-shell lobsters, and sometimes they are the only type available, you may wish to use three lobsters instead of two.

2 live 1-pound chicken lobsters	freshly ground black pepper
1 pound ripe red tomatoes, any size or variety	1 heaping tablespoon drained capers
	5 or 6 fresh basil leaves, coarsely chopped
8 ounces spaghetti	2 tablespoons unsalted butter
2 tablespoons olive oil	kosher or sea salt
1 large clove garlic, finely chopped	

1. Parboil the lobsters (page 30), drain and let cool at room temperature. Use a cleaver to crack and remove the meat from the claws, knuckles and tails. Remove the cartilage from the claws and the intestine from the tail. Cut the lobster meat into ¾-inch dice. Cover and refrigerate. You have the option of cracking open and picking the carcass for meat to be added to the diced meat or reserving it to make soup.

2. Score each tomato with an X on the bottom. Blanch in boiling salted water for 30 seconds to 1 minute until the skins begin to loosen. Remove and submerge in ice water immediately to stop the cooking. Peel off the skins, quarter the tomatoes and cut out the seedy centers. Cut the flesh into 1-inch dice.

3. Fill a 6- to 8-quart pot with 4 quarts water and add 4 tablespoons salt. Bring to a rolling boil. Before you add the spaghetti, organize the other ingredients. There will be no time to spare once you start cooking the pasta. Add the spaghetti to the boiling water. It will take about 10 minutes to cook.

4. Heat a large sauté pan (10 inches) over medium heat. After the pasta has cooked for 5 minutes, add the olive oil, garlic and diced lobster meat to the sauté pan. It should be sizzling. Grind a little pepper over the lobster. Sauté the lobster for about 2 minutes, turning the pieces with tongs. The oil will turn red. Stir the garlic so that it browns lightly but does not burn. Add the diced tomatoes, capers and basil. Lower the heat and cook for 2 minutes more.

5. Drain the pasta in a colander, shaking the colander well so that the pasta is as free of water as possible, and add it to the sauté pan. Add the butter and toss or stir the spaghetti so that it becomes coated with the pan juices. Season lightly with salt and adjust the pepper. Place in a large bowl or divide evenly among warmed bowls. Serve at once.

Serves 4 as a first course or 2 as a hearty main course

Pappardelle with Lobster, Mushrooms, Shallots & Cream—Autumn

Pappardelle is a long, wide noodle that is often found fresh but can also be purchased dry. You will most likely need to shop for an imported brand of pasta; Del Verde is excellent. If you cannot locate pappardelle, substitute fettuccine or another wide egg noodle. This recipe uses fresh domestic mushrooms with a small amount of dried porcini. If you are lucky enough to find chanterelles, fresh porcini (cèpes) or other wild mushrooms, omit the dried mushrooms and substitute a quarter cup Savory Lobster Broth (page 54), Quick Lobster Stock (page 57), chicken stock, white wine or water for the mushroom soaking liquid.

2 live 1-pound chicken lobsters	¼ cup heavy cream
½ ounce dried porcini mushrooms	kosher or sea salt
½ cup hot water	freshly ground black pepper
6 ounces fresh button, cremini and/or shiitake mushrooms	8 ounces dried pappardelle
4 tablespoons unsalted butter	4 sprigs Italian parsley, leaves picked and coarsely chopped
2 shallots (1 ounce), finely diced	

1. Parboil the lobsters (page 30), drain and let cool at room temperature. Use a cleaver to crack and remove the meat from the claws, knuckles and tails. Remove the cartilage from the claws and the intestine from the tail. Cut the lobster meat into ¾-inch dice. Cover and refrigerate. You have the option of either cracking open and picking the carcass for meat to be added to the diced meat or reserving it to make soup.

2. Soak the dried porcini in the water until tender. Drain, reserving the soaking liquid, and coarsely chop. Slice the fresh mushrooms about ⅓ inch thick.

3. Fill a 6- to 8-quart pot with 4 quarts water and add 4 tablespoons salt. Bring to a rolling boil. (You can start the pasta now, but if time is not an issue and you would like to concentrate on making the mushroom sauce first, you can wait until you remove the sauce from the heat.)

4. Meanwhile, in a large sauté pan (10 inches), melt 3 tablespoons of the butter over medium heat. Add the lobster pieces and sauté, turning the pieces with tongs, about 2 minutes until fully cooked. Lift the lobster out of the butter, letting it drain over the pan before putting it on a plate. Cover to keep warm. Add the shallots to the butter and cook for about 1 minute. Add the fresh mushrooms and cook for another 2 to 3 minutes until the mushrooms are soft. Add the dried mushrooms, the soaking liquid and the cream. Bring to a boil, season with salt and pepper and remove from the heat.

5. Add the pappardelle to the boiling water and cook until al dente (firm to the bite). It will take about 8 minutes.

6. About 2 minutes before the pasta is done, return the mushroom mixture to a boil. Drain the pasta in a colander, shaking the colander well so that the pasta is as free of water as possible, and add it to the sauté pan. Add the lobster meat, the remaining 1 tablespoon butter and the parsley. Mix thoroughly over the heat. When the noodles are well coated, place in a large bowl or divide among individual plates. Serve at once.

Serves 4 as a first course or 2 as a hearty main course

Orecchiette with Lobster, Savoy Cabbage, Onion & Bacon—Winter

This is a robust winter dish, rich with deep, smoky flavors and thick, chewy orecchiette. "Orecchiette" translated from Italian means "little ears." They are made fresh by slicing a tube of dough and shaping it over your thumb, but they can be purchased dried (imported only). If you cannot locate this shape, substitute another small, hearty pasta such as penne or shells. If you want this dish to be more authentic Italian, use pancetta instead of bacon.

2 live 1-pound chicken lobsters	1 small onion (4 ounces), cut into ¾-inch dice
¼ head Savoy cabbage (6 ounces), cut into 1-inch dice	kosher or sea salt
8 ounces orecchiette	freshly ground black pepper
3 ounces slab bacon or pancetta, cut into ½-inch slices or cubes	2 tablespoons unsalted butter

1. Parboil the lobsters (page 30), drain and let cool at room temperature. Use a cleaver to crack and remove the meat from the claws, knuckles and tails. Remove the cartilage from the claws and the intestine from the tail. Cut the lobster meat into ¾-inch dice. Cover and refrigerate. You have the option of either cracking open and picking the carcass for meat to be added to the diced meat or reserving it to make soup.

2. Fill a 6- to 8-quart pot with 4 quarts water and add 4 tablespoons salt. Bring to a rolling boil. This will be used to cook both the cabbage and the pasta. Add the cabbage and boil for 1 minute. Using a slotted spoon or a strainer so that you can reuse the water for the pasta, remove the cabbage to a bowl and cover to keep warm. Before you add the orecchiette, prepare and organize the other ingredients. There will be no time to spare once you start cooking the pasta. Add the orecchiette to the boiling water and cook, stirring often so that it doesn't stick together, for 12 to 14 minutes.

3. As soon as you add the pasta, heat a large sauté pan (10 inches) over medium heat. Add the bacon and cook for about 4 minutes until crisp but not dry. Add the onion and cook for another 4 to 5 minutes until lightly browned. Add the diced lobster and cabbage and cook for 2 minutes. Season with salt and pepper.

4. Drain the pasta in a colander, shaking the colander well until the pasta is as free of water as possible, and add it to the sauté pan. Add the butter. Stir over the heat until the orecchiette are well coated. Place in a large bowl or divide evenly among individual plates. Serve at once.

Serves 4 as a first course or 2 as a hearty main course

ABOUT DRIED PASTA

One of my first cooking jobs was for Marenzi's, an Italian restaurant in San Francisco. Luigi Marenzi was a passionate and masterful chef who worked every day until he died in 1978. I was given the honor of cooking his lunch every day after service. On the menu at Marenzi's we offered homemade fettuccine, gnocchi, ravioli and many other fresh pastas, but Luigi always asked me to cook spaghetti or another dried pasta. When I finally had the courage to ask him why he always ate dried pasta, he replied, "Jasper, the fresh pasta is for tourists." I have been skeptical of fresh pasta ever since. Fresh pasta can be magnificent and is necessary to make ravioli, tortelli and other stuffed pastas, but I love the texture of dried pasta. Of course, its quality varies from brand to brand, so be careful when choosing. My favorite imports are Del Verde, Rustichella d'Abruzzo and De Cecco. My favorite domestic brand is Prince, which is made right here in New England.

Pasta needs a lot of water to cook properly. The large volume of water allows for a quick return to a boil and also lets the noodles move around the pot freely, which helps them cook evenly. Use about 4 quarts water for every 8 ounces pasta. The water should always be salted, with about 1 tablespoon salt per quart of water. At home I usually serve pasta on a large warmed platter. A good way of warming the platter is to place it under the colander in your sink; when you drain the pasta water, it will warm the platter. If you are serving the pasta in individual plates or bowls, warm them briefly in the oven.

Creamy Lobster Succotash

Succotash is the anglicized Narragansett word "msickquatash," a dish of corn and beans that was a staple of Native Americans from New England to Mexico. The dish varied from tribe to tribe, cook to cook and season to season. Some versions added game birds and venison, some added seafood. Succotash is best made with fresh neutral-flavored beans. In New England, shell beans—also called cranberry or horticultural beans—are the most widely available fresh beans during the summer and are my absolute favorite. If no fresh beans are available, dried large white limas, produced in Maine and sold under the label A-1, are an excellent substitute, but any small to medium dried bean will work. If you are using dried beans, remember to soak them in water overnight.

Lobster succotash is a wonderful side dish to serve with a seafood dinner. It is great served under a piece of cod, monkfish or bass dredged in cornmeal and then pan-fried or roasted. It is also fantastic with grilled fish and shellfish. If you want to serve it as a side dish with grilled or steamed lobster, or even Lobster Sausage (page 107), omit the garnish of diced lobster meat.

The recipe can be doubled. As always, feel free to increase the amount of lobster meat used for garnish.

2 pounds fresh lima or shell (horticultural or cranberry) beans, shelled (1½ cups), or 6 ounces dried white lima, shell, navy or other dried beans	¾ cup Savory Lobster Broth (page 54) or Quick Lobster Stock (page 57)
1 live 1-pound chicken lobster, or 3 to 4 ounces fully cooked lobster meat	¼ cup heavy cream
4 ounces green beans	1 teaspoon cornstarch
2 large or 3 small ears sweet corn	1 tablespoon cold water or lobster broth
2 tablespoons unsalted butter	kosher or sea salt
1 small onion (3 ounces), finely diced	freshly ground black pepper
	cayenne pepper

1. If using fresh beans, shell them and then blanch in lightly salted water until tender. Drain and reserve. If using dried beans, soak them overnight in water, then simmer in unsalted water until tender. Drain and reserve. The cooking time for beans will vary: Fresh beans will take as little as 10 minutes for small limas (butter beans); fresh shell beans, 20 to 30 minutes; dried beans, 30 minutes to 1 hour. Cook dried beans well in advance to avoid any problems with timing.

2. If using live lobster, steam (page 32), microwave (page 33) or boil (page 29) it. Let cool at room temperature. Use a cleaver to crack and remove the meat from the claws, knuckles and tail. Remove the cartilage from the claws and the intestine from the tail of the cooked lobster meat. Cut the lobster meat into ½-inch chunks. Cover and refrigerate until ready to serve the succotash.

3. Trim the green beans and boil in lightly salted water until tender. Drain the beans and rinse with cold water to stop the cooking. Drain again and cut into ½-inch pieces.

4. Husk the corn and remove all the silk. Cut the kernels off the cobs and scrape the cobs with the back of the knife. Combine the milky scrapings with the corn kernels. You should have about 1½ cups.

5. Use a heavy saucepan (2 quarts) to make the succotash. Melt the butter over medium heat, add the onion and cook for about 5 minutes until tender. Add the corn, lobster broth and cream and bring to a boil. Turn down the heat and simmer for 10 minutes. Add the cooked shell or dried beans and simmer for another 5 minutes. Stir the cornstarch with the cold water until smooth and add it to the corn mixture. Bring back to a boil and season with salt, pepper and cayenne. The succotash can be kept warm for up to 20 minutes or can be cooled and refrigerated for up to a day before serving. When you are ready to serve the succotash, add the cooked lobster meat and green beans. Reheat thoroughly, check the seasonings and serve at once.

Serves 4 to 6 as a side dish

Risotto with Lobster

Risotto, a creamy dish of rice cooked in broth and finished with butter and cheese, is a gem of Northern Italian cuisine. It is made with highly glutinous arborio rice, available in most supermarkets. The rice is first sautéed in butter and olive oil, and then hot broth is added to it in small amounts. The rice is stirred continuously during the cooking, and more broth is added only after all the previous broth has been absorbed. After the rice is cooked al dente—firm to the bite—it is removed from the heat and finished by stirring in butter and cheese, though cheese is not always used. The cooking time from start to finish is about seventeen minutes.

The broth, which is usually chicken, plays an important role in the final taste of risotto, serving as the canvas on which all the other flavors are blended. When made with lobster, the broth moves a step ahead, becoming the defining characteristic of the dish. Lobster broth produces such exquisitely flavored rice that even lobster meat as a garnish is optional.

I have created a master recipe for making risotto with lobster broth; it is purposely simple, intended to feature the flavorful Savory Lobster Broth without such competing flavors as cheese, mushrooms or vegetables. The variations following the recipe demonstrate the broth's ability to integrate beautifully with other ingredients. You may substitute Quick Lobster Stock for the broth, but the flavors will be less intense.

Equipment: You will need a heavy 2-quart saucepan, a small pot to heat up 2 cups broth, a ladle and a wooden spoon. The 2-quart pot allows for fast and even cooking and gives you plenty of room to stir the rice. The wooden spoon prevents the rice from absorbing any metallic flavor.

4 ounces fully cooked lobster meat, or 1 live 1¼-pound lobster	2 tablespoons unsalted butter
2 cups Savory Lobster Broth (page 54) or Quick Lobster Stock (page 57)	1 small onion (3 ounces), finely diced
2 tablespoons olive oil	1 cup Arborio rice
	kosher or sea salt
	freshly ground black pepper

1. If using live lobster, boil (page 29) or steam (page 32) it. Let cool at room temperature. Use a cleaver to crack and remove the meat from the claws, knuckles and tail. Remove the cartilage from the claws and the intestine from the tail of the cooked meat. Cut the lobster meat into chunks about ½ to ¾ inch thick. Cover and refrigerate until you are ready to cook the risotto.

2. Heat the lobster broth in a small pot and keep hot but not boiling.

3. Before making the risotto, remove the lobster meat from the refrigerator and let stand at room temperature. Preheat the oven to 200°F to warm the serving platter or plates.

4. Heat the olive oil and 1 tablespoon of the butter in a heavy 2-quart saucepan over medium heat until the butter is melted. Add the onion and cook gently for 4 to 5 minutes until golden. Add the rice and stir continuously, using a wooden spoon, for 1 minute. Ladle in about ⅓ cup hot broth. Stir constantly and gently until the broth is absorbed. Add another ladleful of broth and stir constantly until the broth is absorbed; repeat until the rice is cooked al dente. Stir in the lobster meat and remove from the heat. Season with salt and pepper. It should require very little seasoning because the lobster broth is already highly seasoned. Stir in the remaining butter and spoon the risotto onto the warmed platter or individual plates. Serve at once.

Serves 4 as a first course

COOK'S NOTE: *You can transform Risotto with Lobster into spectacular variations by simply adding one or two ingredients to the original recipe.*

Risotto with Lobster & Parmigiano-Reggiano

Add to the fully cooked risotto ¼ cup grated Parmigiano-Reggiano cheese along with the last tablespoon butter.

Risotto with Lobster & Fresh Peas

Cook ½ cup shucked fresh peas in a small pot of boiling salted water until tender (8 ounces fresh garden peas will make about ½ cup shucked). Remove the peas from the boiling water and submerge in ice water immediately to stop the cooking. Drain and reserve. Before you add the last ladleful of lobster broth to the risotto, combine 1 tablespoon lobster broth with the last tablespoon butter and the blanched peas in a small skillet (6 inches). Warm the peas over medium heat. Gently stir the peas with the buttery sauce into the fully cooked risotto.

Risotto with Lobster, Asparagus & Parmigiano-Reggiano

Unless they are very thin "pencils," peel 4 to 6 ounces asparagus and cut on a diagonal into ¾-inch pieces. Boil in lightly salted water until tender. Drain and rinse with cold water to stop the cooking. Drain again and reserve at room temperature. Add the asparagus pieces to the risotto just before you add the lobster meat. Gently stir in ¼ cup grated Parmigiano-Reggiano cheese along with the last tablespoon butter.

Risotto with Lobster & Butternut Squash

For this variation, you will need a small piece of peeled butternut squash that weighs between 6 and 8 ounces. Cut the squash into ½-inch cubes and simmer in lightly salted water until tender but still firm. Drain and rinse with cold water to stop the cooking. Drain again and reserve. Add the squash right after you add the final ladleful of lobster broth. When the risotto is fully cooked, remove it from the heat and gently stir in the last tablespoon butter.

Risotto with Lobster & Mushrooms

Use about 8 ounces fresh button, cremini, chanterelle or porcini (cèpes) mushrooms, cut into ⅓-inch-thick slices. Each will impart its own flavor, and all taste great. After the onion has cooked for about 1 minute, add the mushrooms and sauté until tender. Add the rice and cook for 1 minute more. Add the first ladleful of broth and proceed with the recipe as specified.

Risotto with Lobster & Dried Porcini

Soak 1 ounce dried porcini in ½ cup warm lobster broth. When tender, remove the porcini from the broth and cut into ½-inch pieces. After you have sautéed the onion and rice, add the porcini and the soaking liquid along with the first ladleful of broth. Proceed with the recipe as directed.

MULTIPURPOSE LOBSTER FORCEMEAT

I created my version of lobster sausage in an effort to use the "sleepers," nearly dead lobsters that a restaurant serving lobster will inevitably come across. This dish became so popular that soon after I put it on the menu, I found myself ordering massive amounts of lobster every day to keep up with the demand. I used large culls, which we steamed and picked for every drop of meat, making the dish about as economical as lobster dishes go.

Over the years I have refined the recipe so that it is relatively easy to prepare. It takes time but can be a lot of fun, and the reaction you'll get from your guests is enough to make the effort worthwhile. I have found that the stuffing—forcemeat—for the sausage is incredibly versatile, making a delicious filling for ravioli and other pastas as well as for wontons, phyllo dough, crêpes and, my favorite, cabbage rolls. I recently used it quite successfully to re-create a one-hundred-year-old recipe for lobster cutlets originally published in 1896 in *The Boston Cooking School Cookbook* by Fannie Merritt Farmer (page 120).

My lobster forcemeat is a mixture of cooked diced lobster meat, finely diced vegetables and a small amount of butter and seasonings, bound with a thick puree of raw shellfish. I use a shellfish puree because the only part of the lobster dense enough to use for the puree is the tail meat. While this is fine in a restaurant, it is just not economical at home. Fresh raw shrimp is a great substitute. If not available, raw scallops or frozen shrimp can be used.

The recipe calls for live 1-pound chicken lobsters, which are almost always available and economical, but the equivalent weight of other sizes or of culls will give you equally good results. Find the best deal and adjust the cooking times. For this recipe you should use every bit of meat from the lobster, including the walking legs and carcass. (To review the technique for extracting meat, see page 36.) The texture and appearance of the sausage will be greatly enhanced by these odd bits. That said, if you wish to buy cooked lobster meat instead, you can still make an excellent forcemeat.

The recipe that follows, Lobster Forcemeat #1, makes 2 pounds; I feel it is hardly worth the effort that making sausage entails for a lesser amount. For dishes that use a smaller amount of forcemeat, half the recipe is more practical. I have halved the recipe for your convenience and refer to it as Lobster Forcemeat #2 (page 111). The method is identical, but Lobster Forcemeat #2 calls for a smaller dice of lobster meat, better for stuffing items such as ravioli.

Lobster Forcemeat #1

4 live 1-pound chicken lobsters or
4 pounds other live lobsters, or
1 pound fully cooked lobster meat

8 ounces peeled and deveined fresh
shrimp, fresh scallops or frozen peeled
shrimp

1 small carrot (2 ounces), finely diced

1 rib celery (2 ounces), peeled and finely
diced

½ small red bell pepper (1½ ounces),
finely diced

8 tablespoons unsalted butter

1 large egg white

1 bunch chives (1 ounce), finely chopped

6 tablespoons dried white bread crumbs

kosher or sea salt

freshly ground black pepper

cayenne pepper

1. If using live lobster, steam (page 32) or boil (page 29) it. Let cool at room temperature. Use a cleaver to crack and remove the meat from the claws, knuckles and tails. Pick all the meat from the carcass and remove all meat from the walking legs. Remove the cartilage from the claws and the intestine from the tail of the cooked lobster meat. Cut the lobster meat into ½-inch chunks. Add the tomalley to the meat. If there is any roe, finely chop it and add it to the meat as well. Cover with plastic wrap and refrigerate.

2. If using shrimp, check to see that there are no fragments of shell and that they are cleanly deveined. If using scallops, pick them over, looking for pieces of shell as you remove the strap, the stringy little hard piece of flesh on the side of the scallop. Cover with plastic wrap and refrigerate.

3. Combine the carrot, celery and red pepper with the butter in the smallest pot you have. Place the pot over low to medium heat and cook for 5 to 7 minutes. The vegetables should be cooked but still have a little crunch. Remove from the heat and let cool to room temperature.

4. Puree the shrimp or scallops and egg white in a food processor until very smooth. Put the puree in a mixing bowl. Fold in the room-temperature vegetable mixture. Add the chives, diced lobster and bread crumbs. Gently mix and season to taste with salt, pepper and cayenne.

Makes 2 pounds

COOK'S NOTE: *When making this forcemeat for sausage, you will want to have the sausage casings and equipment ready to go. It is essential that you make the sausages immediately after the forcemeat is prepared, because it sets very firmly and quickly, making it difficult to work with if allowed to sit. For other uses, the forcemeat should be refrigerated.*

Lobster Sausage

The rustic and familiar look of sausage adds drama to the unexpected flavors and textures of this dish. Although seafood sausages are not quite as unusual as they were when I first created this dish more than eighteen years ago, they still provide an element of surprise and delight.

Grill or pan-fry these sausages and serve one as an appetizer or two as a main course. Autumn and winter vegetables such as fennel, squash, cabbage and mushrooms complement their hearty nature and have a special affinity with the flavor of the sausages. Potatoes, sweet potatoes and beans are also great accompaniments. My absolutely favorite side dishes for the lobster sausages are Hot Cabbage Slaw (page 109) and Roasted Sweet Potatoes (page 110).

When thoroughly chilled, lobster sausage will keep well for three days after you make it. Feel free to make them a day in advance of serving and do not worry if you cannot use them all at one meal, for I have never known them to stick around long enough to go bad.

Equipment: You will need a "pig stuffer" (the real name), also called a sausage nozzle. Purchase this odd piece of equipment through a restaurant-supply company or through your local butcher shop. Make sure to specify "pig," because it refers to the size of the nozzle, which is designed for pork casings. There is no need to use a grinding machine to produce this sausage. You will need a pastry bag, cut at the tip to fit the nozzle. Order casings from your butcher shop in advance, since they are not always kept on hand. Casings are naturally tough and need tenderizing. Papaya enzymes are used commercially; papaya juice and pineapple juice, more readily available, work well. In addition to tenderizing the casings, these tropical juices remove any taste of meat that may be present in them. Let soak eighteen to twenty-four hours for optimal results.

5 feet pork casings	kosher or sea salt
1 small can pineapple juice	3 tablespoons unsalted butter, olive oil or
ingredients for 1 batch Lobster	vegetable oil
Forcemeat #1 (page 106)	

1. One day before you plan to make the sausages, rinse the casings thoroughly in cold water and place them in a small bowl with enough pineapple juice to cover. Let soak for 18 to 24 hours, no longer. (If they become too tender, they will split open during cooking.) After they have soaked, rinse thoroughly in cold water and keep refrigerated until ready for use.

2. Prepare the lobster forcemeat and leave at room temperature as you quickly fit the pig stuffer into the pastry bag; you will most likely have to cut off a little of the bag at the bottom. Slip the casings over the nozzle. Be sure that the smooth side of the casing is on the outside—they are sometimes inside out. Fill the pastry bag about half full and squeeze a bit of forcemeat through the nozzle. Tie a knot in the casing and proceed to fill the casings by squeezing the bag. Fill the casings loosely. Add more filling to the bag before it runs out, or you will get air pockets in the sausage. Continue until all the forcemeat is used up. You will need to push the last bits of forcemeat through the nozzle with the handle of a wooden spoon. Twist off the sausages at 4-inch intervals, spinning in the opposite direction each time. Lay them out on a baking sheet and refrigerate, uncovered, until ready to use. I recommend 4 hours minimum; this lets them set completely and allows time for the flavors to blend. If you do not intend to cook them within 8 hours, cover them with plastic wrap so that the casings do not get a dry skin on them.

3. Whether you intend to pan-fry or grill the sausage, you must gently poach them first. Because of their high moisture content, these sausages will explode if taken from the refrigerator and exposed to high heat. To poach all the sausages at the same time, you will need a 12- or 14-inch sauté pan; you can use a smaller pan to poach in batches. Fill the pan about two-thirds full with water and lightly salt it, using about 1 teaspoon salt per cup of water. Put the pan over low heat and wait until you see the first signs of vapor released at the surface. The temperature should be about 180°F. Cut the sausages into single links and gently lower them into the poaching water. Let them sit for about 8 minutes, never allowing the water to boil or simmer. At this point the sausages are almost fully cooked. Carry the pan to the sink and pour off the water, using a spatula to keep the sausages from spilling out. They can now be either grilled or fried. You could cook the sausages fully in water, but the texture of the casings is not nearly as good without the final step.

4. *To grill:* Have a charcoal fire prepared so that it is at a moderate or even low heat. Brush the sausages lightly with melted butter or oil and place on the grill. Cook for 3 to 4 minutes to lightly mark and crisp the sausage as well as complete the cooking. Serve at once. *To pan-fry:* Melt the butter or heat the oil over medium heat in a skillet large enough to hold the amount of sausage you are cooking. You will need a large pan (12 to 14 inches) to cook them all at once. Place the sausage in the pan and cook for 4 to 5 minutes, gently turning once so that they become lightly browned on all sides. Serve at once.

Makes 12 sausages about 4 inches long and 2½ ounces each

Hot Cabbage Slaw

In winter, when most green vegetables look and taste pretty ragged, Savoy cabbage comes into its own. Like other cabbages, it has a remarkable capacity for storage and a robust flavor. This hot slaw is the perfect complement to lobster sausage but is also magnificent with other seafood dishes as well as chicken and pork.

1 small head Savoy cabbage (about 1 pound)	1 small carrot (2 ounces), peeled and grated
3 tablespoons unsalted butter	¼ teaspoon celery seeds
1 medium onion (4 ounces), thinly sliced	1 tablespoon apple cider vinegar
1 small red bell pepper (4 ounces), thinly sliced	kosher or sea salt
	freshly ground black pepper

1. Discard the tough or damaged outer leaves of the cabbage. Quarter the cabbage and cut away the core. Slice the cabbage crosswise into ¼-inch slices. Fill a 6-quart pot two-thirds full with water and lightly salt it. Bring to a rolling boil and add the cabbage. Cook for 1 minute, then drain the cabbage. Rinse with cold water to stop the cooking.

2. Heat a 12-inch skillet over medium heat and add the butter, onion, bell pepper and carrot. Cook for 6 to 8 minutes until the vegetables are soft and beginning to brown lightly. Add the cabbage and celery seeds. Cook, stirring often, for another 6 to 8 minutes until the cabbage is very hot. Add the cider vinegar and season to taste with salt and pepper. Serve hot.

Serves 4 to 6 as a side dish

Roasted Sweet Potatoes

As demonstrated in many recipes in this book, mildly sweet flavors complement lobster by echoing the lobster's own natural sweetness. This simple dish of sweet potatoes roasted in a small amount of butter is excellent with Lobster Sausage (page 107) and Hot Cabbage Slaw (page 109). It can also be served as a side dish with pan-roasted or steamed lobster, as well as with many other seafood, poultry, game or meat dishes.

4 or 5 medium sweet potatoes (about 2½ pounds)

2 tablespoons unsalted butter, melted

kosher or sea salt

freshly ground black pepper

1. Preheat the oven to 375°F.

2. Place a medium roasting pan (12 x 9 inches) in the preheating oven while you prepare the sweet potatoes.

3. Rinse the sweet potatoes. Without peeling them, cut into 2-inch chunks. You will get 4 to 6 pieces from each potato, depending on its shape and weight. Do not fuss with making the chunks perfect; just try to keep them fairly uniform in size. Using a paring knife, trim away the outer peel. Try to give the potatoes an oval shape as you do this, but again, do not fuss.

4. Place the sweet potatoes in a mixing bowl and pour in the melted butter. Season to taste with salt and pepper. Mix the potatoes so that they are coated lightly with the butter and seasonings. Open the oven and slide the potatoes into the hot pan. You will hear them sizzle. Cook for 45 minutes, turning the potatoes twice at 15-minute intervals. They will have dark brown spots where the natural sugar in the sweet potatoes has caramelized, and their centers will be creamy and luscious. Serve as soon as possible.

Serves 4 to 6 as a side dish

Lobster Forcemeat #2

2 live 1-pound chicken lobsters or 2 pounds culls, or 8 ounces fully cooked lobster meat

4 ounces peeled and deveined fresh shrimp, fresh scallops or frozen peeled shrimp

½ small carrot (1 ounce), finely diced

½ rib celery (1 ounce), peeled and finely diced

¼ small red bell pepper (¾ ounce), finely diced

4 tablespoons unsalted butter

1 small egg white

½ bunch chives, finely chopped

3 tablespoons dried white bread crumbs

kosher or sea salt

freshly ground black pepper

cayenne pepper

1. If using live lobsters, steam (page 32) or boil (page 29) them. Let cool at room temperature. Use a cleaver to crack and remove the meat from the claws, knuckles and tails. Pick all the meat from the carcass and remove all meat from the walking legs. Remove the cartilage from the claws and the intestine from the tail of the cooked lobster meat. Cut the lobster meat into ¼- to ⅓-inch chunks. Add the tomalley to the meat. If there is any roe, finely chop it and add it to the meat as well. Cover with plastic wrap and refrigerate.

2. If using shrimp, check to see that there are no fragments of shell and that they are cleanly deveined. If using scallops, pick them over, looking for pieces of shell as you remove the strap, the stringy little hard piece of flesh on the side of the scallop. Cover with plastic wrap and refrigerate.

3. Combine the carrot, celery and bell pepper with the butter in the smallest pot you have. Place over low to medium heat and cook for 5 to 7 minutes. The vegetables should be cooked but still have a little crunch. Remove from the heat and let cool to room temperature.

4. Puree the shrimp or scallops and egg white in a food processor until very smooth. Put the puree in a mixing bowl. Fold in the room-temperature vegetable mixture. Add the chives, diced lobster and bread crumbs. Gently mix and season to taste with salt, pepper and cayenne. Cover with plastic wrap and refrigerate.

Makes 1 pound

Savoy Cabbage Rolls with Lobster Stuffing, Braised in Savory Lobster Broth with Mushrooms

I stumbled upon this dish one day when making Lobster Sausage. My butcher had sent me the wrong casings, which I did not notice until it came time to stuff the sausages. I had already made the forcemeat and had Savoy cabbage to make slaw, so in a moment of inspiration born of pure panic, I stuffed the sausage forcemeat into cabbage leaves and braised them in lobster broth. It was delicious! The lobster broth, which is also served as the sauce, adds a robust dimension. If you have none on hand and are not inclined to make it, you may substitute Quick Lobster Stock, chicken or fish stock with excellent results. Serve one roll as a hearty appetizer or main course or two rolls as a main dish with boiled small potatoes or roasted sweet potatoes.

ingredients for 1 batch Lobster Forcemeat #2 (page 111)

1 large head Savoy cabbage (about
1 pound)

1 small onion (3 ounces), thinly sliced

5 tablespoons unsalted butter

kosher or sea salt

freshly ground black pepper

2 shallots (1½ ounces), finely diced

1 small carrot (2 ounces), peeled and cut
into ¼-inch dice

6 ounces fresh chanterelle, shiitake or
other mushrooms, thinly sliced

1 cup Savory Lobster Broth (page 54),
Quick Lobster Stock (page 57) or chicken
or fish stock

a few sprigs chervil, parsley and/or
chives, leaves picked and coarsely
chopped

1. Make the lobster forcemeat and keep chilled. Meanwhile, remove 9 of the best outer leaves from the Savoy cabbage to make the rolls. (You need only 8, but I like to keep an extra one handy just in case.) Cut the remaining cabbage in half and remove and discard the core. Thinly slice the cabbage no more than ¼ inch thick. Fill a 6-quart pot two-thirds full with water and lightly salt it. Bring to a rolling boil and add 3 cabbage leaves. Cook for about 3 minutes until tender and, using a slotted spoon, carefully remove the leaves to a tray where they can drain and cool. Repeat this step until all 9 leaves are cooked. Put the thinly sliced cabbage in the boiling water and cook for 1 minute. Drain the cabbage and rinse with cold water to stop the cooking. In a medium sauté pan (9 or 10 inches), cook the onion in 1 tablespoon of the butter over medium heat for 6 minutes until browned. Add the sliced cabbage and cook, stirring often, for 2 minutes to allow the flavors to blend. Season lightly with salt and pepper and remove from the heat. Let cool.

2. Preheat the oven to 350°F.

3. Cut out the heavy rib from the cabbage leaves and place them on a work surface with the best-looking side facing down. Place one-eighth of the forcemeat in the center of each leaf and shape the forcemeat into a log about 3 inches long.

4. Divide the onion and cabbage mixture into 8 even portions and place a portion beside the forcemeat on the side where the rib was cut away. Fold the sides toward the center and roll up each cabbage leaf. Use 1 tablespoon of the butter to grease a baking dish about 11 x 9 inches. Line the cabbage rolls 6 down and 2 sideways in the pan, leaving a little room between each for heat and liquid to circulate. The dish can be made up to this point well in advance (up to a day ahead) and kept, covered, in the refrigerator until ready to cook.

5. Put a medium sauté pan (9 or 10 inches) over medium-high heat and add 1 tablespoon of the butter. Add the shallots, carrot and mushrooms and sauté for about 6 minutes until lightly browned. Add the lobster broth and bring to a boil. Pour over the cabbage rolls. Cover the dish with aluminum foil and bake for 25 to 30 minutes.

6. Remove the cabbage rolls with a slotted spoon or spatula, allowing them to drain over the baking dish before placing on a platter or individual plates. Cover to keep hot. Pour the broth and vegetables into a small pot and bring to a boil. Stir in the remaining 2 tablespoons butter to make a creamy broth. Spoon the broth over the cabbages. Sprinkle with the chopped chervil and serve at once.

Makes 8 cabbage rolls; serves 4 as a main course or 8 as a fish course

Pan-Fried Lobster Dumplings with Dipping Sauce

These dumplings, made with wonton wrappers, are great fun at a casual gathering with friends and family. Make them up to two hours in advance if you wish, but it is even more fun to make the stuffing ahead and let your friends wrap the dumplings while you cook them in small batches. The stuffing, big in lobster flavor but neutral in spices, blends terrifically with the Asian flavors in the dipping sauce. If you live near an Asian market, buy freshly made egg wontons, which have an excellent texture and flavor. Otherwise, use any frozen variety available at your supermarket. These dumplings are best served as an hors d'oeuvre. Cook them in batches of six or eight and serve as soon as they are ready. The recipe can be doubled or tripled for a big party.

ingredients for 1 batch Lobster Forcemeat #2 (page 111)	**kosher or sea salt**
3 dozen wonton wrappers (3 x 3 inches)	**peanut oil for frying**
	Chinese Dipping Sauce (recipe follows)

1. Prepare the lobster forcemeat. Cover with plastic wrap and chill thoroughly.

2. Lay out 6 or 8 wonton wrappers at a time. Keep the others covered, or they will dry out. Place about 1½ teaspoons forcemeat in the center of each wonton. Keep a small bowl of water nearby. Wet the tip of your finger and run it along the edge of one wrapper to moisten it. Fold the wrapper diagonally in half, making a triangular shape. Be careful to avoid an air pocket in the center. Use your fingers to crimp the edges, creating a tight seal. Repeat with the remaining wrappers.

3. Fill a 6- or 8-quart pot about two-thirds full with water and lightly salt it. Bring to a boil. Add 6 to 8 dumplings and boil for 2 minutes. Remove with a slotted spoon and drain well. Repeat until all the dumplings are boiled.

4. Heat a large skillet (9 or 10 inches) over medium-high heat. Add enough peanut oil (about ⅛ inch) to coat it well and heat until hot. Place 6 to 8 dumplings, flat side down, in the hot oil and cook for about 1 minute until browned and crisp. Serve the dumplings, crisp side up, on a plate or small platter with a small bowl of dipping sauce. Repeat this process, adding more oil as needed, until all the dumplings are cooked.

Makes about 32 dumplings

Chinese Dipping Sauce

1 small piece ginger (½ to ¾ ounce),
peeled and finely minced

2 to 3 scallions (white and green parts),
very thinly sliced

½ cup rice vinegar

1 scant cup regular soy sauce (Kikkoman)

¼ cup sugar

2 tablespoons dark sesame oil

1. Combine all ingredients and mix well. Cover with plastic wrap. Let stand at room temperature for at least 1 hour before serving.

Makes about 1½ cups (enough for 32 dumplings)

COOK'S NOTE: *For a stronger sesame flavor, add 1 tablespoon sesame oil to the peanut oil each time you add oil to the pan when frying the dumplings. If you choose this method, omit the sesame oil from the dipping sauce.*

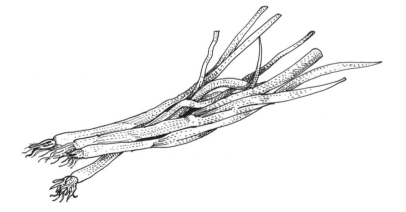

Lobster Ravioli

Ravioli stuffed with lobster meat is the most heavenly pasta I can think of. Every fragrant bite is worth the time and effort that goes into its making. I serve these elegantly delicious ravioli for my most cherished holidays, such as Christmas Eve. Ravioli can be made a day ahead but is really best the same day it is made. For special equipment you will need a hand-cranked (manual) pasta machine, imported from Italy. These are available at most gourmet shops. Pasta dough can be rolled by hand but never as thin as by machine. The very thin dough causes a lighter, more refined texture. The oil in this recipe makes the dough slightly more flexible, making it easier to roll at the thinnest setting on the machine without tearing. I have intentionally created a recipe that yields about a quarter more dough than needed for the amount of stuffing in order to allow for mistakes. You can always cut the remaining dough into noodles and cook them the next day. A tool that is nice but not absolutely necessary is a crimper-cutter, a cutting wheel that seals and cuts the edge of the ravioli in a zigzag pattern.

ingredients for 1 batch Lobster
Forcemeat #2 (page 111)

2½ cups all-purpose flour, plus extra for
rolling the pasta

kosher or sea salt

3 large eggs

2 teaspoons olive oil

1. Prepare the lobster forcemeat. Cover with plastic wrap and chill. This can be made up to a day ahead.

2. Combine the flour and ½ teaspoon salt in a large bowl and mix well. Beat the eggs and oil together in a small bowl with a fork. Make a well in the middle of the flour and pour in the egg mixture. Using the fork, mix the egg and flour, working from the center out. When well mixed, it will look crumbly, not like dough. Using your hands, try to bring it together to form a dough, adding a few drops of water if necessary. Be very careful, though; it is much easier to add a little more water to a dry dough than it is to add flour to a wet one. Try to work with as dry a dough as possible.

3. Turn the dough out onto a work surface and knead by pushing it with the palm of your hand and giving it a quarter turn after each kneading motion. This is hard work, but it must be done. Knead for 10 to 15 minutes until a smooth and very strong dough is made. Wrap the dough tightly in plastic wrap and let it sit for 45 minutes. The dough will relax during this period and become much easier to work with. Set up your pasta machine during this time. Clamp it to the side of the counter and make sure the counter is bone-dry and very clean.

4. After the dough has rested, divide it into 4 pieces. Rewrap 3 pieces so that they do not dry out. Shape the remaining piece into a small rectangle about ½ inch thick. Roll this through the widest setting of the machine (#1 on most machines) and then make it into a smaller rectangle by folding it into thirds. Repeat this step twice more. This step is really a final kneading done by the machine, and it produces a stronger and smoother dough.

5. Turn the dial of the machine to the next notch, which is slightly thinner, and roll again. Keep one hand under the pasta to keep it from tearing while the other hand cranks the handle. If at any time the dough begins to stick or tear, dust it very lightly with flour. Turn to the next thinnest setting and roll again. Repeat this process, moving up a notch each time, until the dough is rolled through the thinnest setting. Most machines have 6 or 7 settings. *Do not skip a notch*; each rolling improves the texture of the dough.

6. Remove the lobster forcemeat from the refrigerator. Eight heaping teaspoonfuls will be used for each rectangle.

7. Lay the sheet of pasta on your work surface and cut the sheet into 2 rectangles about 18 x 4½ inches. At this point it is very important to work quickly with no interruptions. On half of each rectangle, place a heaping teaspoon of lobster forcemeat every 2 inches, 4 across and 2 down. Have a small bowl of water handy. Dip your finger in the water and wet the edges and the area in between the stuffing (see diagram on page 118). Do not use too much water; it is not needed and will ruin the ravioli. Fold the empty half of the dough over the filled half. Working from the side that is folded, mold the dough over the stuffing, being careful to avoid air pockets. When the dough covers the stuffing completely, press down with your fingers to seal the 8 individual ravioli. Using a crimper-cutter or a knife, cut the 8 ravioli and place them on a lightly floured tray or baking sheet.

8. Cover the ravioli loosely with plastic wrap and refrigerate while you make the next batch. Repeat this entire process with the remaining dough and filling. You should need only 3 of the 4 pieces of dough, but if you need more for any reason, you have it. Cover the ravioli with plastic wrap and keep chilled until ready to cook.

9. The size of the pot you need to cook the ravioli will depend on how many you are going to cook at one time, although I recommend cooking no more than 24 at a time. Allow 4 quarts water for each 12 ravioli and add 1 tablespoon salt for each quart of water. Bring to a rolling boil and add the ravioli. If you are cooking the ravioli the same day you made them, they will take 3 to 4 minutes to cook. If they are a day old, add an extra minute of cooking time. Sacrifice one ravioli by removing it from the pot and biting into it—the only really accurate test for doneness. The dough should be cooked through but slightly chewy, and the center should be piping hot. Use a strainer basket to gently remove the ravioli from the pot.

Makes about 48 small ravioli (2 x 2 inches); serves 8 as a light pasta course, 6 as a more substantial pasta course and 4 as a main course

Making lobster ravioli

COOK'S NOTE: *Lobster Ravioli is so exquisite that complicated garnishes or strong-flavored sauces only detract from its perfection. Keep your sauce simple. Let the ravioli speak for themselves.*

Lobster Ravioli with Butter

For each 12 ravioli, melt 1 tablespoon unsalted butter with 2 teaspoons of the pasta water in a sauté pan. After the ravioli are cooked and very well drained, add them to the pan. Grind a bit of black pepper over and toss gently. Serve on a warmed platter or in warmed individual bowls or plates and sprinkle with a little freshly chopped Italian parsley.

Lobster Ravioli with Lemon, Capers & Butter

For each 12 ravioli, heat in a sauté pan 1 tablespoon unsalted butter, 1 teaspoon lemon juice, 1 teaspoon of the pasta water and 2 teaspoons rinsed and drained small capers. After the ravioli are cooked and very well drained, add them to the pan. Grind a bit of black pepper over and toss gently. Serve on a warmed platter or in warmed individual bowls or plates and sprinkle with a little freshly chopped Italian parsley.

Lobster Ravioli with Truffles

For each 12 ravioli, melt 1 tablespoon unsalted butter with 2 teaspoons of the pasta water in a sauté pan. Shave 8 or 10 thin slices of fresh white or black truffle into the butter and warm the truffle in the butter. After the ravioli are cooked and very well drained, add them to the pan. Grind a bit of black pepper over and toss gently. Serve on a warmed platter or in warmed individual bowls or plates and sprinkle with a little freshly chopped Italian parsley. If you wish, you may add a few more truffle shavings on top. Good but not as good: Add 1 teaspoon white truffle oil to the butter and water mixture and omit the fresh truffle.

Lobster Ravioli in Brodo

Each portion should have 6 ravioli and ¾ cup Savory Lobster Broth (page 54). Quick Lobster Stock (page 57) can be substituted for the Savory Lobster Broth. The flavor is not as intense, but it is still good.

To serve 4 people, place a small pot over medium heat and add 1 tablespoon unsalted butter, 2 tablespoons finely diced leek and 2 tablespoons finely diced carrot. Simmer for about 2 minutes until the vegetables are tender. Add 3 cups broth and bring to a boil. Season with salt and pepper if needed and keep very hot. After the ravioli have been well drained, divide them evenly among 4 warmed soup plates. Ladle the hot broth evenly over the ravioli and serve at once.

Fannie Farmer's Lobster Cutlets

The only American cookbook my Italian grandmother, Aida Padagrosi (Ida White), ever owned was a 1924 edition of The Boston Cooking School Cookbook *written by Fannie Merritt Farmer in 1896. She left this to me many years ago when she died. I was fascinated by the book and have since acquired several other editions, each revised to reflect the tastes of the time in which it was published. Later editions—after 1950—were called* The Fannie Farmer Cookbook *and were revised by Marion Cunningham. The books document the history of American cooking, showing the progression from coal and wood to gas and electric as a source of heat for cooking, the introduction of frozen and convenience foods, new equipment and devices and new knowledge concerning nutrition and diet.*

In 1996, Larry Forgione, chef and owner of An American Place in New York City and guru of down-home American cooking, and I re-created a twelve-course dinner from Fannie's original 1896 cookbook as a way of celebrating its one-hundredth anniversary. We chose the lobster cutlet, a funny and old-fashioned type of entrée, as the seventh course. The term "entrée" in Fannie's time referred to a small course of fish or light meat that was diced or pureed and usually prepared like croquettes. Larry and I tried to keep the menu true to her recommendations, taking liberties only when we thought the dish would be too rich or heavy for modern palates. We substituted my lobster forcemeat for the cream sauce–based stuffing called for in 1896.

The lobster filling in this dish is shaped to resemble a small lamb chop. It is then breaded and pan-fried, and a walking leg from the lobster is stuck into the top, playfully simulating the bone of a meat chop. Serve one cutlet as an appetizer or two as a main dish with Summer Vegetable Slaw. The light, crunchy and acidic salad serves to cut the richness of the dish. When you serve the cutlet, do not forget to tell the story of its origins.

8 ounces (½ loaf) good-quality dense white bread

ingredients for 1 batch Lobster Forcemeat #2 (page 111), using 2 live 1-pound chicken lobsters

2 large eggs

¼ cup milk

1 cup all-purpose flour for dredging

peanut oil for frying

1 batch Summer Vegetable Slaw (page 135)

8 wedges lemon

8 sprigs parsley

1. Trim the crust off the bread and make fine bread crumbs of the interior loaf in a food processor. Cover to keep fresh.

2. Prepare the lobster forcemeat, breaking off and refrigerating the cooked lobsters' 4 front walking legs (with the little claws attached) and increasing the amount of bread crumbs to ¾ cup. Cover the forcemeat and chill for 1 hour.

3. Divide the chilled forcemeat into 8 portions. Shape into small cutlets resembling the shape of a lamb chop and place on a tray or baking sheet. Cover with plastic wrap and chill again for another hour. (Make this up to 6 hours in advance if desired.)

4. Beat the eggs and milk together with a fork. Set up bowls of flour, egg wash, and bread crumbs. A few minutes before you are ready to cook the "cutlets," dip each one individually in the flour first, then in the egg wash, and last in the bread crumbs. They should be evenly coated with bread crumbs.

5. Heat a large skillet (12 inches) or two smaller skillets (8 or 9 inches) over medium heat. Add ¼ inch oil to the pan(s) and heat until hot enough to seal the breaded cutlet when it is put in the pan, but not so hot as to brown it instantly. If the oil is not hot enough, the breading will absorb the oil; if it is too hot, it will brown or darken the breading before the filling is fully cooked. Cook for 3 minutes until golden brown. Gently turn the cutlets, using a spatula, and cook for 3 minutes more. Remove the cutlets to a platter with paper towels to absorb the excess oil.

6. Drop the walking legs in the oil for 30 seconds to warm them and make them shiny. Stick a leg into the top of each cutlet.

7. Lean the cutlet on a mound of vegetable slaw and garnish with lemon wedges and parsley sprigs. Serve at once.

Serves 4 as a main course or 8 as a fish course

Frittata with Lobster & Leeks

Frittata is a unique Italian egg dish that resembles something between an omelet and a quiche with no crust. It is tasty, easy to make and versatile. Frittata can be served hot, cold or at room temperature. It can be cut into small wedges and served as part of an antipasto or cut into larger wedges and served as a main dish. For a wonderful light lunch or supper, serve a warm wedge of this lobster frittata with a few fried potatoes and a tossed green salad.

2 live 1-pound chicken lobsters or
2 pounds other live lobsters, or 8 ounces
fully cooked lobster meat

1 medium leek (6 to 7 ounces)

3 tablespoons olive oil

8 large eggs

2 tablespoons finely grated Parmigiano-Reggiano (½ ounce)

2 sprigs Italian parsley, coarsely chopped (1 tablespoon)

kosher or sea salt

freshly ground black pepper

1. If using live lobsters, steam (page 32) or boil (page 29) them. Let cool at room temperature. Use a cleaver to crack and remove the meat from the claws, knuckles and tails. Remove the cartilage from the claws and the intestine from the tail of the cooked meat. Freeze the carcass for future use. Cut the meat into ½-inch chunks. Add the tomalley to the meat. If there is any roe, finely chop it and add it to the meat as well. Cover and refrigerate.

2. Preheat the oven to 450°F.

3. Remove the tough outer leaves of the leek, as well as the dark green tips. Cut the leek in half lengthwise and then cut straight across about ⅓ inch wide. Soak the leek in water to remove any dirt or grit, then drain thoroughly.

4. Heat a small sauté pan (6 inches) over medium heat and add the leek with 1 tablespoon olive oil. Simmer for about 10 minutes until tender. Set aside and let cool a bit.

5. Break the eggs into a large mixing bowl. Add the cheese and whip the eggs to a smooth batter. Stir in the lobster, leek and parsley. Season to taste with salt and pepper (about ½ teaspoon salt and ¼ teaspoon pepper).

6. Heat a 9- or 10-inch sauté pan over medium-high heat. When the pan is hot, add the remaining 2 tablespoons of olive oil. Pour in the batter, using a wooden spoon to distribute the lobster meat evenly throughout the frittata. Cook for 1 minute until the edge begins to set. Place the frittata in the hot oven and bake for about 8 minutes: The top should be lightly browned and the eggs should be firmly set. Remove from the oven and invert a plate over the top of the pan. Quickly but carefully turn the frittata over onto the plate. If you are going to serve it hot, let it sit at least 1 minute before cutting it into wedges. If not, let the frittata cool to room temperature. Cut into wedges just before serving.

Makes 6 large or 12 small wedges

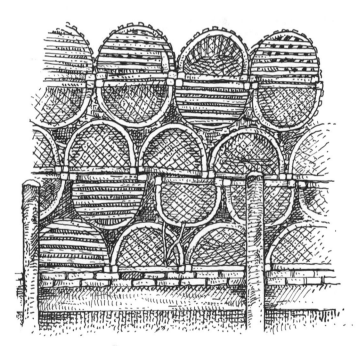

Lobster Hash

Hash, a venerable Yankee dish, is usually made with the leftovers from Boiled Dinner (Corned Beef) or Roast Beef Dinner. In keeping with the humble origins of hash, my version of Lobster Hash uses a modest 2 ounces of lobster meat per person. Serve this as a satisfying main dish for lunch, brunch or even a hearty breakfast.

2½ pounds live lobsters, or 8 ounces fully cooked lobster meat

1 pound large red Bliss potatoes, unpeeled

2 ounces sliced smoked bacon, cut into ½-inch slices

1 medium onion (4 ounces), cut into ½-inch dice

1 small red bell pepper (4 ounces), cut into ½-inch dice

3 sprigs fresh thyme, leaves picked and chopped

½ teaspoon Hungarian paprika

kosher or sea salt

freshly ground black pepper

white vinegar for poaching

4 to 6 tablespoons vegetable oil

4 large eggs

2 scallions, thinly sliced

1. If using live lobsters, steam (page 32) or boil (page 29) them. Let cool at room temperature. Use a cleaver to remove the meat from the claws, knuckles and tails. Freeze the carcass for future use. Remove the cartilage from the claws and the intestine from the tail of the cooked meat. Cut the meat into ½-inch chunks. Cover and refrigerate.

2. Boil the potatoes in lightly salted water until thoroughly cooked, about 30 minutes. Drain and let cool. Cut the potatoes, with their skins, into ½-inch dice. Place in a mixing bowl.

3. Cook the bacon in an 8- or 9-inch sauté pan over medium heat until browned and crisp. Remove the pan from the heat and, using a slotted spoon, remove the bacon from the pan, leaving the fat in the pan. Add the bacon to the potatoes. Return the sauté pan to the heat and add the onion and pepper. Turn up the heat and cook for 5 to 6 minutes until browned. Add the thyme and paprika, mix well and remove from the heat.

4. Add the onion and pepper (including the fat) to the potatoes. Mix in the lobster meat and season with salt and pepper. Mix very well, mashing the potato a bit so that the mixture sticks together. Divide the mixture into four 8-ounce portions and shape into 5-inch cakes. Refrigerate until ready to cook.

5. Fill a deep pan with water for poaching the eggs. Lightly salt the water and add 1 tablespoon white vinegar for each cup of water. Bring to a boil, then lower the heat so that it barely simmers.

6. Heat the oil in a well-seasoned 12- to 14-inch skillet over medium-high heat. Cook the hash "cakes" (they should sizzle when you add them to the pan) for about 5 minutes until the sides are crisp and brown. Using a spatula, turn the cakes over. If they break when turning, don't worry; just use the spatula to reshape them in the pan. Meanwhile, break the eggs one at a time into a small bowl and slide each into the poaching liquid. Do this quickly so that all the eggs cook in about the same amount of time. It will take only 2 minutes for a loose poached egg: whites barely set and yolks runny. Center each hash cake on a medium plate and, using a slotted spoon, gently place a poached egg on top. Grind a bit of pepper over each egg and sprinkle the scallions over the entire dish. Serve at once.

Serves 4 as a main course

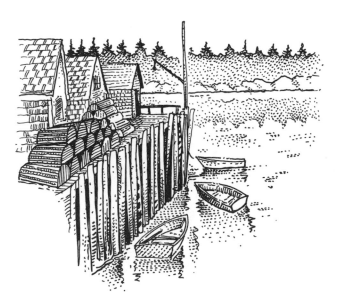

CHAPTER 5

Lobster Salads, Sandwiches,

Cold Plates & Composed Salads

CHILLED LOBSTER, LIKE chilled crab, has a luscious flavor and sumptuous texture. The rich flavor of the lobster paired with its natural leanness creates what could very well be the perfect food. The dishes in this chapter emphasize the opulent nature of lobster, concentrating on presentation as well as flavor, but they are relatively simple to prepare. All call for cooked lobster meat, so if you are not yet ready to boil, split, crack or otherwise hone your lobster cooking skills, you will find plenty of opportunities here to create splendid lobster dishes without facing a live one eye to eye. In all recipes I have given the weight of cooked lobster meat you will need when you go to the fish store. If you decide to purchase live lobsters, remember to look for the best price. It will usually be chicken lobsters, but consider buying culls and even larger lobsters if they are priced advantageously.

Traditional Lobster Salad

This classic mayonnaise-based lobster salad reminds me of Fourth of July picnics on the Maine coast. Its beautiful colors and rich taste, as well as the many ways it can be presented—set it out at a family-style buffet or use it for sandwiches—make it a favorite with my family. My recipe strays from the standard by substituting cucumber and scallion for the usual chopped celery and onion. I like the crunch of the cucumber, and the scallions don't leave the bitter taste that raw onion can. The recipe gives you the option of using bottled mayonnaise or making Special Tarragon Mayonnaise, which is also excellent for other cold seafood salads such as crab, salmon and tuna.

Fresh tarragon melds beautifully with sumptuous lobster meat but should not be overdone—do not use more than the recommended amount. If fresh tarragon is unavailable, omit it; dried tarragon is a poor substitute. This salad is best eaten a few hours after it is made, but it will keep, covered and refrigerated, for up to 2 days.

1 pound fully cooked lobster meat, or 5 pounds live lobsters	3 small scallions (white and most of the green parts), thinly sliced
1 medium cucumber (5 to 6 ounces), peeled, seeded and finely diced	kosher or sea salt
½ cup Special Tarragon Mayonnaise (recipe follows) or bottled mayonnaise	freshly ground black pepper

1. If using live lobsters, steam (page 32) or boil (page 29) them. Let cool at room temperature. Use a cleaver to crack and remove the meat from the claws, knuckles and tails. Remove the cartilage from the claws and the intestine from the tails of the cooked meat. Cut the meat into ½-inch dice. You may pick all the meat from the carcass and add it to the meat or freeze the carcass for soup or broth.

2. Place the cucumber in a colander for at least 5 minutes to drain the excess liquid.

3. Combine the lobster, cucumber and mayonnaise. If the salad is to be served within the hour, add the scallions. If not, add them 30 minutes before serving. Season with salt if needed and pepper. Cover with plastic wrap and chill for at least 30 minutes before serving.

Serves 6 for sandwiches or as a light entrée

Special Tarragon Mayonnaise

Covered and refrigerated, this mayonnaise will keep for up to three days.

1 large egg yolk

1 tablespoon Dijon mustard

2 teaspoons chopped fresh tarragon leaves

1 cup salad oil, such as safflower, sunflower or peanut (avoid full-flavored oil)

juice of ½ large lemon

1 tablespoon ice water

kosher or sea salt

freshly ground black pepper

cayenne pepper or Tabasco sauce

By Hand

1. Place a stainless-steel mixing bowl on a damp cloth to keep the bowl from sliding around. Add the egg yolk, mustard and tarragon to the bowl and whisk until blended.

2. Drizzle the oil into the bowl while whisking constantly. Be sure that the mixture is smooth and well blended at all times. Stop adding the oil periodically to allow yourself time to catch up; when there is no oil visible, continue adding and whisking. When half the oil is added, add 1 teaspoon of the lemon juice. Alternate between the remaining oil and lemon juice, whisking all the while, until both are incorporated.

3. Whisk in the ice water. (The water stabilizes the mayonnaise, which prevents separating, a common flaw of homemade mayonnaise.) Season to taste with salt, pepper and cayenne. Whisk. Store in a small container, covered and refrigerated, until needed.

Using a Food Processor

1. Place the egg yolk, mustard and tarragon in the bowl of a food processor. Put the lid on and pulse the machine for a few seconds to blend the ingredients.

2. With the machine on, add half the oil by pouring it in at a slow but steady speed. Alternate the last half of the oil with the lemon juice until both are incorporated.

3. Add the ice water and pulse for a few seconds. Season to taste with salt, pepper and cayenne. Pulse. Store in a small container, covered and refrigerated, until needed.

Makes 1 cup

COOK'S NOTE: *To make this a sauce for chilled lobster, add 2 tablespoons water or 3 tablespoons heavy cream for each ½ cup mayonnaise. Even better, add chopped cooked roe (2 tablespoons per ½ cup), finely diced tomato (4 tablespoons per ½ cup) or chopped hard-boiled egg (1 egg per ½ cup). One tablespoon freshly chopped Italian parsley tastes good with any of the added ingredients.*

The World-Famous Maine Lobster Roll

A trip along the Maine coast in summer is incomplete unless you stop to eat a lobster roll at one of the many roadside stands, restaurants or clam shacks. This warm, buttery, griddled bun wrapped around a cool fresh lobster salad is quintessential Maine in style and flavor. It is usually served in a paper hot dog container with no garnish other than a small bag of potato chips. I love the humor expressed in the startling contrast between the cheap, relaxed presentation and the excellence of flavor, texture and temperature of this dish.

The longer I live in New England, the more I realize how peculiar we Yankees are. Even our hot dog buns are different! New England hot dog buns are cut on the sides, not in the middle, permitting them to be buttered, toasted or griddled. A lobster roll without this type of bun is just not a proper lobster roll. If you do not live here, you can bake your own New England–Style Hot Dog Buns (page 132).

ingredients for 1 batch Traditional Lobster Salad (page 128)

6 New England–style hot dog buns

6 tablespoons unsalted butter, softened

pickles and potato chips

1. Prepare the lobster salad and chill for at least 30 minutes.

2. Preheat a large heavy skillet (12 or 14 inches) over medium-low heat. (A black cast-iron pan is perfect.)

3. Lightly butter both sides of each bun. Place in the pan and cook for about 2 minutes until golden brown. Turn the buns over and toast the other side. Or toast the buns under a broiler instead.

4. When the buns are ready, stuff them with the chilled lobster salad. Place each roll on a small paper or china plate; garnish with pickles and potato chips. Serve at once.

Makes 6 lobster rolls

Jasper's Deluxe Lobster Roll

The flavor of the Maine Lobster Roll cannot be improved upon but is limited by being appropriate only for informal occasions. I felt compelled to dress it up in order to broaden its appeal.

I start my fancified version by baking fresh New England–Style Hot Dog Buns, adding saffron to the dough (recipe, including this variation, is on page 132). I also make home-made potato chips or even *pommes soufflé,* a classic French potato chip that is fried twice in order to puff and create a hollow center. I serve it with Pickled Beets (page 136) or an-other homemade pickle and hard-boiled eggs. And in summer I serve a light vegetable slaw called Summer Vegetable Slaw (page 135).

Presentation: Butter and toast the saffron bun. Place it on a plate and fill with lobster salad. Put two halves of a perfect hard-boiled egg next to it, then spoon a little more of the lobster salad over so that it spills out of one end of the roll and partially drapes over the egg. Place a small mound of pickled beets (3 or 4 wedges), Summer Vegetable Slaw and warm potato chips behind the roll. The lobster roll has now been transformed into an ele-gant cold plate. It has lost its sense of humor and authenticity, but if you can't drive to a lob-ster shack in Kennebunkport and order the traditional Down East version, I can't think of a more delicious substitute.

New England–Style Hot Dog Buns

Rich in eggs and butter, this dough is soft and tender and does not require excessive kneading. It is easy to make by hand and even easier if you have an electric mixer with a dough hook.

1 teaspoon active dry yeast	3 large eggs
1 teaspoon granulated sugar	½ cup warm milk
½ cup warm water	4 tablespoons unsalted butter
1 teaspoon salt	2 tablespoons salad oil
4 cups all-purpose flour, sifted after measuring, plus additional for dusting	2 tablespoons water

1. Combine the yeast and sugar with ¼ cup of the warm water in a large bowl or in the bowl of an electric mixer. Let stand for 5 to 10 minutes until the mixture becomes frothy. (This allows the yeast to "bloom.")

2. Add the salt and flour. Lightly beat 2 of the eggs with the milk and add this mixture to the bowl. Melt 3 tablespoons of the butter and add this as well. Have the remaining ¼ cup warm water ready. If you are mixing by hand, add some of the water and begin to mix, adding the water as needed. If using an electric mixer, attach the dough hook and jog the machine (turn it on and off) until the dough begins to form. This prevents the flour from jumping out of the mixing bowl. Add the remaining warm water as needed; the dough usually takes the full amount. When a soft dough has formed, knead for 5 minutes by machine or about 8 minutes by hand. This is a soft bread and does not require as much kneading as chewier types. The finished dough should be soft but dense and should not be sticky.

3. Shape the dough into a ball and lightly oil it with the salad oil. Place it in a large bowl. Cover with plastic wrap or a slightly damp towel and let rise in a warm place for about 1 hour until doubled in bulk.

4. Punch the dough down and move to a work surface. Lightly dust the work surface with flour. Shape the dough into a square. Using a knife, cut the dough into 13 equal pieces. This is best done by cutting 12 pieces and using scraps to make the thirteenth. If there is not enough dough for the thirteenth piece, steal a little pinch off the others.

5. With the remaining 1 tablespoon butter, lightly grease a baking sheet that is at least 15 inches long. Shape the dough into uniform 7-inch-long tubular pieces. It is important that all the pieces be the same length. Place the tubes in a line, side by side, down the center of the baking sheet, leaving a ½-inch gap between them (see diagram on page 134). Put the pan in a warm place and let rise a second time.

6. Prepare a thick egg wash by mixing the remaining egg with 2 tablespoons water. After 15 to 20 minutes, the tubes of dough will have risen enough that they will be touching. Generously brush the tubes with egg wash, return the pan to the warm spot and let the dough rise until almost doubled in size, 10 to 15 minutes.

7. Preheat the oven to 350°F.

8. Place the buns in the oven and bake for about 30 minutes until deep golden brown.

9. Let the buns cool on the baking sheet for at least 15 minutes, then run a spatula under them to make sure they are not sticking to the pan. Using 1 or 2 spatulas, carefully lift the baked dough in one piece onto a rack to cool. It is crucial that you not let the buns break or tear apart. After an hour, when the baked dough is completely cooled, move it in one piece to a cutting board. Using a serrated knife, slice down the center of each tube. You will lose half a tube on each end (which is why you need 13 tubes to make 12 buns). The place where the tubes met is now the center of each bun. They will open naturally when it comes time to stuff them, but you can make a small incision to ensure that this happens.

10. Wrap the buns in plastic wrap until ready to use. If you do not intend to use all 12 buns, freeze the extras and defrost when needed.

Makes 1 dozen sliced buns

COOK'S NOTE: *To infuse the dough with the delicate flavor of saffron, chop 1 teaspoon saffron threads and add to ¼ cup water in a small pan. Bring the mixture to a boil over medium-high heat, then remove from the heat. Let cool to lukewarm and substitute for the ¼ cup water added for mixing. Since the dough will be golden to start with, look for a dark brown top before removing from the oven.*

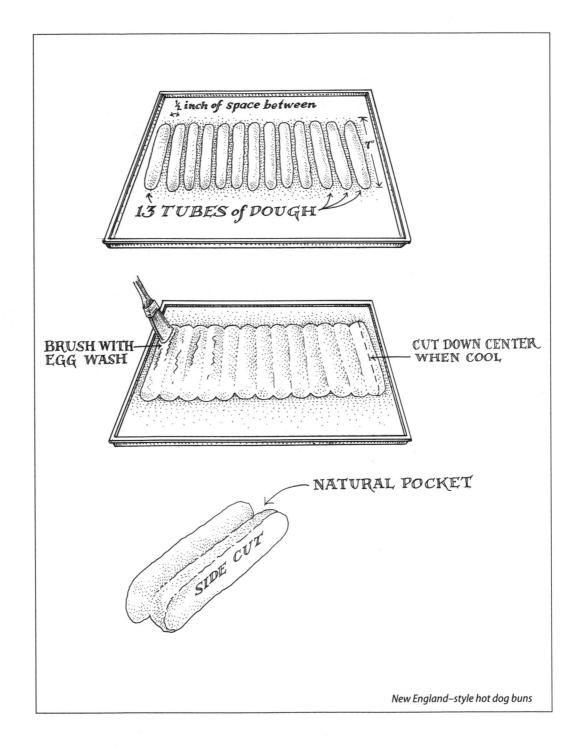

½ inch of space between

T"

13 TUBES of DOUGH

BRUSH WITH
EGG WASH

CUT DOWN CENTER
WHEN COOL

NATURAL POCKET

SIDE CUT

New England–style hot dog buns

Summer Vegetable Slaw

This light, refreshing slaw is wonderful with fresh vegetables from your garden or local farmer's market. Think of the recipe as a guideline: The only constants are that half of the mixture should be cabbage and the amount of onion should always be the same. The rest is up to you. Fennel, peas, cucumbers and summer squash work well here. If you like it spicy, throw in a few slivers of fresh hot chiles. This slaw is perfect with chilled lobster and many other summer foods.

3 tablespoons white wine or champagne vinegar

2 tablespoons granulated sugar

1 small or ½ large red onion (4 ounces)

1 ear sweet corn

½ head green cabbage (1¼ to 1½ pounds)

1 red bell or other sweet pepper (5 to 6 ounces)

1 handful snow peas (2 to 3 ounces)

1 medium carrot (4 ounces)

2 small zucchini or other summer squash (8 to 10 ounces)

3 or 4 jalapeño peppers or a lesser amount of a hotter fresh chile, seeded and sliced (optional)

¼ teaspoon celery seeds

¼ cup peanut or other salad oil

about 2 teaspoons kosher or sea salt

freshly ground black pepper

1. In a bowl large enough to hold the entire slaw, mix the vinegar and sugar. Thinly slice the onion and add it to the vinegar. Let the onion slices "pickle" for a short time while you prepare the remaining vegetables. This process gives the slaw a sweeter flavor.

2. Husk the corn and remove the silk. Boil in lightly salted water for about 3 minutes until tender. Let cool. Cut off the kernels with a knife.

3. Scrub, peel and/or clean the vegetables you have selected. Very thinly slice the cabbage and the other vegetables using a mandoline, a kitchen utensil for slicing or shredding, to save time. Otherwise, use a sharp knife.

4. Add the corn, sliced vegetables, jalapeño peppers, celery seeds and oil to the pickled onion. Toss, season with salt and pepper and toss again. Cover and chill. It is best to make the slaw at least 1 hour before serving to permit the different flavors to mingle. Check the seasonings before serving, adjusting the vinegar, salt and pepper if necessary.

Makes about 3 quarts

Pickled Beets

My Irish grandmother, Mary Josephine Donoghue, from Ballyroan in County Laois, taught me to appreciate pickled beets during one of my yearly visits. In Ireland, where beets (called beetroot) are grown in every garden, extra beets are often pickled and served as a side dish. During one visit, my grandmother, knowing my passion for lobster, invited me to a very special Sunday tea. To my delight I found slices of chilled lobster served along with cold meats, homemade breads, jams and pickled beets. The lobster and beets were a perfect combination of rich flavors and contrasting textures and colors. In the west of Ireland, near Galway, and in the south, near Cork, the European lobster (Homarus gamarus) *is found in enough abundance to support a small lobster industry. Because they are so expensive, they are served only on special occasions. Most are exported to mainland Europe.*

4 pounds medium beets, scrubbed	**¼ cup granulated sugar**
1 cup apple cider vinegar	**1 heaping tablespoon mixed pickling spice**
5 cups water	
2 tablespoons salt	**1 medium onion (6 ounces), cut into ¼-inch slices**

1. In a 4- or 5-quart pot, cover the unpeeled beets with water and bring to a slow boil. Lower the heat, cover and simmer until the beets are tender. Medium beets will take almost 1 hour; you will need to add water once or twice during the cooking. To test for doneness, stick a small paring knife into the beet; it should go in without resistance. If you think the beets are done, cut the biggest one in half and check that the center is cooked. Pour off the hot water and rinse the beets with cold water. Let stand until cool enough to handle, then peel them; the skins will almost fall off.

2. Cut the beets in half and then into wedges ¾ to 1 inch wide, about 10 wedges per beet.

3. Combine the vinegar, 5 cups water, salt, sugar, pickling spice and onion in the same pot in which the beets were cooked. Bring to a boil over medium-high heat and continue to boil for 5 minutes. Now add the beets; the liquid should completely cover them. Remove the pot from the heat and let cool at room temperature. Store the beets and their liquid in quart jars. Refrigerated, they will keep for 3 months.

Makes 3 quarts

COOK'S NOTE: *If you want to "can" the pickled beets (hermetically seal them in jars in a water bath), follow the instructions given with purchased canning jars. They will keep for 2 years in dry storage.*

Lobster Melt

This is the tuna melt's wealthy cousin, a variation of the very American, very 1960s sandwich. I especially like nibbling on the crisp, lacy bits of cheese that stick to the baking sheet after it melts off the sandwich. The recipe below makes eight very rich open-faced lobster melts, which are usually served two to a person. Most kids love them but can barely eat one. If you serve a cup of soup first, you might get away with serving one per person, but despite its richness, people adore this sandwich. I have never seen them left over.

White Cheddar, preferably Vermont, or Colby cheese—a cousin of Cheddar that is a great melting cheese—are my first choices. Use a cheese knife to slice the cheese thinly; it will melt more evenly than grated cheese.

ingredients for 1 batch Traditional Lobster Salad (page 128)	1 to 2 ripe tomatoes (4 ounces), sliced ⅓ inch thick (optional)
4 English muffins	10 ounces Cheddar or Colby cheese, thinly sliced

1. Prepare the lobster salad. Chill for at least 30 minutes.

2. Position a rack in the top third of the oven. Preheat the oven to 425°F.

3. Split and toast the English muffins. Since the muffins will be baked in the oven, do not toast them too much—light brown is ideal.

4. Top the toasted muffin halves with lobster salad and spread evenly. Top with a slice of ripe tomato. Cover completely with thin slices of cheese. Place the muffin halves on a baking sheet and bake for about 8 minutes until the cheese is bubbly and beginning to brown. Flashing the sandwiches under the broiler gives them a nice crisp finish. A good way to do this is to switch your oven from bake to broil after the first 4 minutes of cooking. The broiler will heat up just in time to "gratinée" the top.

Makes 8 open-faced lobster melts; serves 4 or more

Lobster Club Sandwiches

Club sandwiches, built upon the flawless combination of bacon, lettuce and tomato and forti-
fied with an extra layer of bread and, traditionally, a layer of sliced turkey, are the culinary safe
haven of travelers—filling, found almost anywhere in the States and hard to mess up. As with
many classic dishes, there is plenty of room to improvise. The simple variation that follows is
mine, but I must salute Anne Rosenzweig, talented chef and owner of Arcadia Restaurant in
New York City, for popularizing this sandwich. In fact, Anne recently opened another restaurant
in New York called The Lobster Club, a tongue-in-cheek reference to her well-known creation.

You already know how to prepare an excellent lobster salad, so let's start with the
BLT combination. My favorite bacon is Harrington's slab bacon from Vermont (mail-order
information, page 230), cut into thick slices and fried. It is a very smoky country-style
bacon, and I heartily recommend that you look for a similar type. Only crunchy iceberg lettuce will do for this sandwich—any other lettuce is an affectation. The tomato is easy—
choose the ripest reds available. If you are making Special Tarragon Mayonnaise for lobster
salad, you will have extra to spread on the toast. The toast itself should be made from high-
quality, fairly dense white bread baked in a Pullman loaf. Bearing in mind that each sandwich has three slices of bread, the slices should be ⅓ to ½ inch thick. The standard
commercial slice is perfect. Have all the ingredients lined up and ready to go so that you
can construct the sandwiches quickly. The toast should still be slightly warm when you
are finished. Serve with pickles and olives. Potato chips and coleslaw, while delicious complements to the sandwich, are strictly optional—remember the substantial nature of
this sandwich.

Long toothpicks or short skewers are required to hold a club sandwich together. Special toothpicks are available, but unfortunately, most have silly multicolored plastic frills—
a presentation that detracts from this classic sandwich. A nicer presentation is to cut
8-inch bamboo skewers in half; you can use both halves. For a festive touch, color the
skewers a bright yellow by boiling them in a small pot of water with a tablespoon of
turmeric.

ingredients for 1 batch Traditional
Lobster Salad (page 128)

2 ripe medium tomatoes (5 ounces)

1 head iceberg lettuce

12 ounces smoky country bacon

12 slices dense white bread

extra Special Tarragon Mayonnaise
(page 129) or bottled mayonnaise

kosher or sea salt

freshly ground black pepper

pickles and olives for garnish

1. Prepare the lobster salad. You will need only three-quarters of the salad, so you can make it with 12 ounces lobster meat and scale back the other ingredients by a quarter or save the bit of leftover salad for a late-night snack. Chill the salad for at least 30 minutes.

2. Slice the tomatoes about ⅓ inch thick.

3. Remove the stringy outer leaves of the lettuce and discard. Tear the other leaves into pieces about the size of the bread. You will need 3 or 4 pieces per sandwich (12 to 16 pieces total).

4. Slice the bacon about ¼ inch thick. Either spread the bacon on a baking sheet and bake at 375°F for 12 minutes or fry it in a skillet. I prefer my bacon limp, but most people like theirs crisp; go with your personal preference. Drain on a plate lined with paper towels and cover to keep warm.

5. Before toasting the bread, organize the ingredients so that they are within reach. You must work fast if you intend to serve this even slightly warm. Toast all the bread either under the broiler or in a toaster. If using a toaster, have 8 slices ready before you start. The last 4 slices can toast while you are constructing the sandwiches.

6. Line up 4 slices of toasted bread. Cover them evenly with the lobster salad. Spread a little mayonnaise on the side of 4 other slices of toast and cover the lobster salad with these slices, mayonnaise side up. Place the lettuce on top of the toast. Distribute the bacon evenly on top of the lettuce and cover with the tomato slices—2 or 3 slices per sandwich, depending on the size of the tomatoes. Sprinkle with salt and a grind of black pepper. Spread mayonnaise on one side of the remaining 4 slices of toast and place them on top, mayonnaise side down. Place toothpicks or skewers in the center of what will be each quarter, then cut each sandwich into quarters. I recommend squares over triangles because they hold together better. Place the pieces on a large platter or individual plates. If you wish, rest them on their sides, allowing a view of the interior of the sandwich. Garnish with pickles and olives and serve at once.

Makes 4 substantial sandwiches

Hot Lobster & Cheddar Cheese Canapés

My dear friend Lydia Shire, owner of the restaurants Biba and Pignoli in Boston, first made these for me almost twenty years ago. In direct rebellion against the Mediterranean-inspired snacks that are almost mandatory these days, they are pure New England, a classic pairing of dairy and shellfish. Their hearty style is best appreciated when they are not immediately followed by a meal. Serve them at teatime or as an hors d'oeuvre for a cocktail party.

ingredients for 1 batch Traditional Lobster Salad (page 128)	8 slices (½ inch thick) white, wheat or dark rye bread
10 ounces white Cheddar or Colby cheese	

1. Prepare the lobster salad, cutting the lobster meat into ⅓-inch dice. Chill for at least 30 minutes.

2. Grate the cheese and keep chilled.

3. Preheat the broiler.

4. Toast the bread. Trim off the crusts if you wish. Cut each piece of toast into 4 squares and top each with a big spoonful of lobster salad. Cover with a generous amount of grated cheese. Place on a baking sheet and broil 6 to 8 inches from the heat for about 4 minutes until bubbly and lightly browned. Transfer to a platter and pass the napkins. Napkins are a must because the warm, creamy lobster salad and cheese tend to ooze—one of the treats of this dish!

Makes about 2 dozen canapés

OTHER SANDWICH IDEAS

Almost any type of sandwich can be made with lobster salad. You can make "pockets" with pita bread or fill warm flour tortillas with lobster salad, avocado, tomato and a sprinkling of hot sauce. Use your imagination. Croissant sandwiches, po' boys, open-faced sandwiches, subs, rolled sandwiches—the possibilities are endless.

Lobster Salad with Vinaigrette

My kids call this lighter alternative to the mayonnaise-based Traditional Lobster Salad "See Through" Lobster Salad. The flavor is similar to that of the traditional salad, but the texture is less creamy. Both salads can be used interchangeably in the cold plates that follow, but stick to the traditional salad for sandwiches, because its texture is far more suited to that type of preparation. Use Lobster Salad with Vinaigrette for stuffing vegetables and fruits for refreshing cold appetizers or main dishes. You can also set it out in a family-style buffet meal, in which case I recommend cutting both the lobster and the cucumber into thin slices rather than dice. Do not substitute dried herbs in this recipe; if fresh tarragon or chervil is unavailable, it is better to substitute Italian parsley or simply omit it.

1 pound fully cooked lobster meat, or 5 pounds live lobsters	juice of ¼ to ⅓ large lemon (about 2 tablespoons)
1 teaspoon Dijon mustard	kosher or sea salt
2 teaspoons chopped fresh tarragon or chervil leaves	freshly ground black pepper
2 shallots (1½ ounces), finely diced	1 medium cucumber (5 to 6 ounces), peeled, seeded and finely diced
⅓ cup peanut oil	

1. If using live lobsters, steam (page 32) or boil (page 29) them. Use a cleaver to crack and remove the meat from the claws, knuckles and tails. Remove the cartilage from the claws and the intestine from the tails of the cooked meat. Cut the meat into ½-inch dice.

2. Combine the mustard, tarragon, shallots, oil and lemon juice in a small bowl. Whisk thoroughly and season to taste with salt and pepper. Let stand for at least 10 minutes. It can be made well in advance and refrigerated if you wish.

3. Place the cucumber in a colander for at least 5 minutes to drain the excess liquid.

4. In a large mixing bowl, combine the lobster meat and cucumber. Drizzle the vinaigrette over and toss. Chill for at least 20 minutes. Check the seasoning before serving.

Serves 4 to 6 as a light entrée

LOBSTER COLD PLATES

An infinite variety of chilled lobster dishes, lovely and refined as main dishes in warm weather or as appetizers throughout the year, can be made with either the vinaigrette or the mayonnaise type of lobster salad. Avocados, papayas, ripe tomatoes and other fruits make delicious containers for the salad. Sweet peppers, cucumbers, summer squash and zucchini are also terrific. Probably the most pleasing receptacle for lobster salad is its own shell. Accompaniments for cold plates are really your choice. Summer Vegetable Slaw (page 135) and Pickled Beets (page 136) are both excellent. Go ahead and substitute them for the vegetables specified in the recipe if you wish. My recipes are intended as guidelines. The strength of cold dishes lies in their flexibility; substitution of ingredients is necessary for making absolutely fresh summer food.

Avocado & Lobster Salad with Toasted Almonds

The pairing of chilled lobster and avocado seems at first to be light and refreshing, but in fact it is luscious and special—a perfect marriage of creamy texture and rich flavors. The avocado can be stuffed with Traditional Lobster Salad or Lobster Salad with Vinaigrette. I like to use crunchy garnishes—romaine, carrots, bean sprouts and almonds, which contrast nicely with the soft avocado. To ensure that your avocados are perfectly ripe, purchase them a few days in advance. Refrigerate only after they have ripened. I prefer this dish as a main course; it is a little too rich for an appetizer. For another main-course lobster and avocado combination, see Rick Bayless's Grilled Lobster with Sweet Toasted Garlic, Avocado and Red Chile, page 196.

ingredients for 1 batch Traditional Lobster Salad (page 128) or Lobster Salad with Vinaigrette (page 141)

¼ cup sliced blanched almonds

kosher or sea salt

1 head romaine lettuce

2 ounces soybean sprouts

½ medium carrot (2 ounces), peeled, grated or very thinly slivered (julienne)

3 scallions (white and some green parts), very thinly sliced on a diagonal

¼ cup peanut, avocado or almond oil

2 tablespoons white wine or champagne vinegar

1 teaspoon sugar

freshly ground black pepper

½ pint cherry or pear tomatoes, red and/or yellow

6 fresh basil leaves, coarsely chopped

2 ripe large avocados

1. Prepare the lobster salad. Cover and chill for at least 30 minutes. Chill the plates you will be using as well.

2. Preheat the oven to 300°F. Spread the almonds on a small baking sheet and toast for about 20 minutes until they begin to turn golden. Remove from the oven and immediately sprinkle generously with salt. Let cool, then wrap tightly in plastic wrap. This can be done several hours in advance.

3. Remove the dark, tough outer lettuce leaves and discard. Choose 8 beautiful yellow leaves from the heart. Rinse, drain, cover and refrigerate. Rinse and dry the remaining lettuce and cut into thin strips about ¼ inch wide (chiffonade). Mix with the bean sprouts, carrot and scallions. Cover and refrigerate until ready to use.

4. Combine the oil, vinegar and sugar to make a vinaigrette. Season to taste with salt and pepper. Halve the tomatoes and combine with the basil and 2 tablespoons of the vinaigrette in a bowl. Let stand while you prepare the salads.

5. Halve the avocados and carefully remove the pits. Using a large serving spoon, scoop the avocado out of its skin. Keep the spoon pressed against the skin so that you do not mar the avocado halves. This job can also be done by simply peeling the skin off with your fingers.

6. Place 2 lettuce leaves on each of 4 plates so that they stick up slightly over the lip of the plate, looking like a pair of rabbit ears. Drizzle a few drops of vinaigrette on each leaf. Combine the lettuce mixture with the remaining vinaigrette and spread it around each plate, leaving a little nest in the center. Place an avocado half in the center and fill with lobster salad. Try not to be perfect; the salad looks better when the lobster salad spills over a little, leaving some of the avocado showing. Spoon the tomatoes around the avocado and sprinkle with toasted almonds.

Serves 4 as a main course

VARIATIONS

Instead of stuffing the avocado, you can slice it, fan the slices on the plates and then top with the lobster salad.

Instead of the toasted almonds, corn tortillas make a nice crispy garnish. Cut them into strips about ⅓ inch wide and bake or fry until crisp. Salt lightly and sprinkle over the salad.

Use the recipe as a prototype and substitute the following fruits and vegetables for the avocado. Feel free to use different lettuces, vegetables and fruits as garnish.

Papaya: Cut 2 papayas in half and remove the seeds. Using a paring knife, carefully peel away the skin. Purchase papayas a few days in advance, for they must be absolutely ripe to be enjoyed. Replace the tomato garnish with grapefruit or orange sections.

Melon: Ripe cantaloupe or other melons are sensuous and refreshing when paired with lobster salad. One melon will be more than enough for 4 salads. Cut the melon in wedges and cut away the rind. Slice the melon so that it can be fanned. Place the melon toward the front of the plate, covering the center. Mound the lobster salad in the center, spilling over the melon. Replace the tomato garnish with orange sections.

Tomato: Use 4 ripe medium tomatoes, any variety. Cut away part of the center of the tomatoes, creating a basket, but be careful not to hollow out the tomato too much, or there will not be much to enjoy. Fill the tomatoes with lobster salad and allow some salad to spill over. Replace the tomato garnish with cubes or slices of avocado or cucumber. Crumbled crisp bacon is a great replacement for the toasted almonds.

Cucumber: Peel 2 medium cucumbers and slice in half lengthwise. Use a teaspoon to scoop out the seeds and fill with lobster salad.

Summer squash or zucchini: Choose 4 small summer squash or zucchini about 6 inches long. Cutting lengthwise, remove the top third of each squash. Using a teaspoon, scoop out some of the center. Brush with olive oil and sprinkle with salt and pepper. Bake at 350°F for 20 minutes. Chill before stuffing.

Roasted red pepper: Over an open flame or under a broiler, roast 4 medium red bell peppers until the skins blister. Put in a small bowl or pan, cover with plastic wrap and let cool. Carefully peel away the skins. Make a slice up the side of each pepper and remove the seeds and stem. Use the lettuce to help prop up the peppers and fill the peppers with lobster salad.

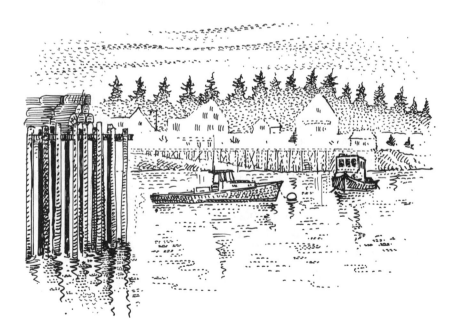

Stuffed Lobster Cold Plate

Because this dish is presented with lobster shells, you will need to buy live lobsters. After you cook and carefully split the lobsters, you will extract enough meat to make half a recipe of either Traditional Lobster Salad or Lobster Salad with Vinaigrette, whichever you like. Serve this dish on beautiful plates or on a large platter to make a dazzling display of chilled lobster salad that has been stuffed back into the lobster's own shell.

2 live 1¼- to 1½-pound hard-shell lobsters

4 small to medium new potatoes (8 ounces)

1 handful fresh green beans (2 ounces)

8 red and/or yellow cherry tomatoes, or 1 large or 2 small ripe tomatoes (4 ounces)

¼ cup good-quality extra-virgin olive oil

2 tablespoons balsamic or red wine vinegar

1 tablespoon finely diced shallot

kosher or sea salt

freshly ground black pepper

8 ounces Bibb, red leaf and/or other leafy lettuce, rinsed and drained

2 eggs, hard-boiled and coarsely chopped

12 chives (about ¼ bunch), cut into 1-inch pieces

1. Steam (page 32) or boil (page 29) the lobsters until fully cooked. Let cool at room temperature. Use a medium Chinese cleaver or large chef's knife to cut off the knuckles where they attach to the carcass. Crack the claws and knuckles and remove the meat. Do not forget to remove the cartilage from the claws. Split the lobsters in half lengthwise (page 34). Remove the head sac and discard. Remove the tomalley and reserve for Tomalley Toasts (page 88) or discard it. If any roe is present, chop it and add it to the meat. Remove the pieces of tail meat and pull out the intestine. You will have about 8 ounces meat. Cut it into ½-inch dice. Make it into either Traditional Lobster Salad (page 128) or Lobster Salad with Vinaigrette (page 141). Cover and chill. Also chill the empty lobster shells and the platter or plates you will be using.

2. Boil the potatoes in a small pot of lightly salted water until tender. Chill thoroughly and cut into slices about ⅓ inch thick.

3. Trim the green beans and boil in salted water until tender. Cool quickly in ice water or with cold running water.

4. Halve the cherry tomatoes or cut the tomatoes into wedges.

5. In a small bowl, mix together the olive oil, vinegar and shallot. Season lightly with salt and pepper and let stand.

6. When you are ready to assemble the cold plates or platter, dress the potatoes, green beans and tomatoes separately with just enough vinaigrette to lightly coat them. You will need about 2 tablespoons for the potatoes and 1 tablespoon each for the green beans and tomatoes.

7. Present the split lobsters on a platter for family-style dining or on individual plates. Stuff the lobster salad equally into the 4 empty shells. Line the platter or plates with lettuce leaves. Place the stuffed lobster shells in the center and arrange the vegetables in individual piles around the shells. Sprinkle the chopped eggs and chives all around the platter or plates and drizzle the remaining vinaigrette over the vegetables and lettuce. Serve at once.

Serves 4 as an appetizer or 2 as a main course

Chilled Split Lobster

To me, plain chilled lobster, served in its shell, is perfection. I must confess that I am just as happy eating this simple treat as I am with any of the more complicated cold dishes. But be careful: In order for this heavenly dish to have its full effect, the lobster must be of excellent quality and it must be served in its shell. This dish is a marriage of appearance and flavor. The presentation alone is enough to stimulate one's appetite, and even more important, storing lobster in its original container keeps it moist and flavorful.

Any lobsters will work for this recipe, depending on availability and the occasion for which you plan to serve them. If you are serving the chilled lobster as a starter, half of a 1-pound chicken lobster or 1¼-pound lobster will suffice. For a more substantial meal, you might offer two halves of a small (1- to 1½-pound) lobster or half of a large (2- to 3-pound) lobster. I have had parties where I just split a bunch of chilled lobsters and put them on a big platter for my friends to help themselves.

Fully cook the lobsters by either steaming (page 32) or boiling (page 29) them. Chill them thoroughly—this may be done up to eight hours ahead of time. Split the lobsters in half lengthwise (page 34) and remove the head sac and tomalley. If roe is present, chop it and add it to the accompanying sauce. Either crack the claws to make it easy for your guests to remove the meat or, if you really want to pamper them, remove the meat from the claws and knuckles and stuff it back into the carcass.

The split lobsters can be served on a large platter of crushed ice garnished with rockweed that has been blanched in boiling water. When the seaweed has been boiled for as little as thirty seconds, it turns bright green—a beautiful and appropriate, if inedible, garnish. Sprigs of parsley, chervil and/or cilantro can be used instead. Lemons and limes cut in wedges are also a great addition to the platter. A little squeeze of juice brightens the flavor of the chilled lobster. If you want to serve the lobsters individually, use large high-sided plates filled with crushed ice and garnish with small strands of rockweed or sprigs of fresh herbs, as well as lemon and lime wedges.

Sauce is nice with chilled lobster but should be kept separate. Let your guests decide how much, if any, they would like. My favorite sauce for chilled lobster is Special Tarragon Mayonnaise (page 129), thinned and enriched with chopped roe. Following is another sauce that is superb with chilled lobster.

"Postmodern" Green Goddess Dressing

Also wonderful with chilled crab, this dressing is another way to enjoy the luxurious combination of avocado and lobster. My recipe does not have much to do with the original "green goddess," but I love the name. You will need a food processor or blender to make this creamy sauce.

½ ripe medium avocado, cut or broken into chunks

juice of 1 lemon

2 sprigs Italian parsley, leaves picked and coarsely chopped

2 scallions (white and green parts), finely chopped

⅓ cup extra-virgin olive oil

¼ cup water

kosher or sea salt

freshly ground black pepper

green Tabasco sauce

1. Combine the avocado, lemon juice, parsley and scallions in the bowl of a food processor or blender. Pulse the machine until the avocado is broken up. With the machine running, add the oil slowly and then the water, also slowly. Scrape down the container with a rubber spatula to be sure you have a very smooth puree.

2. Season to taste with salt, pepper and green Tabasco sauce. (Green Tabasco is mild, so be generous.) Adjust the dressing with a bit more lemon if necessary. Scrape into a small bowl, cover and refrigerate until needed.

Makes 1 heaping cup

COOK'S NOTE: *You can add chopped roe to this sauce. You will barely be able to see it, but it will add great flavor.*

COMPOSED SALADS

Salads in which greens play a secondary role to other ingredients are known as composed salads. Prior to the introduction of nouvelle cuisine, the French cooking revolution that reached America in the 1970s, our exposure to this type of salad was limited to Chef's, Niçoise and Greek. Then, like an explosion, slices of rare duck breast, baked goat cheese, grilled tuna, seared foie gras, fried calamari, warm lobster—of course—and all sorts of marvelous treats arrived as main-course salads in restaurants and homes across the country. In addition to expanding our concept of what goes well with salad, the French gave us a needed reminder of the wonderful variety of lettuces and greens that can be used for salad. Small composed salads are delightful appetizers and fit in well with the American custom of eating salad before the entrée. Larger composed salads are perfect main courses for lunch or a light dinner.

Summer Salad of Lobster, Ripe Tomatoes & Mint

Luscious ripe tomatoes are the essential ingredient in this recipe. Without them, it is rendered meaningless. You can buy cooked lobster meat for this salad if you do not want to cook lobster on what may be a very hot summer day. This salad is simple and easy to prepare.

It is important to rinse the salad greens properly. If you are using a small head of lettuce, pick the tender leaves apart and tear into large bite-size pieces. If you are using a mix of lettuces, either a mix from your garden or a mesclun mix available in many markets now, pick through and discard any tough stems or bruised leaves you may find. Fill a large bowl or small sink with cold water and add the lettuce. Use your hands to gently toss the greens in the water. Allow a few minutes for the dirt to settle. Lift the greens out of the water and place in a colander or salad spinner. Drain or spin the greens until completely dry. I highly recommend using a salad spinner; wet or even damp greens do not allow the vinaigrette to coat the salad evenly.

8 ounces fully cooked lobster meat, or 2½ pounds live lobsters	kosher or sea salt
6 sprigs fresh mint	freshly ground black pepper
½ small red onion (2 ounces), thinly sliced	2 ripe medium tomatoes (8 ounces), red and/or yellow
2 teaspoons balsamic or good red wine vinegar	1 small head lettuce, or 8 ounces mixed lettuces, torn into large bite-size pieces, rinsed, dried and chilled
2 tablespoons olive oil	

1. If you are using live lobsters, fully cook them by steaming (page 32) or boiling (page 29). Let cool at room temperature. Remove the meat from the tails, claws and knuckles. Reserve the carcass for soup. Cover and refrigerate the cooked lobster meat; this will make it easier to slice. Depending on how fancy you want the slices, either make a slit along the top of the tail to remove the intestine or try to remove it with tweezers (page 38). Carefully cut the tails into slices about ⅓ inch thick. Remove the cartilage from the claws and do your best to slice them into 2 pieces. Do not worry if you tear the claw when you remove the cartilage. Place the meat in a small mixing bowl, cover and refrigerate.

2. Pick 4 of the most beautiful sprigs of mint and set aside. Remove the remaining mint leaves and coarsely chop: you should have about 3 tablespoons. Combine the mint with the red onion, vinegar and oil. Season lightly with salt and more generously with pepper. Let stand for 5 minutes.

3. Meanwhile, cut the tomatoes into 6 slices each and spread on a large plate. Drizzle the vinaigrette over the tomatoes. Cover and refrigerate for 10 to 15 minutes. Chill your plates if you have not already done so.

4. When ready to serve the salad, place the lettuce in a bowl and put the bowl of lobster meat next to it. Holding your hand on the sliced tomatoes so that they do not slide, pour a little vinaigrette off the plate onto the lobster and the greens. Toss the greens and divide evenly among the 4 chilled plates. Arrange 3 tomato slices in the center of each plate, leaving a little space in the middle for the lobster. Toss the lobster meat and place the slices in the center. Garnish each plate with a sprig of mint and serve at once.

Serves 4 as an appetizer

ASIAN FISH SAUCE FROM LOBSTER?

Fish sauce is made by grinding fish bones, heads and other remains, then mixing them with salt. The ratio is approximately ½ pound salt to 1 pound fish. It is then put into vats or barrels and allowed to ferment for six months. The strained liquid is then bottled. My friend Nam Van Tran tells me the smell of a fish sauce factory would knock you down. This was recently confirmed by Steward Blackburn, owner of Stache Foods in Medomac, Maine. His company successfully manufactured fish sauce using ground-up lobster carcasses. Unfortunately, he was forced to discontinue this product due to an onslaught of complaints from neighboring businesses. He confessed to me that even he could not stand the smell!

Fish sauce is used in small quantities to add a pungent underlying flavor to dishes, much the way anchovies are used in Mediterranean cuisine. Like anchovies, it adds salt to dishes and should be added before a final seasoning with salt.

Vietnamese Cabbage Salad with Lobster

I first tasted this spicy salad many years ago at the home of my dear friend Nam Van Tran. Nam was the bartender at my restaurant for twelve years, and during this time he introduced me to many of the exotic flavors of Vietnam. His father was the manager of a fish sauce company in Saigon. Fish sauce is an important ingredient in this salad and in many Vietnamese dishes. You will need to plan a trip to an Asian market before making this salad. Your shopping list should include fish sauce, chili paste, rice wine vinegar and Chinese ham. The Chinese ham is similar to dry-cured cappicola; if you cannot locate it, substitute thinly sliced cappicola or prosciutto.

You can make this salad with Chinese cabbage, but if you do, it must be served within an hour, or the salad will be limp. I prefer to use green head cabbage, which stays crunchy even when made as long as eight hours in advance. The ingredients in this salad are exotic, but the preparation is quite easy.

The classic version of this salad is made with shrimp, which may be substituted for the lobster in an equal amount. I have also made this salad without any seafood garnish and then served it as a side dish for grilled lobster or other fish. However you make it, it's great!

8 ounces fully cooked lobster meat, or 2½ pounds live lobsters

½ head green cabbage (12 ounces), finely shredded (3 heaping cups)

1 small carrot (2 ounces)

3 ounces Chinese ham, imported cappi-cola or prosciutto, thinly sliced

1 bunch cilantro

⅓ cup rice wine vinegar

2 tablespoons Asian fish sauce

3 tablespoons peanut oil

2 teaspoons Asian chili paste (*sambal olek*)

1 tablespoon granulated sugar

freshly ground black pepper

½ cup roasted peanuts (3 ounces), chopped

1. If you are using live lobsters, fully cook them by steaming (page 32) or boiling (page 29). Let cool at room temperature. Remove the meat from the tails, claws and knuckles. Reserve the carcass for soup. Cover and refrigerate the cooked lobster meat; this will make it easier to slice. Depending on how fancy you wish to make the slices look, either make a slit along the top of the tail to remove the intestine or try to remove it with tweezers (page 38). Carefully cut the tails into slices about ⅓ inch thick. Remove the cartilage from the claws and do your best to slice them into 2 pieces. Do not worry if you tear the claw when you remove the cartilage. Place the meat in a small mixing bowl, cover and refrigerate.

2. Place the shredded cabbage in a large mixing bowl. Peel the carrot and continue using the peeler to make long paper-thin slices. Cut the slices into thin strips and add to the cabbage. Cut the sliced ham into very thin strips and add it as well.

3. Rinse and dry the cilantro. Pick out 8 of the nicest sprigs for garnish. Lay the rest on a cutting board as a bunch. Slice across the leaves and stems of the bunch, cutting the stems into very small pieces (the stems are important for flavor). You will have about ½ cup. Add the sliced cilantro to the cabbage mixture.

4. Add the vinegar, fish sauce, oil, chili paste and sugar to the bowl and toss. Season with pepper, cover and refrigerate. No salt is needed because the fish sauce is so salty. Allow at least 30 minutes for the flavors to combine. You can prepare this up to 8 hours in advance. Chill the bowls, plates or platter you plan to serve the salad on.

5. When you are ready to serve, remove 3 tablespoons chopped peanuts and set aside. Add the remaining peanuts and the lobster to the salad and toss. Check the final seasoning. Divide this among individual plates or small glass bowls or serve on a large platter or in a large bowl. Garnish each mound of salad with cilantro sprigs and sprinkle with the remaining peanuts.

Serves 4 to 6 as an appetizer or side dish

COOK'S NOTES: *Peanuts taste best if you buy them raw and roast them yourself. Preheat the oven to 325°F. Toss 3 ounces raw peanuts in 1 teaspoon peanut oil. Spread in a baking dish or roasting pan and bake for about 20 minutes until golden. Let cool completely, then coarsely chop with a knife or in a food processor. If you use store-bought roasted peanuts, which are usually salted, use a little less fish sauce when you season the salad. Check the seasoning again after you add the peanuts.*

It is traditional to serve fried shrimp chips with this salad. They can be purchased in Asian markets. One bag is enough for twenty-five people. These thin little chips are about the size of a quarter, but they quadruple in size when you fry them! Unless you want to be authentic for authenticity's sake, these chips are more trouble than they are worth. If you do want to serve them, avoid the multicolored chips and buy the plain white ones. Follow the directions on the box.

Warm Green Salad with Lobster, Mineola Oranges & Citrus Vinaigrette

This exquisite appetizer, both satisfying and refreshing, is perfect on a chilly winter night. The flavors of citrus, lobster and greens are all intensified by warming. Think of this salad as a kind of stir-fry that requires you to be well organized before you start. The actual cooking time is less than six minutes, and timing is crucial.

Three parts of the oranges are used here: zest, segments and juice. The lemon oil, made by my friend John Boyajian, is not an infused oil but is the real oil squeezed from the skins of lemons. It takes hundreds of lemons to make a pint of this oil, which functions the way a flavor extract does; a few drops add a beautiful brightness to vinaigrettes, sauces and desserts. Boyajian Lemon Oil can be purchased from Williams-Sonoma or other specialty-food stores. Grated lemon zest can be substituted for the lemon oil if necessary.

2 live 1¼- to 1½-pound hard-shell lobsters	⅓ cup peanut or safflower oil
	freshly ground black pepper
2 seedless oranges, Mineolas or navel	¼ teaspoon lemon oil, or grated zest of 1 lemon
4 shallots (2 ounces)	
12 fresh basil leaves	3 tablespoons aged sherry vinegar
10 ounces mixed hearty salad greens (frisée, radicchio, mizuna, spinach and/or Belgian endive), torn into bite-size pieces	kosher or sea salt

1. Parboil the lobsters using the timing chart on page 30. Using tongs, remove the lobsters from the boiling water and let cool at room temperature. Remove the meat from the claws and knuckles; try to leave them whole. Break the carcass off from the tail and freeze the carcass for another use. Split the tail in half lengthwise and remove the meat from the tail. Remove the intestine. Cut each tail half into 3 nice chunks. Cover the lobster meat and refrigerate until ready to use.

2. Prepare the oranges by first peeling the zest from one of the oranges. This can be done by using either a zester or a paring knife. Be sure to remove the white pith, then cut into thin strips. Next, using your paring knife, trim the skin and white pith from both oranges. Slice the oranges into sections, then squeeze the juice from the remains; you should get about ¼ cup. Reserve the zest, sections and juice separately.

3. Chop the shallots and slice the basil leaves. Rinse and dry the salad greens. Have all the other ingredients lined up and ready to go before you start the dish.

4. About 6 minutes before serving the salad, heat the peanut oil in a large sauté pan (12 inches) over medium heat. Lightly pepper the lobster meat and place it in the oil. There should be a little sizzle but not much. Cook the lobster pieces about 3 minutes, turning and moving them with tongs so that they cook evenly. Remove the meat to a plate and let sit while you finish the salad.

5. Add the shallots and orange zest to the oil, which will now be tinted red from the lobsters, and cook for 1 minute. Remove the pan from the heat and add the basil, lemon oil, sherry vinegar and orange juice. Add the juices that have accumulated on the dish with the lobster meat. Mix well and season with salt and pepper.

6. Return the pan to the heat and add the salad greens. Using tongs, continuously toss the salad until the greens are warmed but not cooked. This takes about 1 minute. When the greens are warm, lift them out of the pan and divide evenly among 4 plates. Work very quickly. Place a lobster claw on top of each salad and arrange the remaining lobster meat (1 knuckle and 3 chunks from the tail per plate) and the orange sections around the salad. Spoon the dressing from the pan over the salad and serve at once.

Serves 4 as an appetizer or a light lunch

Millionaire's Salad: Warm Greens with Lobster, Foie Gras & Papaya

The cooks at my restaurant rightfully dubbed this "millionaire's salad," because everything about it is rich: the flavor, the texture, the color—not to mention the price. I usually reserve this dish for special dinners or events, such as New Year's Eve. The papaya adds a brilliant color, but a perfectly ripened mango can be substituted with equally dazzling results. Purchase it a few days earlier so that you know it will be ripe. If you cannot find fresh moulard (duck) foie gras in a specialty store, you can order it from Hudson Valley Foie Gras (see page 230 for mail-order information).

    Like the preceding warm salad, this can be thought of as a stir-fry. For best results, it is essential that all the ingredients be organized and ready to go before you start.

2 live 1-pound chicken lobsters	freshly ground black pepper
4 slices moulard (duck) foie gras (1½ to 2 ounces each)	½ small red onion (2 ounces), thinly sliced
8 ounces hearty salad greens (frisée, radicchio, mizuna, spinach and/or Belgian endive), torn into bite-size pieces	3 tablespoons sherry vinegar
	1 tablespoon finely sliced or grated lemon zest
1 ripe large papaya or mango	kosher or sea salt
⅓ cup peanut oil	all-purpose flour for dusting

1. Parboil the lobsters using the timing chart on page 30. Using tongs, remove the lobsters from the boiling water and let cool at room temperature. Remove the meat from the claws and knuckles; try to leave them whole. Break the carcass off from the tail and reserve the carcass for soup. Split the tail in half lengthwise and remove the meat from the tail. Remove the intestine. Cut each tail half in half again. Cover the lobster meat and refrigerate until ready to use.

2. Look over the foie gras and, using tweezers, remove any veins that might be present.

3. Rinse and dry the salad greens. Peel, seed and cut the papaya into uniform 1-inch chunks. Have all the other ingredients organized and ready to go.

4. About 10 minutes before serving the salad, place your pans on the burners: a 12-inch sauté pan over medium heat and an 8- to 10-inch nonstick skillet over medium-high heat. Add the oil to the 12-inch pan. Lightly pepper the lobster and add it along with the red onion to the pan. Cook the lobster and onion for about 3 minutes, turning and moving them with tongs so that they cook evenly. Remove the meat to a plate and let it sit while you finish the salad. Leave the onion in the pan and remove the pan from the heat. Add the sherry vinegar and lemon zest and season with salt and pepper. Add any juice that has accumulated on the plate with the lobster meat.

5. Salt and pepper the slices of foie gras and dust with flour, shaking off any excess. Place the pieces in the dry nonstick skillet. In a few seconds, you will hear them begin to sizzle. Cook for about 45 seconds on each side to form a nice brown crust. Remove the foie gras immediately and cover to keep warm.

6. Return the 12-inch pan to medium heat and add the mixed salad greens. Using tongs, continuously toss the salad greens until they are warmed but not cooked. This takes about 1 minute. When the greens are warm, lift them out of the pan and divide evenly among the 4 plates. Work very quickly. Place the foie gras on top of the salad and lean a lobster claw against each slice. Garnish the salad with the remaining chunks of lobster (1 knuckle and 2 tail pieces per plate) and the papaya. Spoon the dressing from the pan over the salad and serve at once.

Serves 4 as an appetizer or lunch

CHAPTER 6

Classic Main Courses

NEWBURG, THERMIDOR, FRA DIAVOLO—this chapter is dedicated to the famous lobster classics, all main dishes created and traditionally prepared only in the kitchens of hotels and restaurants. These recipes call for generous portions of lobster and are perfect for celebrating the most special occasions. These rich, often elaborate dishes are most suitable in the autumn and early winter when appetites are robust, high-quality hard-shell lobsters are abundant and the darkening season calls for greater reserves of inner joy. Most of the recipes in this chapter are for two to four people, and although they can be doubled, the expense of the large portions of lobster and the intricacy of the preparations make them more appropriate for intimate gatherings. Varying degrees of effort and time are required, but rest assured that the gasps of pleasure from your guests will make it well worth the energy you put into it. Do not be intimidated by the number of steps in some recipes. If you follow each step carefully and think of it as a process unto itself, you will find the entire recipe quite manageable. After all, as the great French chef and restaurateur Fernand Point once said, "Success is the sum of a lot of small things correctly done." Enjoy!

Baked Stuffed Lobster

Baked stuffed lobster, filled with fresh briny seafood, broken crackers and sweet butter and then baked until crisp and golden, is a legendary New England classic that has been served for most of this century in the great Boston hotels such as Parker House and Copley Plaza. When particular care is taken in preparing the stuffing, it is a spectacular dish. But be careful: If the stuffing is made ahead of time, it risks becoming soggy. Always mix your stuffing very gently at the last minute. My favorite stuffing is made with fresh Maine shrimp in the winter and rock crab during the rest of the year, although scallops are also wonderful. The crumbled crackers that bind the stuffing are common crackers, oyster crackers or Ritz crackers; to be honest, Ritz crackers work best. A nontraditional but excellent stuffing can also be made with dried, crumbled corn bread. Bread crumbs are not a good choice because they tend to become soggy.

The seafood you choose for the stuffing will determine the exact preparation. For lobster and crabmeat, both of which are precooked, the onions are cooled before the stuffing is mixed. Shrimp or scallops are cut into dime-size pieces and partially cooked by sautéing with the onions. The recipe accounts for this difference. Lobsters weighing between 1½ and 2½ pounds are best here. Smaller ones overcook, and bigger ones cook unevenly.

For a medium main course, serve half of a 2-pound lobster to each guest. For a large portion, serve a whole 1½- to 1¾-pound lobster.

Equipment: You will need a medium Chinese cleaver or large chef's knife, a small mixing bowl, a pastry brush, a 9-inch skillet and a large baking sheet or roasting pan that measures at least 24 x 16 inches.

8 tablespoons unsalted butter, plus 3 tablespoons, melted, for brushing	kosher or sea salt
1 medium onion (5 to 6 ounces), finely diced	freshly ground black pepper
2 sprigs tarragon, leaves picked and coarsely chopped (2 teaspoons)	2 live 1½- to 2½-pound hard-shell select lobsters
2 sprigs Italian parsley, leaves picked and coarsely chopped (2 tablespoons)	3 ounces Ritz crackers, common crackers (page 75), oyster crackers or dried corn bread, crumbled
4 ounces peeled raw Maine shrimp or raw scallops or cooked crabmeat or lobster meat, cut into ½-inch dice	

1. Preheat the oven to 425°F.

2. Melt 8 tablespoons butter in a 9-inch skillet over medium heat. Add the onion and cook for 5 minutes until soft but not browned. Stir in the tarragon and parsley. If using raw shrimp or scallops, add them with the herbs and cook for 1 minute. Remove from the heat and let cool slightly. If using cooked lobster or crabmeat, remove the pan from the heat as soon as you stir in the herbs, let cool and then add the lobster or crabmeat. Season with salt and pepper.

3. With a cleaver or chef's knife, split the lobsters in half lengthwise (page 34). Remove and discard the head sac and intestine. Remove the tomalley and the roe if present and place in a small bowl. Break into small pieces using a fork. With the back side of a knife, crack the center of each claw on one side only. Season the lobsters lightly with salt and pepper. On a large roasting pan or baking sheet, place the halves together to resemble a butterfly.

4. The tomalley and roe are optional for the stuffing. If you want to include them, mix them into the seafood mixture. Gently fold the crumbled crackers into the mixture. Divide the mixture evenly between 2 lobsters. If you are serving 1 lobster per person, spread the stuffing over the center so that the lobsters look whole again. Do not pack the stuffing tightly, or it will affect the even baking of the lobster. Brush the 3 tablespoons melted butter over the exposed tail meat, stuffing and claws. Bake until the lobster is cooked through and the stuffing is crisp and golden. (Use the following chart as a guideline for cooking times.) Serve at once.

Makes enough stuffing for 2 big lobsters

BAKED STUFFED LOBSTER COOKING TIMES IN A PREHEATED 425°F OVEN

1½ pounds	17 minutes
1¾ pounds	20 minutes
2 pounds	24 minutes
2½ pounds	30 minutes

Lobster Potpie

The potpie dates back to colonial New England, when pies of every description were made at harvesttime and stored frozen in an outdoor shed. During the lean winter months they were defrosted and eaten as needed. The crust, made of lard and flour, sealed the different foods and acted as an antioxidant, retarding bacterial growth and preventing freezer burn. In the 1800s a chicken potpie was as popular for Thanksgiving dinner as turkey is today.

I love cracking open the top of a steaming potpie to see and smell the bubbly hot filling. And I love the texture of the crisp, flaky crust coated with creamy sauce. I have made all types of potpies: rabbit and mushroom, pheasant and turnip, chicken and oyster and even one with porgies and mussels, but lobster potpie is definitely my favorite. The recipe I created for this delectable lobster dish has a shortened cooking time to avoid the problem of overcooking usually found with seafood potpies. This potpie has a wonderfully crisp, light crust that covers a luscious stew of lobster and vegetables. You can prepare the potpies in the morning and bake them for dinner. Served with a salad of lightly dressed mixed greens, they make a complete meal and an exciting treat for guests that requires almost no effort at dinnertime. You will need to buy individual potpie dishes, sold at specialty stores and restaurant-supply stores. The most common size is 10 ounces, which makes a hearty portion. A 10-ounce ramekin can also be used.

This recipe calls for two 2-pound lobsters. You may substitute four 1-pound chicken lobsters, but the larger chunks of meat that the bigger lobsters produce are less apt to overcook than pieces from a smaller lobster. The recipe calls for mushrooms; use buttons, shiitakes, chanterelles or almost any type, but avoid mushrooms such as cremini or trumpet because they will discolor the sauce. You can also use a sweet potato for the potato here if you'd like.

The recipe for the crust, really a "cream biscuit," can also be used for quick and tasty biscuits.

2 live 2-pound hard-shell select lobsters	2 cups Savory Lobster Broth (page 54) or Quick Lobster Stock (page 57)
1 large potato (12 ounces), peeled and cut into ¾-inch dice	½ cup heavy cream
5 tablespoons unsalted butter	3 tablespoons cornstarch
1 medium red bell pepper (4 ounces), cut into ¾-inch dice	3 tablespoons water
1 medium onion (5 to 6 ounces), cut into ¾-inch dice	kosher or sea salt
	freshly ground black pepper
6 ounces fresh mushrooms, stems trimmed, cut into ¾-inch dice	cayenne pepper (optional)
	ingredients for 1 batch Biscuit Dough for Potpies (page 166)

1. Set up a steamer in a large (4- to 5-gallon) pot with a rack. Add 1 inch water and ¼ cup salt. Bring to a rolling boil. With your hand on the carapace of the lobsters, place them inside the steamer and cover tightly with a lid. Steam for 12 minutes and then, using tongs, remove them and let cool at room temperature. The lobsters will be slightly undercooked. If you are steaming different-size lobsters, refer to the chart on page 32 but shorten cooking time by 25 percent. If you prefer to boil them, refer to the chart on page 29, but again, shorten the cooking time by 25 percent. Remove the meat from the claws, knuckles and tails; remove the cartilage from the claws and the intestine from the tails. Pick all the meat from the carcass and remove all the meat from the walking legs. Cut the meat into ¾- to 1-inch chunks. Add the tomalley to the meat, and if there is any roe, finely chop it and add it to the meat. Cover with plastic wrap and refrigerate.

2. Simmer the potato in salted water until tender. Drain and reserve.

3. Heat 3 tablespoons of the butter in a 9-inch skillet over medium heat. Add the bell pepper and onion and cook for 5 minutes. Add the mushrooms and cook for about 5 minutes until the mushrooms are thoroughly cooked.

4. Drain the liquid, if any, from the sautéed vegetables into a small saucepan (2 quarts). Add the lobster broth and cream and bring to a slow boil. Dissolve the cornstarch in the water and whisk it in. Cook, whisking vigorously, until the sauce returns to a boil. It will be very thick. Combine the sauce with the hot vegetables and cooked potato in a mixing bowl. Let cool at room temperature, stirring gently to facilitate the cooling. When the mixture is no longer hot, add the lobster meat and season with salt, pepper and cayenne. Divide the mixture evenly among the 4 potpie crocks and refrigerate while you prepare the dough.

5. Prepare the dough for potpies as instructed.

6. Melt the remaining 2 tablespoons butter and brush over the top of each crust. Return the pies to the refrigerator. This can be done as much as 8 hours in advance. The pies should be well chilled before baking.

7. Preheat the oven to 350°F. Place the pies on a baking sheet. Prick each pie top about 6 times with a fork to allow steam to release while baking; otherwise, they may explode. Bake for about 25 minutes until golden brown and bubbling hot. They can sit for up to 10 minutes before serving.

Makes four 10-ounce potpies

Biscuit Dough for Potpies (or Cream Biscuits)

This recipe cooks much more quickly than pie dough and is excellent for seafood potpies because it avoids the danger of overcooking. It makes enough dough to cover four individual potpies and can also be used to make traditional cream biscuits—perfect with chowder or as bread at the dinner table. This recipe makes about a dozen medium biscuits. They are so good, you'll probably want to double it!

2 cups pastry flour, plus extra for dusting	1 teaspoon salt
2 teaspoons baking powder	about 1 cup heavy cream
1 teaspoon sugar	

For Potpies

1. Combine the flour, baking powder, sugar and salt in a mixing bowl and stir well to mix. Add the cream slowly and mix gently by hand until a soft dough forms. This may take more cream or a little less, depending on the starch in the flour and the butterfat in the cream. Remove the dough to a lightly floured surface and gently knead until the dough is smooth. Try not to overwork the dough.

2. Divide the dough into 4 balls and roll each one out to make a lid that allows an overhang of ½ to ¾ inch on the pie dish. The dough should be about ⅓ inch thick. Place a lid on each pie and mold to overlap the rim of the dish (this keeps the crust from pulling away as it bakes). Return to step 6 of the potpie recipe.

For Cream Biscuits

1. Preheat the oven to 375°F.

2. Add 4 tablespoons melted unsalted butter to the list of ingredients. Lightly grease a baking sheet about 15 x 10 inches with 1 tablespoon of the melted butter.

3. Combine the flour, baking powder, sugar and salt in a mixing bowl and stir well to mix. Add the cream slowly and mix gently by hand until a soft dough forms. This may take more cream or a little less, depending on the starch in the flour and the butterfat in the cream. Remove the dough to a lightly floured surface and gently knead until the dough is smooth. Try not to overwork the dough.

4. Roll the dough out into a rectangle about 10 x 6 inches and about ¾ inch thick. Dust the work surface lightly with extra pastry flour if it is needed. Cut the dough crosswise in half (5 x 6 inches) and brush one half with half of the remaining melted butter. Place the other half on top of the buttered half and gently roll your pin over the top so that the pieces stick to each other. Shape the sides of the rectangle and brush the top with the remaining butter. Cut into 1½-inch squares by cutting 3 rows across the 5-inch side and 4 rows across the 6-inch side. Place on the buttered baking sheet about 1 inch apart and bake for about 15 minutes until golden brown.

Makes 4 individual potpie crusts or 1 dozen cream biscuits

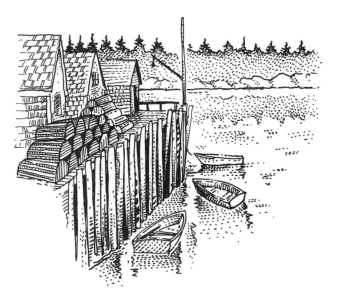

Broiled Lobster with Whiskey Butter

The dry, smooth flavor of whiskey is a wonderful complement to moist, sweet broiled lobster, made famous at steak houses like The Palm and Peter Luger's in New York. Any high-quality, smooth-tasting Scotch, Irish, American or Canadian whiskey will do. Cognac and Armagnac can also be used, but the sweet flavor they produce does not offset the flavor of the lobster the way drier whiskies do.

This recipe calls for two hard-shell select lobsters weighing 1¾ pounds each. The chart on page 169 gives the approximate cooking times for broiling lobsters between 1½ and 2½ pounds. Stay with these sizes. Home ovens do not produce enough heat to broil jumbo lobsters successfully, and small lobsters tend to overcook when broiled.

Equipment: You will need a medium Chinese cleaver or large chef's knife, a broiler pan measuring about 16 x 12 inches, a small whisk, a saucepan and a pastry brush.

8 tablespoons unsalted butter	1 teaspoon fresh lemon juice
2 shallots (1½ ounces), finely diced	kosher or sea salt
⅓ cup plus 2 tablespoons good-quality whiskey	freshly ground black pepper
	2 live 1¾-pound hard-shell select lobsters

1. Position the rack below the broiler so that the lobsters are 6 to 8 inches from the heating element. Preheat the broiler.

2. Place 2 tablespoons of the butter in a small saucepan (1 quart). Cut the remaining butter into ½-inch cubes and set aside. Add the shallots and cook over low to medium heat for about 2 minutes, allowing them to brown very lightly. If you are cooking over a gas fire, remove the pan from the heat and add ⅓ cup whiskey. Tilt the pan as you place it back on the burner and ignite the whiskey. Stand back! If you are cooking on an electric burner, use a match to ignite the whiskey. Let the flames die and continue to simmer the whiskey until just 3 to 4 teaspoons liquid remain. Turn the heat to low and whisk the reserved cubes of butter, a few at a time, into the reduction. Wait for the butter to melt after each addition before adding more. Move the saucepan on and off the heat every now and then in order to maintain a temperature of about 180°F (hot but not boiling); the sauce will separate if it becomes too hot. When all the butter has been whisked into the sauce, add the lemon juice and season with salt and pepper. The sauce should be silky smooth and pale yellow in color. Keep the sauce in a warm place while you prepare the lobster.

3. With a cleaver or chef's knife, split the lobsters in half lengthwise (page 34). Remove and discard the head sac and intestine. Remove the tomalley and the roe if present and place in a small bowl. Break into pieces using a fork. With the back side of a knife, crack the center of each claw on one side only. Arrange the lobsters so that they fit on a broiler pan without overlapping; the lobster must be completely exposed in order to cook evenly under the broiler. Divide the tomalley and roe among the cavities and season the lobsters lightly with salt and pepper.

4. Sprinkle the 2 tablespoons whiskey over the lobster pieces and then lightly brush the lobster with the whiskey butter sauce; brush the big claws as well as all exposed meat and tomalley. Broil for 5 minutes. Remove the pan and quickly baste the lobster with the whiskey butter sauce. It is not necessary to baste the claws this time, only the exposed meat. Return the pan to the broiler, reversing the original position to help all parts cook evenly. Warm the butter sauce over low heat without letting it boil. If it seems too thick, thin it with a few drops of water. Broil for 5 minutes more; the lobster should be thoroughly cooked (total cooking time: 11 minutes). To check for doneness, take a peek at the tail meat where it enters the lobster carcass. If the lobster is cooked through, the tail meat will be creamy white.

5. Remove the lobsters from the broiler and place the pieces on a platter or individual plates. Lightly brush the lobsters with the sauce one last time. Serve immediately with the remaining whiskey butter sauce poured into small bowls or ramekins for dipping.

Serves 2 as a main course or 4 as a fish course

APPROXIMATE COOKING TIMES FOR BROILED LOBSTER

Begin timing the lobsters as soon as they are first put under the broiler. It is necessary to remove the pan from the broiler halfway through the broiling. Baste the lobster and reverse the direction of the pan before returning it to the oven. This should take less than one minute and is included in the cooking times below.

1½ pounds	10 minutes
1¾ pounds	11 minutes
2 pounds	13 minutes
2¼ pounds	15 minutes
2½ pounds	17 minutes

Lobster with Vanilla Butter Sauce

When I told my nine-year-old son J.P. that I was making lobster with vanilla, he asked, "Can we eat it now, or do we have to wait for dessert?" I laughed, but he was quite serious. He could only imagine using vanilla to flavor sweets. Vanilla is so popular in ice cream and other sweets that it is hard to think why anyone would want to use it in a savory dish. But this flavor combination, created by Alain Senderens at his famous three-star Paris restaurant L'Archestrate is brilliant. It has become a classic of contemporary French cuisine and has been widely copied by chefs around the world. I first tasted this dish at Maurice, a restaurant at the Meridien Hotel in New York, which was under the supervision of Mr. Senderens in 1982. The original dish consisted of a bed of sautéed spinach and watercress topped with warm pieces of lobster coated in a silky, pale yellow butter sauce speckled with tiny bits of vanilla bean. The natural sweetness of the lobster mingled beautifully with the tangy vanilla sauce—it was sublime.

I have modified the original recipe to make this complex dish manageable for the home cook. In my recipe the lobster is broiled and the vanilla sauce is used for basting and for dipping, in the same way the whiskey butter sauce is used in Broiled Lobster with Whiskey Butter (page 168). In keeping with the original dish, sautéed spinach or a spinach salad can be served as an accompaniment.

Equipment: You will need a medium Chinese cleaver or large chef's knife, a broiler pan about 16 x 12 inches, a small whisk, a saucepan and a pastry brush.

8 tablespoons unsalted butter	1 vanilla bean (4 inches long), split lengthwise and pulp scraped out
2 shallots (1½ ounces), finely diced	kosher or sea salt
⅔ cup dry white wine	freshly ground black pepper
1 tablespoon white wine vinegar	2 live 1¾-pound hard-shell select lobsters

1. Position a rack under the broiler so that the lobster is 6 to 8 inches from the heating element. Preheat the broiler.

2. Put 2 tablespoons of the butter in a small saucepan (1 quart). Cut the remaining butter into ½-inch cubes and set aside. Add the shallots and cook over low to medium heat for about 2 minutes, allowing them to brown very lightly. Add the white wine and vinegar and turn the heat to medium-high. Boil until just 3 to 4 teaspoons liquid remain. Remove the pan from the heat and add the vanilla bean pulp. Return the pan to the heat and turn the heat to low. Whisk the cubes of butter, a few at a time, into the reduction. Wait for the butter to melt after each addition before adding more. Move the saucepan on and off the heat every now and then in order to maintain a temperature of about 180°F (hot but not boiling); the sauce will separate if it becomes too hot. When all the butter has been whisked into the sauce, season it with salt and pepper. The sauce should be silky smooth and pale yellow with specks of vanilla. Keep it warm while you prepare the lobster.

3. With a cleaver or chef's knife, split the lobsters in half lengthwise (page 34). Remove and discard the head sac and intestine. Remove the tomalley and the roe if present and place in a small bowl. Break into pieces using a fork. With the back side of a knife, crack the center of each claw on one side only. Arrange the lobsters so that they fit on a broiler pan without overlapping; the lobster must be completely exposed in order to cook evenly under the broiler. Divide the tomalley and roe among the cavities and season lightly with salt and pepper.

4. Lightly brush the lobster with the vanilla butter sauce; brush the big claws as well as all exposed meat and tomalley. Broil for 5 minutes. Remove the pan and quickly baste the lobster with the vanilla butter sauce. It is not necessary to baste the claws this time, only the exposed meat. Return the pan to the broiler, reversing the original position to help all parts cook evenly. Warm the butter sauce back over low heat without letting it boil. If it seems too thick, thin it with a few drops of water. Broil for 5 minutes more; the lobster should be thoroughly cooked (total cooking time: 11 minutes). To check for doneness, take a peek at the tail meat where it enters the lobster carcass. If the lobster is cooked through, the tail meat will be creamy white.

5. Remove the lobsters from the broiler and place the pieces on a platter or individual plates. Lightly brush the lobsters with the sauce one last time. Serve immediately with the remaining vanilla butter sauce poured into small bowls or ramekins for dipping.

Serves 2 as a main course or 4 as a fish course

COOK'S NOTE: *If you wish to substitute a different-size lobster, use the chart on page 169. Stick to sizes between 1½ and 2½ pounds.*

Lobster Thermidor

Lobster Thermidor is one of the greatest lobster dishes of classic French cuisine. Although its origin has been lost, the recipe is well documented in three books: Auguste Escoffier's Guide Culinaire, La Repertoire de la Cuisine *and* Larousse Gastronomique. *Pieces of cooked lobster are mixed with Mornay sauce, a rich cheese sauce, and then flavored with Dijon mustard and a Bercy reduction (wine and lobster broth cooked down to a flavoring essence). The mixture is then stuffed back into the lobster's shell, topped with grated cheese, drizzled with butter and baked until crisp and golden. Forget your concerns about fat for one night. This is a dish for a special occasion when you drink expensive wines and throw caution to the wind. Start with caviar and Champagne. Move on to a consommé made with game birds and truffles while you drink chilled dry sherry. Serve the Lobster Thermidor with a beautiful mix of salad greens tossed lightly with olive oil and a squeeze of fresh lemon. Drink a big, creamy white burgundy such as Chassagne-Montrachat or Meursault with the lobster. For dessert: fresh fruit.*

Lobster Thermidor can be fully prepared up to the point when it is baked, as much as eight hours in advance. Serve half of a 2-pound lobster per person—the portion will satisfy without overwhelming.

Equipment: You will need a medium Chinese cleaver or large chef's knife, a large pot for boiling, two small saucepans, a small whisk, a cheese grater and a baking sheet. In a professional kitchen, Lobster Thermidor would be baked and then flashed under a broiler to gratinée (become crisp and golden brown). This can be duplicated at home by turning the oven setting to broil halfway through the cooking; the oven remains hot while the broiler heats up just in time to finish the dish. If your oven does not have a broiler, set the temperature at 500°F instead of 450°F. Check the lobsters for doneness in 8 minutes—the hotter oven should effectively gratinée the top of the lobster.

2 live 1¾- to 2-pound hard-shell select lobsters

4 shallots (2 ounces), finely chopped

1 cup dry white wine

1 cup Savory Lobster Broth (page 54) or Quick Lobster Stock (page 57)

freshly ground black pepper

4 tablespoons unsalted butter

3 tablespoons all-purpose flour

1½ cups milk

2 ounces Parmigiano-Reggiano cheese, grated

6 ounces Emmentaler or Gruyère cheese, grated

1 large egg yolk

¼ cup heavy cream

2 tablespoons Dijon mustard

juice of ½ lemon

kosher or sea salt

cayenne pepper

1. Parboil the lobsters using the timing chart on page 30. Using tongs, remove the lobsters from the boiling water and let cool at room temperature. Remove the claws with the knuckles attached. Remove the meat from the knuckles and claws and the cartilage from the claw meat. Using a cleaver or large knife, split the lobsters in half lengthwise (page 34). Leaving the halved lobsters intact, remove the tail meat. Remove the intestine from the tail meat and cut all the lobster meat into ¾- to 1-inch chunks. Chop the tomalley and the roe if present and add to the lobster meat. Cover both the lobster meat and empty lobster shell halves with plastic wrap and refrigerate.

2. In a small saucepan (1 quart), combine the shallots, wine, broth and ½ teaspoon black pepper. Simmer until just ⅓ cup liquid remains (this is a Bercy reduction).

3. Melt 2 tablespoons of the butter in a small heavy saucepan (1 quart) over low heat. Stir in the flour and cook for about 1 minute until the mixture gives off a nutty smell. Do not allow it to pick up any color. Add the milk a little at a time, whisking constantly; allow the sauce to thicken before adding more milk. After all the milk has been added, simmer the mixture slowly for 15 minutes, stirring it often to prevent scorching.

4. While the sauce is simmering, mix together the cheeses and divide them in half—half for the sauce and half for topping. Add the cheese to the sauce and stir over low heat until the cheese is completely melted. In a small bowl, whisk together the egg yolk and cream, then whisk about 2 tablespoons of the hot cheese sauce into the egg yolk mixture. Remove the sauce from the heat and stir in the egg yolk mixture. Immediately strain the sauce, called Mornay, into a mixing bowl. Add the Bercy reduction, mustard and lemon juice to the bowl. Stir and season with salt and more pepper, if needed, and a pinch of cayenne. When the mixture is tepid, fold in the reserved lobster meat.

5. Position a rack in the top third of the oven. Preheat the oven to 450°F.

6. Place the empty lobster shell halves on a baking sheet and spoon the lobster mixture evenly among the 4 shells, which will fill generously. Sprinkle the remaining grated cheese over the stuffed lobsters. Melt the remaining 2 tablespoons butter and drizzle over the cheese. If you are not going to cook the stuffed lobsters immediately, cover them loosely with plastic wrap and refrigerate; they can be prepared to this point up to 8 hours in advance.

7. Ten minutes before serving, place the pan of lobsters in the oven and bake for 5 minutes. Switch the oven from bake to broil. The broiler will be hot just in time to give a nice crispy brown gratinée. Serve at once.

Serves 4 as a main course

Lobster Newburg with Toast Points

Lobster Newburg, which belongs to the family of classic toast dishes that were immensely popular at the turn of the century, has become obscured by its own widespread popularity. The title "Newburg" has been used for every haphazard combination of seafood and cream under the sun. The authentic Newburg is perfect for a buffet where your guests can help themselves to as little or as much as they'd like of this luscious treat.

Lobster Newburg was originally made with Madeira, but sherry has become the more commonly used fortified wine for this dish. I prefer top-quality Amontillado sherry, but Fino (dry) sherry and Pineau des Charentes, a Cognac-based aperitif, are also wonderful. Because the lobster meat is sliced, you will need to take care to extract the tail meat in one piece and remove the intestine as well. Review the procedures on page 36. Bake or buy an *unsliced* Pullman loaf of good white bread so that you can cut extra-thick slices. If you do not have any lobster broth or stock on hand, you can substitute fish stock.

Lobster Newburg requires detailed attention during its preparation and must be served immediately after it is made. Have all the ingredients organized and ready to go before you start.

2 live 1¾- to 2-pound hard-shell select lobsters

6 hand-cut slices white bread (Pullman loaf), ¾ to 1 inch thick

4 tablespoons unsalted butter

kosher or sea salt

freshly ground black pepper

¼ cup Amontillado or Fino sherry

⅓ cup Savory Lobster Broth (page 54), Quick Lobster Stock (page 57) or fish stock

⅔ cup heavy cream

1 large egg yolk

1. Parboil the lobsters using the timing chart on page 30. Using tongs, remove the lobsters from the pot and let cool at room temperature. Remove the claws with the knuckles attached. Remove the meat from the knuckles and claws, taking care to remove the cartilage from the meat. With one hand on the carapace and one on the tail, break the tail away from the carcass. Break off the tail fins, and from the back of the tail, push the tail meat out in one piece. Use surgical or other tweezers to remove the intestinal tract—try to pull it out in one piece. Slice the tail into nice coins, cut on a slight diagonal, about ½ inch thick. Slice the claw meat into similar-size pieces. Chop the roe if present and add it to the meat. Cover with plastic wrap and refrigerate. Reserve the carcass with the tomalley for soup.

2. Cut the crusts off the bread slices and cut the slices in half diagonally to make 2 large triangles from each. Melt 2 tablespoons of the butter and lightly brush over both sides of the bread. Arrange the buttered triangles on a baking sheet.

3. Preheat the oven to 400°F. Have all your ingredients measured and ready to go.

4. Heat a large sauté pan (10 inches) over medium heat for 2 minutes. Put the bread in the oven right before you start the lobster. Add the remaining 2 tablespoons butter to the pan. As soon as it sizzles, add the pieces of lobster meat with the roe. Season lightly with salt and pepper. After 2 minutes, turn the lobster pieces over; the pieces will redden, as will the butter. Cook for 2 minutes more, for a total cooking time of 4 minutes. Leaving the pan on the burner, use tongs to remove the lobster meat to a large plate. Cover the meat so that it stays warm.

5. Add the sherry and swirl it around the pan, loosening any particles stuck to the bottom with a wooden spoon. Raise the heat and add the lobster broth and cream. Let the sauce reduce rapidly until you have about ¾ cup light pink sauce that is thick enough to coat the back of a spoon. Turn the heat to low.

6. Check your toast points. If they are golden, remove them: otherwise, leave them to cook for 1 to 2 minutes more. Set your timer so that you do not burn the toast.

7. Whisk the egg yolk and 1 tablespoon of the sauce together; add another tablespoon sauce and whisk again. Add the lobster and any juices from the lobster to the pan and slowly stir in the egg yolk mixture. Stir gently but constantly until the sauce is thickened. Adjust the seasoning with a bit more salt and pepper if needed.

8. Arrange the warm toast points around a platter or on individual plates and spoon the lobster and sauce into the center and over the tips of the toast. Serve at once.

Serves 6 to 8 as a starter or 4 as a main course

Lobster Fra Diavolo

Lobster Fra Diavolo is made by cutting up and searing lobsters in olive oil and then simmering them in a spicy tomato sauce. Diavolo, which translates as "devil," refers to the fiery nature of the sauce. The traditional accompaniment to this dish is pasta, but I find it a messy, if fun, distraction to the lively marriage of the spicy tomato sauce and the luscious white meat. My favorite accompaniment is long, thick slices of crusty baguette brushed with olive oil and toasted in the oven until crisp and golden. The toasted slices—crostini—are great dipped in the sauce. Plain white beans, such as cannellini, tossed with a bit of olive oil and salt are also a good accompaniment. The sauce can be made well in advance and refrigerated.

1 medium onion (4 ounces), peeled

1 small carrot (2 ounces), peeled

6 cloves garlic (about ½ head), peeled

6 tablespoons olive oil, plus extra for brushing

1 bay leaf

1 teaspoon dried red pepper flakes

1 teaspoon dried oregano

2 cups Savory Lobster Broth (page 54), Quick Lobster Stock (page 57), fish stock or clam broth

2 tablespoons tomato paste

1 can (28 ounces) Italian plum tomatoes with their juice

freshly ground black pepper

1 French baguette

2 live 1¾- to 2-pound hard-shell select lobsters

½ cup dry white wine

6 sprigs Italian parsley, leaves picked and coarsely chopped

1. To make the sauce, cut the onion, carrot and garlic into medium dice. Place in a food processor and pulse to finely chop without pureeing. If you do not have a food processor, chop by hand. Combine with 3 tablespoons of the olive oil in a heavy 2-quart saucepan and place over medium heat. Cook for about 10 minutes until the vegetables are browned, stirring only to prevent scorching. Add the bay leaf, red pepper and oregano. Stir and cook for 1 minute. Add the lobster broth and tomato paste. Drain the tomato juice from the can into the pot. Coarsely chop the tomatoes and add them as well. Season to taste with black pepper; I use about 1 teaspoon. Bring to a boil, lower the heat and simmer until the sauce is cooked down to about half its original volume and very thick, about 45 minutes. Either keep the sauce warm while you cook the lobsters or refrigerate until ready to use.

2. Preheat the oven to 375°F.

3. Cut the baguette on a diagonal into slices about 1 inch thick. Brush the slices on both sides with olive oil and arrange on a baking sheet. Place in the oven just before you start cooking the lobster; the bread will be ready when the lobsters are cooked. If your sauce was made ahead of time and chilled, reheat it before you toast the bread and cook the lobsters.

4. With a medium Chinese cleaver or large chef's knife, split the lobsters in half lengthwise (page 34). Remove and discard the head sac and intestine. Remove the claws and knuckles, leaving them attached to each other. This is done by cutting the knuckle close to where it meets the carcass. With the back side of your knife, crack the center of each claw on one side only. Remove the tomalley and the roe if present and place in a small bowl. Break into small pieces using a fork and cover with plastic wrap. Quarter the lobster by cutting down in one swift motion where the tail and carcass join. Place the pieces of lobster on a plate, shell side down, so that you can slide them into the hot pan.

5. Heat a 12-inch sauté pan over high heat for a few minutes until the pan is very hot. Add the remaining 3 tablespoons olive oil and then slide in the lobster pieces; they should sizzle. Using tongs, move the pieces around to sear the shells evenly. Because of their shape, you will have to hold them in the hot oil to accomplish this. Sauté for about 4 minutes until all the shells have turned bright red. Add the white wine, using a spoon to loosen any pieces that have stuck to the pan. Lower the heat and add the tomato sauce along with the tomalley and roe. Stir the lobster, then cover the pan loosely. Simmer for 5 minutes, then move the pieces around to ensure even cooking. Cover again and simmer for 5 minutes more. Check to see how the toast is doing; it should be ready. Use tongs to remove the pieces of lobster to a warm platter. Put the sauce back on the heat and add the chopped parsley. Stir the sauce well and spoon over the lobster. Place the warm, crispy toasts around the platter and serve at once.

Serves 2 or 3 as a hearty main course or more when served with pasta

VARIATIONS

One teaspoon dried red pepper flakes will make the sauce spicy hot. If you like it really fiery, add more.

To serve the lobster over pasta, omit the toast and cook linguine or spaghetti instead. Figure on 3 to 4 ounces dried pasta per person. After draining the pasta, toss it with a little sauce and place it on a warmed platter. Arrange the pieces of lobster over the pasta and spoon on the remaining sauce.

To make this dish with leftover lobster, make the sauce as described but add the ½ cup wine to the sauce at the same time you add the tomatoes. Do not reduce the sauce as much as when using live lobsters. Cut up the cooked lobster and discard the head sac and intestine. Remove the tomalley and roe, chop it and add it to the sauce along with any juices and blood (the white stuff) that may be present. Simmer for a few minutes, then add the cut-up lobster. Turn off the heat and let the lobster sit in the sauce for 15 minutes. Reheat the lobster and sauce. Serve over linguine or spaghetti.

Lobster & Cod Braised with Leeks & Mushrooms in a Savory Broth

The vivid aroma, potent flavor and contrasting textures of this dish make for a thoroughly sat-isfying, healthful meal, perfect for a chilly night. Savory Lobster Broth, which can be made well in advance, is the soul of this preparation. Shiitake mushrooms have an excellent taste and tex-ture for soup, but you may substitute almost any variety, from the cultivated button to wild chanterelles, cèpes or lobster mushrooms. The type of mushroom used will affect the final fla-vor in its own unique way.

A beautiful and simple presentation of this dish is to place two thick slices of the crunchy, toasted garlic bread on a wide soup plate so that they stick out from the plate like rabbit ears. The seafood and vegetables are then stacked in the center and surrounded by piping-hot broth.

Equipment: It is best to make this dish in a large pan (12 to 14 inches) that has high sides (3 to 4 inches) and a lid. This type of pan allows the seafood to cook in the broth without moving around and breaking up. If you do not have a lid, aluminum foil will do the trick. You will also need a medium Chinese cleaver or large chef's knife, tongs, a baking sheet, a slotted spoon and a ladle.

1 large French baguette	2 small carrots (4 ounces), peeled and thinly sliced on a diagonal
4 cloves garlic, finely chopped	
4 tablespoons unsalted butter, softened	2 medium leeks (white and light green parts only), rinsed, drained and thinly sliced
kosher or sea salt	
freshly ground black pepper	6 ounces fresh shiitake mushrooms, wiped clean and thinly sliced
2 live 1½-pound hard-shell select lobsters	
1 pound skinless cod fillets, cut into 4 pieces 1 inch thick	3 cups Savory Lobster Broth (page 54)
2 tablespoons olive oil	2 tablespoons chopped Italian parsley

1. Preheat the broiler.

2. Cut eight ¾-inch-thick slices from the baguette on a sharp diagonal, using about half of the baguette. Place the slices on a baking sheet and toast under the broiler until lightly browned; turn the slices and repeat.

3. Mix the garlic and butter together and season with salt and pepper. When the toast is cool, spread one side of each piece with garlic butter and return to the baking sheet. Cover loosely with plastic wrap and set aside.

4. Parboil the lobsters using the timing chart on page 30. Using tongs, remove the lobsters from the pot and let cool at room temperature. Remove the meat from the knuckles and claws, trying to keep each claw in one piece. With one hand on the carapace and one on the tail of the lobster, break the tail away from the carcass. Using a cleaver or chef's knife, split the tails in half lengthwise. Remove the intestine from the tail pieces. Either crack open and pick the carcasses for meat (to be added to the other lobster meat) or reserve them for soup. Combine the meat from the claws and knuckles with the pieces of tail meat in the shell; cover with plastic wrap and refrigerate. This may be done earlier in the day if desired.

5. Trim the fish if needed and check for bones. Keep chilled.

6. Preheat the oven to 350°F. Place the baking sheet with the garlic toasts in the oven.

7. Heat the olive oil in a large sauté pan over medium heat. Add the carrots, leeks and mushrooms, and cook for 6 to 7 minutes, stirring occasionally, until the vegetables are softened. Add the lobster broth and bring to a boil. Skim any foam off the top and lower the heat for a slow simmer. Season the fish fillets with salt and pepper and add them to the pan; they should be surrounded by the vegetables and almost covered with the broth. Cover the pan with a lid or aluminum foil and cook for 5 minutes. Uncover the pan and add the lobster tails, shell side down, as well as the reserved meat from the knuckles and claws. It is not necessary for the lobster to be completely submerged. Cover again and cook for 5 minutes more.

8. Check on the garlic toasts. Remove them when crisp and brown. Put your soup plates in the oven to warm. You can turn the oven off at this point.

9. Check to see if the fish is cooked through—it will be pure white. When it is ready, take the pan off the heat and let sit, covered, for 1 to 2 minutes. Using a slotted spoon, place each piece of fish in a large soup plate. Arrange the vegetables over and around the fish. Place 2 pieces of toast at the top of the plate. Arrange a lobster tail on one side of the fish and a claw and knuckle on the other. Check the broth for seasoning and place over high heat. As soon as it boils, divide it evenly among the bowls. Sprinkle with parsley and serve at once.

Serves 4 as a main course

Lobster Casserole

Big chunks of lobster meat baked in a casserole with any variety of sauces and toppings are sometimes called lazy man's lobster. The name refers to the ease of eating the lobster, but it could also be called lazy cook's lobster, because if you buy the lobster meat already cooked, lobster casserole can be put together in very little time. Forget the thick and gooey casseroles of the past; this dish and its variations are brand-new—still simple but more savory. The dish is not inexpensive, as the master recipe for a plain lobster casserole uses a 1½-pound lobster per person, but you can use a smaller lobster and add mushrooms and other vegetables to stretch the casserole. Some suggestions are given in the variations that follow. If you are looking for a recipe that uses large culls, this is it. Whether you cook large culls or smaller lobsters, pick all the meat out of the carcass; it will add extra flavor to the casserole.

You have a choice of baking this in a large casserole or in individual gratin dishes. A casserole for four people should hold four to six cups; individual gratin dishes should hold eight to ten ounces. Find an underliner to hold the casserole or individual dishes to prevent you and your guests from burning your hands.

6 to 7 pounds live culls or other lobsters, or 1½ pounds cooked lobster meat

1 cup Savory Lobster Broth (page 54) or Quick Lobster Stock (page 57)

1 cup heavy cream

2 tablespoons tomato puree, or 1 tablespoon tomato paste

1 teaspoon finely minced garlic or roasted garlic puree

6 tablespoons butter

kosher or sea salt

freshly ground black pepper

1 heaping cup crumbled oyster or common crackers (page 75)

1 tablespoon chopped parsley

1. If you are using live lobsters, steam (page 32) or boil (page 29) them. Let cool at room temperature. Use your cleaver to crack and remove the meat from the claws and knuckles. If the claws are small, leave whole; if large, cut in half. Remove the meat from the tail in one piece (page 36). Make a small incision along the top of the cooked tail meat and remove the intestine. Small tails should be sliced across in 1-inch chunks; for larger tails, split the tail lengthwise, then cut into 1-inch chunks. Pick all the meat out of the carcass and add it to the other meat. If there is roe, chop it and add to the meat. It is optional to whip the tomalley into the sauce; otherwise, freeze for Tomalley Toasts (page 88) or discard. Cover and refrigerate.

2. Combine the broth with the heavy cream, tomato puree and garlic in a small saucepan (1 quart) over medium heat. Bring to a boil, then lower the heat so that the sauce simmers rapidly; it will boil over if cooked too fast. Reduce by more than half so that you have ¾ cup sauce remaining. Remove the sauce from the heat and whip in the tomalley. Let cool for 10 minutes. Whisk 2 tablespoons of the butter into the warm sauce and season the sauce with salt and pepper. Pour the sauce over the lobster and toss.

3. Melt 3 tablespoons of the butter and combine with the crumbled crackers and parsley in a small bowl. Toss well so that the butter is evenly distributed and season with salt and pepper.

4. Preheat the oven to 400°F. Position the rack in the middle of the oven.

5. Use the last tablespoon of the butter to grease the casserole or individual baking dishes. Place the lobster and sauce mixture in the casserole or divide the lobster and sauce evenly among 4 dishes. The sauce will cover the bottom half of the meat. (The recipe can be made to this point up to 6 hours in advance, covered with plastic wrap and refrigerated. If this is done, remove the casserole from the refrigerator 30 minutes before cooking.)

6. Spread the buttered crumbs evenly over the top of the lobster and place in the oven. Bake until the top has become golden brown and the sauce is bubbling. The casserole will take 15 to 18 minutes, individual dishes 10 to 12 minutes.

Serves 4 as a hearty main course

COOK'S NOTE: *Savory Lobster Broth has a spicy bite to it. If you substitute Quick Lobster Stock, you may wish to add a pinch of cayenne pepper to jazz it up.*

No-Sauce Lobster Casserole

Omit the lobster broth or stock. Use only ½ cup cream. Warm the cream with the tomato puree and roasted garlic. Remove from the heat and let stand for 10 minutes. Whisk in the butter and season with salt and pepper. Proceed with remainder of recipe.

Lobster Casserole with Cheese

Prepare the lobster casserole following the original recipe or no-sauce version until the lobster is placed in the dish. Before adding the cracker topping, sprinkle 1 cup grated cheese (4 ounces) over the lobster. Vermont cheddar, Colby or a good-quality Monterey Jack all work well. Cover with the buttered crumbs and bake as instructed.

Lobster Casserole with Mushrooms & Tomatoes

Reduce the amount of cooked lobster meat to 1 pound or the live lobsters to 4 to 5 pounds. Cook and cut as instructed and place in a bowl. Make the sauce as instructed, but omit the 2 tablespoons butter. Instead, place the butter in a 9-inch sauté pan over medium heat and cook 8 to 12 ounces ½-inch-thick sliced mushrooms (button, exotic or wild) for about 5 minutes until tender. Add 1 cup peeled and diced fresh tomatoes or ½ cup canned tomatoes. Also add 1 teaspoon chopped fresh tarragon leaves and simmer for 5 minutes. Season to taste with salt and pepper, remove from the heat and let cool. Combine with the lobster and sauce and place in the greased casserole or individual dishes. Cover with the buttered crumbs and bake as instructed.

Lobster Casserole with Leeks & Potatoes

Reduce the amount of cooked lobster meat to 1 pound or the live lobsters to 4 to 5 pounds. Cook and cut as instructed and place in a bowl. Make the sauce as instructed, but omit the 2 tablespoons butter. Instead, place the butter in a 9-inch sauté pan over low heat and simmer 2 medium leeks (white and light green parts, cut across in ½-inch pieces, soaked in water and drained) for about 10 minutes until tender. Peel 2 medium all-purpose potatoes (about 12 ounces) and cut into ¾-inch cubes. Boil in lightly salted water until tender. Rinse under cold water and drain well. Combine the lobster, leeks and potatoes in a bowl with the sauce and place in the greased casserole or individual dishes. Cover with the buttered crumbs and bake as instructed.

Lobster with Ginger & Scallions

This dish, taught to me by my good friend C. K. Sau, chef and proprietor of New Shanghai in Boston's Chinatown, is traditionally prepared in China with fresh live crabs. C.K. taught me this version when he was the chef at Sally Ling's, the restaurant next door to Jasper's, on the waterfront in Boston. Ten years ago I was privileged to travel through China with C.K. I witnessed firsthand how his speed, accuracy and "understanding of the fire" earned him the respect of chefs all over China. I have modified C.K.'s technique for cutting and cooking the lobster, building my recipe instead on the technique of "quartering" used for pan-roasted lobster. After the lobster is quartered, each piece is cut in half again, creating eight pieces of lobster from the carcass and tail. The other Chinese classic in this book, Lobster Cantonese (page 226), uses this same technique for cutting the lobsters.

If you do not have a wok and/or a hot gas fire to work with, this dish can be produced in a heavy skillet or sauté pan. You will need a 14-inch pan. Even when the pan is placed over as high a heat as possible, the cooking time will be longer than with a wok. Check for doneness in the pieces of claw, since they take the longest time to cook. This recipe cannot be doubled, but it can be made twice in succession. Serve with steamed rice and a side vegetable such as broccoli, eggplant or snow peas.

Equipment: You will need a medium Chinese cleaver or large chef's knife, a wok or 14-inch skillet, tongs and utensils for stir-frying.

2 live 1¼- to 1½-pound hard-shell lobsters	½ cup light chicken stock
4 tablespoons peanut oil	⅓ cup Chinese cooking wine
1 thumb-size piece fresh ginger (½ ounce), peeled and cut into thin strips (julienne)	2 tablespoons soy sauce
	2 teaspoons sugar
2 cloves garlic, very thinly sliced	½ teaspoon ground white pepper
4 or 5 scallions (2 ounces), cut diagonally into 1-inch pieces and white part cut in half lengthwise	2 teaspoons cornstarch
	1 tablespoon water
	2 teaspoons rice vinegar
	1 teaspoon dark sesame oil

1. With a cleaver or chef's knife, split the lobsters in half lengthwise (page 34). Remove and discard the head sac and intestine. Remove the claws and knuckles, cutting the knuckle close to where it meets the carcass. Break the knuckle away from the claw and cut it with a cleaver on one side so that the cooked lobster meat is easy to extract. With the back side of your knife, crack the center of the claw on both sides. Remove the tomalley and the roe if present and place in a small bowl. Break into small pieces using a fork and cover with plastic wrap. Quarter the lobsters (page 34), then cut each piece of quartered lobster in half, cutting sideways in the same direction as when you quartered it. From each lobster you will have 8 tail and carcass pieces, 2 claws and 2 knuckles—24 pieces in all. Place the lobster pieces on a plate, shell side down, so that you can slide them into the hot wok or pan.

2. Have all ingredients cut, measured and ready to go before you begin. Preheat the wok or pan over very high heat until smoking hot. Add 3 tablespoons of the peanut oil and immediately slide the lobster pieces into the wok. Stir just enough to ensure that all pieces cook evenly; pay special attention to the claws, which take the longest to cook. After 2 to 3 minutes, depending on the heat of the wok, the lobster pieces will be red and slightly charred and will be cooked to about 80 percent of their doneness. Remove the wok from the heat and, using tongs or a slotted spoon, lift the pieces out of the wok onto a platter. Cover to keep warm.

3. Add the remaining 1 tablespoon peanut oil to the wok or pan and heat over high heat. Add the ginger, garlic and scallions and stir-fry for barely 1 minute until cooked but not browned. Add the chicken stock, cooking wine, soy sauce, sugar, pepper and reserved tomalley and roe. Reduce the heat to medium so that the liquid simmers without boiling. Add the lobster pieces and cook for 2 minutes, moving the pieces around so that they cook evenly. Pay special attention to the claws so that they cook thoroughly.

4. Dissolve the cornstarch in the water and slowly add it to the sauce, avoiding pouring it on the lobster and stirring constantly to prevent lumps from forming. Immediately stir in the rice vinegar and sesame oil. Stir the lobster to coat each piece evenly with the sauce as well as with the ginger and scallions. Remove the pieces to a warm platter and spoon any extra sauce and pieces of ginger and scallion over the lobster. Serve at once.

Serves 2 or more

Lobster & Sweet Potato Tempura

Japanese tempura, crispy deep-fried seafood and vegetables, is traditionally eaten at counters in restaurants that specialize in this artful method of frying. Nuances such as the consistency of the batter, the blend of frying oils and the variety of fresh local ingredients available all determine the style of tempura, which in Japan reflects regional as well as individual tastes. The light batter and resulting lightness of the foods cooked makes tempura different from other methods of deep-frying. It also makes the time span between cooking and eating less forgiving than any other method of deep-frying. Tempura is best eaten hot, within seconds of the time it is cooked. When I make this dish, I like to have family and friends hang around in the kitchen with me, drinking beer and talking while I cook. It's fun and relaxing, and they can eat the tempura when it's best—immediately after it's cooked. Tempura is best served with a Japanese salad, such as spinach and sesame seed, or a light mixed green salad. Japanese pickles are a traditional accompaniment.

Making tempura at home is much easier than you might think. I have created a list of ingredients, but feel free to substitute whatever fresh vegetables are available. Your oil should keep a constant temperature of 350°F. It is important not to crowd the pot as you cook, because this lowers the temperature of the oil and causes uneven cooking. The batter, which is put together at the very last minute, is not mixed like other batters; in fact, it's not really mixed at all! It's this lack of mixing that makes the tempura lacy and crisp. The dipping of foods does most of the mixing, but even after you have cooked most of the food, the batter should be lumpy with a ring of raw flour around the outside of the bowl.

Equipment: You will need a medium Chinese cleaver or large chef's knife, a grater, a small pot, a large high-sided sauté pan (10 to 12 inches) for frying, 3 medium mixing bowls, a deep-fry thermometer, a small strainer for skimming the oil during frying and lots of paper towels. I like to use wooden chopsticks for mixing and dipping, and even for removing food from the oil, but if you are not comfortable with chopsticks, you can use tongs or a slotted spoon. Remember, this is supposed to be fun, not frustrating!

2 live 1¼-pound hard-shell lobsters

1 large or 2 small sweet potatoes (14 ounces)

1 small bunch watercress

¼ cup light soy sauce

¼ cup mirin

½ cup Savory Lobster Broth (page 54), Quick Lobster Stock (page 57) or dashi (broth of dried fish and dried kelp, made from instant powder)

2 teaspoons grated fresh ginger

one 3-ounce piece daikon

4 cups pure vegetable oil (soy or
safflower) for frying

2 tablespoons dark sesame oil

2 cups water, chilled with 6 to 8 ice cubes

2 large egg yolks

2 cups all-purpose flour, plus extra for
dredging

1. Parboil the lobsters using the timing chart on page 30. Using tongs, remove the lobsters from the pot and let cool at room temperature. Break away the knuckles and claws from the carcass. Remove the meat from the claws and knuckles; try your best to leave them in one piece (page 36). With one hand on the carapace and one hand on the tail, break the tail away from the carcass. Reserve the carcass for soup. Break off the tail fins and, from the back side of the tail, push the meat out of the tail. Slice the tail meat lengthwise into 4 pieces about ¼ inch thick (they will look like shrimp when they are cooked). Carefully remove the intestine. If you are going to be cooking within 20 minutes, leave the lobster at room temperature; otherwise, cover and refrigerate it.

2. Peel the sweet potato. If the sweet potato is large, cut it in half lengthwise and then slice it diagonally into ¼-inch slices. If you are using 2 small sweet potatoes, cut them in ¼-inch rounds. Pick out 8 nice leafy sprigs of watercress. Set the potatoes and watercress aside until ready to cook.

3. Combine the soy sauce, mirin, lobster broth and ginger in a small pot (1 quart); keep warm over low heat. Grate the daikon (½ cup) and set aside.

4. Fill a 10- to 12-inch sauté pan with 2 inches oil (3 to 4 cups). Add the sesame oil for flavor. Place the pan over medium to medium-high heat and heat the oil slowly to 350°F.

5. Fill a bowl with 2 cups water and 6 to 8 ice cubes. You will be making the batter twice, so set up 2 bowls with 1 egg yolk in each bowl. Lightly beat each egg yolk. In separate 1-cup batches, sift and measure 2 cups flour. Sift extra flour into a bowl for dredging. Set up an assembly line going toward the sauté pan: raw foods, then flour for dredging and the batter last. On the other side of the pan, you should have a small strainer on a small plate and a large plate lined with paper towels.

6. When the oil is at the right temperature, measure 1 cup ice water (from the bowl of ice water) and add it to one bowl with egg yolk. Dump 1 cup sifted flour right on top and lightly stir with 5 or 6 strokes of the chopsticks. Use your hand to dip one slice sweet potato in the dredging flour and then drop into the batter. Using the chopsticks, coat the sweet potato in the batter and then drop into the hot oil. Work quickly. Because the sweet potato takes slightly longer than the lobster to cook, drop 3 or 4 slices sweet potato into the oil first and then add 2 slices lobster for each batch. Stir while frying so that the oil temperature remains even. After about 2 minutes, the tempura will pick up a light golden color. Remove the food from the oil and drain on paper towels. In between batches, skim any loose batter out of the oil with the strainer.

7. Mix the daikon into the warm sauce and divide it among little bowls. Do not dredge the watercress in flour but instead dip directly into the batter and shake off any excess over the bowl before frying. The watercress will take only about 1 minute. Continue to alternate between the different foods, serving them as soon as they are ready. About halfway through the cooking, you will quickly make the second batch of batter—a job that takes 30 seconds. If the batter seems too thick toward the end of cooking , add a few drops of ice water. It will take about 20 minutes to cook all the food in this recipe.

Serves 4

The Maine Lobster Bake

Of all the great American cookouts, surely the lobster bake, known outside of Maine as the clambake, is the most dramatic. The technique, learned from the original Americans, uses a steaming pit either dug in the sand or made from natural rock formations to cook a wide variety of ingredients without relying on forged pots and pans. The presentation, the most spectacular I have ever seen, is a ten-foot-tall burst of steam released upon removal of the tarp. As the steam subsides, bright red lobsters facing back to back on dark green rockweed come into view. Sweet corn surrounds the lobsters. Underneath the seaweed lie buried treasures: softshell clams, rock crabs, a whole fish, mussels, periwinkles, potatoes, boiling onions, sausage and hen or duck eggs. The sights and smells are intoxicating. The lobster bake, much more than a dish or even a feast, embodies a day filled with the wonders of water, fire, food, family and friends.

The most important rule to remember to ensure the festive spirit of a lobster bake is that all who partake must share in the preparation. A lobster bake is an all-day affair, so bring along a midday snack and plenty of beverages. You will also need lots of butter, bread or rolls, salt, pepper, Tabasco and spicy mustard. For dessert, bring watermelon, cantaloupe, peaches, berries and other fresh fruits as well as homemade pies. In Maine, blueberry pie is as good as mandatory.

The Location

Scout out the location well in advance. A rocky beach is superior for cooking, but a sandy beach is better for swimming. Decide which will be more pleasurable for your guests. If you decide on a sandy beach, you will need quite a few large, flat rocks, so choose a spot where you will not have to spend hours dragging them in. If your beach does not have a lot of driftwood, you will need to bring about twenty fireplace-size logs. You will also need newspaper and kindling. Organize your wood supply and set up the pit the day before the bake. Bring along a tarp so that you can cover the wood and keep it dry overnight. Make sure there is plenty of rockweed growing nearby; otherwise, arrange for about seventy-five pounds of it. Most lobster dealers have plenty on hand, but it is wise to order ahead of time. The small oval sacs on the rockweed release the seawater that is essential for creating steam inside the pit. Take note of the foods growing near your location. If there are lots of mussels and periwinkles, count them as part of your ingredients, but be sure to check with the Coast Guard for "red tide alert." You will have lots of time to pick them while you wait for your fire to be ready, provided you have a low tide at that time. If you intend to rake for clams, remember that you need a permit in most places.

The Pit

Build your pit well above the high-tide line. I have heard disaster stories of waves crashing over the pit and ruining the bake. To cook enough food for twelve to sixteen people, the pit should be about 5 x 3½ feet wide and 3 feet deep.

On a rocky beach: I learned how to build a pit on a rocky beach from my friend John Stevens—a lobsterman and great "bake master" from Boothbay Harbor, Maine—when, about eight years ago, we filmed a lobster bake for a PBS series called "Crazy for Food." You will not always be able to create a pit that is 3 feet deep on a rocky beach, but this is okay because the top of the pit does not have to be flush with the ground. Find an area where the stones are less than 1 foot in average size and remove them from the center as you build up the sides. You may even find an area where nature has started the pit. If you clear 2 feet down and build 1 foot up, you will still have a pit that is 3 feet deep. Be sure your tarp is big enough to fold over the sides of the pit and lie flush with the ground. One advantage of a pit built on a rocky beach is that it can reach a very high temperature and cook food more quickly than a pit built on a sandy beach. Another advantage is that you will not get sand in your food.

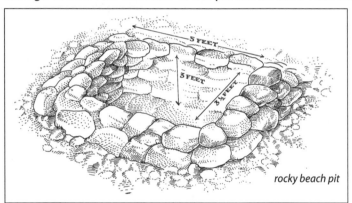

rocky beach pit

On a sandy beach: You will dig the pit 5½ x 4 feet wide and 3½ feet deep. Line the bottom with large stones and the sides with smaller ones. After you add the rocks, the pit will be the same size as that built on a rocky beach. Taper the sides of the pit toward the bottom so that the walls do not collapse. The more stones you use to line the pit, the better it will retain the heat.

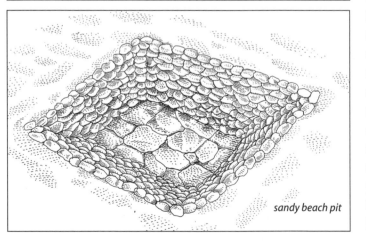

sandy beach pit

Lighting the fire: Have the pit and firewood ready to go. About 3½ hours before you start the lobster bake, stack the kindling in a tepeelike structure with crumpled newspaper underneath. Light the fire; once the kindling is burning well, begin to stoke the fire by adding more kindling, then small logs or driftwood. After they have caught fire, start adding the bigger logs or driftwood; once they catch, use your shovel to spread them around the pit. Continue stoking the fire with more logs until the entire pit is filled with blazing wood. After about 2 hours, when the fire has reached its hottest stage, quit stoking the fire (do not add any more wood) and allow the wood to burn away completely. This should take about 1½ hours. Wet your broom in the ocean and brush away all the coals and ashes; they will settle between the hot rocks.

Equipment

You will need a shovel, a broom, a large canvas tarp that is at least 8 x 6 feet, a couple of big buckets, a few pairs of tongs, two pairs of gloves to protect hands from the steam, a pot to melt butter, a ladle, cheesecloth for wrapping the small food items (such as steamers and periwinkles), twine for tying the cheesecloth bundles and platters for the cooked food. A picnic table is terrific for serving the platters of food but is not absolutely necessary. You will also need plates, cups, bowls for melted butter, eating utensils, lobster crackers, plenty of napkins and several large garbage bags.

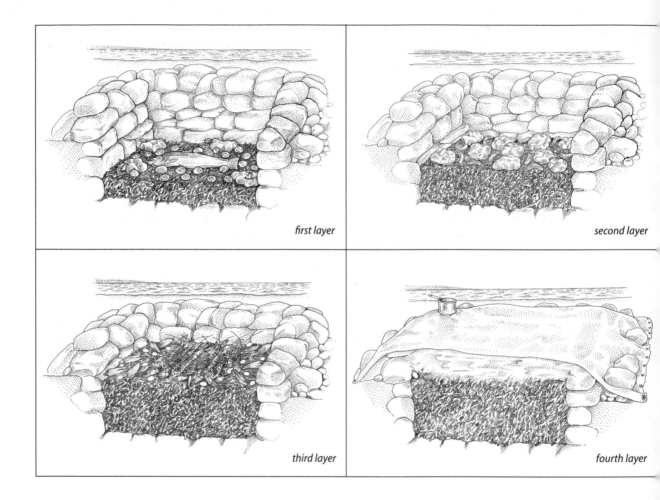

first layer

second layer

third layer

fourth layer

Layering the Pit

75 pounds rockweed

INGREDIENTS AS STACKED FROM BOTTOM TO TOP:

FIRST LAYER OF ROCKWEED

1 whole 6-pound fish (striped bass, salmon, or bluefish, etc.), gutted and scaled

12 large red Bliss or medium Maine potatoes

6 medium sweet potatoes

2 pounds large white boiling onions or small Spanish onions

4 jumbo sea clams (optional; used for flavoring, not eating)

SECOND LAYER OF ROCKWEED

6 to 8 pounds soft-shell clams (steamers)

6 to 8 pounds mussels

4 pounds periwinkles

3 pounds linguica, chorizo or other sausage

THIRD LAYER OF ROCKWEED

12 live 1-pound chicken lobsters

16 ears sweet corn

12 extra-large eggs

LAST LAYER OF ROCKWEED

2 pounds unsalted butter

1. Prepare the pit according to the directions on pages 190 and 191. While the fire is cooking down, start preparing the food. Scrub the potatoes and sweet potatoes in the nearby ocean. Peel the onions, wrap in 4 cheesecloth sacks (so you can have the aroma of onions scattered throughout the pit) and tie the sacks off with twine. Scrub the sea clams and return them to your cooler. Wrap the steamers, mussels and periwinkles in cheesecloth sacks, putting about 2 pounds in each bundle. Tie the bundles together and place temporarily in the ocean—just be sure they are well anchored. Otherwise, return the bundles to the cooler to keep chilled. Divide the sausage into portions. To prepare the corn, carefully pull back the husks without detaching them. Pick away the silk and fold the husks back over the corn. Wet the corn in the ocean a few minutes before you begin the bake.

2. Start the bake as soon as the coals have cooked down and been brushed away. At this point, a single person (the bake master) should take charge of the actual bake. That person should have an assistant. Caution should be exercised around the pit: Master and assistant should take their responsibilities seriously, and children should be kept at least 10 feet away. Gather all the food and bring it close to the pit. Make sure the rockweed is moist. If it is not, give it one last dip in the ocean and bring it close to the pit. Bring the tarp to the ocean and soak it thoroughly. Work carefully but as quickly as possible.

3. Start with an 8-inch layer of rockweed. Place the whole fish in the center and lay the potatoes, sweet potatoes, onions and sea clams around the fish. Cover the food completely with a 4- to 6-inch layer of rockweed and then distribute the bundles of steamers, mussels and periwinkles, with the sausages on top. Add the third layer of rockweed (4 to 6 inches) over the food. Place the lobsters in the center, back to back (actually tail to tail), forming 2 rows. Lobsters can only move backward on land, so by laying them this way, they will stay put. Place the corn around the lobsters and scatter the eggs about. Place one egg very close to the corner of the pit and *remember exactly where it is.* Scatter a last thin layer of rockweed over the corn and eggs but do not cover the lobsters. By now the steam will be rising from the pit fairly vigorously. Cover the pit with the damp tarp and place heavy rocks all around to form a tight seal. Place the butter in a pot and set it on a corner of the tarp to melt.

4. If your pit is on a rocky beach the food could be ready in as little as 50 minutes, but an hour is the norm. If your pit was made in the sand, the food could take up to 90 minutes. Make sure everyone knows the approximate time of unveiling. Have all plates and utensils ready. Bring the platters near the pit; you can even warm them on the tarp. The bake master and assistant should have their gloves on for the next step.

5. Remember the special egg? Lift up the corner of the tarp and pull out the egg. Crack it open. If it is cooked through (hard-boiled), the bake is ready to eat. Gather everyone about 10 feet from the pit. Remove the melted butter and all the rocks that are holding the tarp in place. The bake master should grab one corner and the assistant the other, on the side closest to the gathering of family and friends. Quickly pull back the tarp. There will be a giant burst of steam. When it subsides, the bright red lobsters will come into view. Both the bake master and the assistant will use tongs to remove the food and place it on platters. As the rockweed is removed, it should be spread around the outside of the pit to show that it is still hot. The hot pit cannot be left unattended—a child or dog could be injured. Get a few people to bring buckets of water up from the beach to pour over the rocks to cool them. The others should unwrap the cheesecloth bundles, cut the potatoes in half and set out the food. Put the butter in small bowls for dipping lobsters, steamers, mussels and anything else you want. Allow plenty of time to eat before you bring out the desserts.

6. After the festivities have ended, everyone should help clean up. Cover the pit back up with rocks or sand; be sure there are no hot rocks left on the beach. The rockweed can be left on the beach to decompose, but all other litter must be put in garbage bags and taken away. *The beach must be left as it was found.*

Serves 12 with leftovers or 16 if you add a lobster for each extra person

CHAPTER 7

Great Lobsters from Great Chefs

Like TRUFFLES, foie gras, and wild game, lobster is high on the list of the world's most luxurious foods. For many chefs, lobster creations have become their "signature dishes." When my editor, Maria Guarnaschelli, suggested we include a few recipes from other chefs, I thought they would make a nice addition to the book. But as the book developed, I realized that these recipes were much more than a nice addition—the book would be incomplete without them. It is impossible to pay homage to the lobster without speaking of the magnificent creations of the world's great chefs and food writers.

I am thrilled to offer you a sampling of recipes from some of the most exciting cooks in contemporary cuisine. In this final chapter you will re-create the finesse of Joël Robuchon, the intricate cuisine of Daniel Boulud, the Pan-Asian flavors of Wolfgang Puck and Lydia Shire, the Nuevo Latino style of Douglas Rodriguez, the authentic Mexican flavors of Rick Bayless, the rustic simplicity of Johanne Killeen and George Germon, the exuberant style of Ed Brown, the southwest flair of Stephan Pyles, the fiery Thai spice of Gerald Clare, the rich Chinese cuisine of Nina Simonds, the Creole/Portuguese cooking of Emeril Lagasse and the great American flavors of Larry Forgione and Bob Kinkead. Combined, these chefs' cooking styles span the globe. Each recipe features bold and authoritative flavors. These dishes are filled with explosions of flavors, aromas, textures and colors, each reflecting the genius of its creator. They are not the easiest recipes in the book, but take my word for it: They are worth every moment you put into them.

On a personal note, I would like to thank the award-winning chefs and authors featured in this chapter. By generously sharing their recipes, they have demonstrated the incredible versatility of lobster in the hands of great masters.

Rick Bayless

Grilled Lobster with Sweet Toasted Garlic, Avocado & Red Chile

Rick Bayless has spent his career re-creating the vibrant flavors and spreading the gospel of authentic regional Mexican cuisine. The excellence of his Chicago restaurants Topolobampo and Frontera Grill, which he operates with his wife, Deann Groen Bayless, is now legendary. His understanding of the cooking traditions of Mexico, researched through extensive travel, combined with his deep respect for ingredients have made him the major force in Mexican cooking in America. Through his authoritative books Authentic Mexican *and* Rick Bayless's Mexican Kitchen *(Scribner, 1996), he has enlightened many of us about the variety, contrasts, complexities and sometimes simple goodness of real Mexican food. In 1995 Rick was given the unprecedented honor of being named* Chef of the Year *by both the James Beard Foundation and the International Association of Culinary Professionals. In doing so, he proved not only that he is one of the world's leading chefs, but that Mexico is home to one of the world's greatest cuisines.*

This fairly simple recipe became an instant favorite for me. The soft flavors of toasted garlic and avocado, both excellent with lobster, are heightened with lime, salt and little bursts of spice and flavor from the chipotle chile; the grilled scallion connects the sauce to the grilled lobster—it is masterful. As you start cooking the garlic and oil, keep a close watch that the oil is barely simmering. The slow cooking develops the deep, sweet and gentle flavor of the garlic. The amount of oil may seem excessive at first glance, but Rick is clever, he has provided us with extra-beautifully flavored oil for brushing on the shells and basting the lobster as it grills.

Equipment: You will need a medium Chinese cleaver or large chef's knife, a small saucepan (1 quart), a charcoal grill, a chimney, a wire brush, a cover (pie plate, shallow roasting pan or double-thick aluminum foil), a large spatula and a pastry brush.

1 medium-large head garlic, cloves broken apart and peeled

⅔ cup good-quality, fruity olive oil

1 scant tablespoon fresh lime juice

kosher or sea salt

1 canned chipotle chile *en adobo,* seeded and thinly sliced

½ bunch (about 5) green onions

1 small avocado, peeled, pitted and cut into ⅓-inch dice

¼ cup chopped cilantro, plus a little extra for garnish

2 live 1½-pound hard-shell lobsters

1. Chop the garlic with a knife (not a food processor) into a rough, fine dice (no larger than ¹⁄₁₆-inch pieces). In a small saucepan set over medium-low to low heat, combine the garlic and oil and keep at a bare simmer until the pieces are very soft and beginning to brown, 20 to 30 minutes. Add the lime juice, ½ teaspoon salt and the chile; raise the heat to medium-high and stir for a couple of minutes until the rapid boiling has subsided (indicating that the liquid has evaporated).

2. Prepare a charcoal fire and let it burn until the charcoal is covered with gray ash; if using a gas grill, preheat for about 15 minutes. Set the grill grate in place. Brush the green onions with a little oil from the garlic and grill until soft and nicely browned. Chop into ¼-inch lengths and add to the garlic, along with the avocado and cilantro. Taste and season with additional salt if necessary. Keep warm over very low heat.

3. With a cleaver or chef's knife, split each lobster in half lengthwise (page 34). Remove the head sac and intestine. Crack the claws in the center on the side that will not be exposed directly to the hot coals. With a pastry brush, brush the shells of the lobsters with a little of the garlicky oil. Lift the lobster halves up and brush the undersides. This prevents the loss of the lobster's juices. Also brush any exposed meat. Season the lobsters lightly with salt. Place the lobsters, shell side down, directly over the coals. Cover each lobster loosely with a pie plate, roasting pan or aluminum foil. Cook for 8 to 10 minutes. *Do not turn the lobster over.* Baste the lobster several times during cooking with a little more of the oil. Check for doneness by gently prying around where the tail meat enters the carcass. If it is cooked through, the meat will be a creamy white. Remove from the grill and place on individual plates. Spoon the garlic mixture over the lobster, letting it pool luxuriously around the crustaceans, then sprinkle with a little extra cilantro.

Makes 2 luxurious servings

Daniel Boulud

Chilled Lobster Salad with Mediterranean Vegetables, Cranberry Beans and Coral and Basil Vinaigrettes

Daniel Boulud and his Restaurant Daniel in Manhattan have been awarded enough stars to start their own constellation. A master of modern French cuisine, Daniel, author of Cooking with Daniel Boulud *(Random House, 1993), has been named Chef of the Year by the James Beard Foundation and his restaurant has been rated the best on dozens of lists, among them the* Zagat *Survey, the* Gourmet *magazine poll and* The International Herald Tribune's *list of the ten most outstanding restaurants in the world. In the years that this native of Lyons has been cooking in America, he has trained many talented chefs who have gone on to work at restaurants across the country—one of the reasons the food in America is so good.*

Daniel's lobster salad is a study in balance. The base of the salad is a mix of cranberry beans, Mediterranean vegetables and fresh herbs, the perfect companion to simply cooked lobster, and a handful of peppery arugula. This elegant dish can be made ahead—indeed, the basil oil should be made and refrigerated at least one day and up to one week in advance and the other components must be chilled ahead—so that at serving time you have only to toss them with vinaigrette and stack them attractively.

Be sure to buy female lobsters (see diagram on page 13) for their coral, or roe.

BASIL OIL

½ cup densely packed basil leaves

1 cup grapeseed or other cooking oil

LOBSTER

2 live 1-pound chicken lobsters

CORAL SAUCE

lobster roe

½ cup Savory Lobster Broth (page 54) or Quick Lobster Stock (page 57)

1 teaspoon tomato paste

1 tablespoon extra-virgin olive oil

½ teaspoon sherry vinegar

kosher or sea salt

freshly ground black pepper

BEANS

2 slices bacon

5 cloves garlic, peeled

2 sprigs fresh thyme

1 cup fresh cranberry beans, rinsed, or ⅔ cup dried, soaked overnight and drained

3 cups chicken stock or water

VEGETABLES

1 small zucchini, scrubbed

½ small Japanese eggplant, rinsed and dried

½ rib celery, cut into 1-inch-long x ¼-inch-thick matchsticks

2 tablespoons extra-virgin olive oil

¼ small onion, peeled and cut into small dice

2 cloves garlic, peeled and finely chopped

1 sprig fresh thyme

kosher or sea salt

freshly ground black pepper

1 small red pepper, peeled and cut into 1-inch-long x ¼-inch-thick matchsticks

½ fennel bulb, cut into 1-inch-long x ¼-inch-thick matchsticks

TO FINISH

4 teaspoons extra-virgin olive oil

1 teaspoon freshly squeezed lemon juice

kosher or sea salt

freshly ground white pepper

¼ pound arugula or mesclun, rinsed and dried

4 large basil leaves, cut in chiffonade

2 tablespoons toasted pine nuts

1. *For the basil oil:* Bring a large pot of salted water to a boil. Prepare an ice bath. Place the basil leaves in the boiling water and cook just until tender but still green, 2 to 3 minutes. Drain and immediately place the leaves in the ice bath until cool. Drain and dry the leaves by squeezing out the excess water. Place the basil in a blender and add a bit of the oil; process to chop the leaves. With the blender on, add the remaining oil in a slow, steady stream. When completely blended, pour the oil into a cheesecloth-lined strainer placed over a bowl. Cover with plastic wrap and refrigerate overnight. The next day, pour the oil into a bottle with a tight-fitting cap and refrigerate until needed; discard the basil.

2. *For the lobsters:* Bring water to a boil in the bottom of a steamer. Kill the lobsters by piercing the heads (behind the eyes) with a skewer. Detach the lobster carcasses and separate the claws and the tail. Working with a small spoon, remove the roe from the carcasses; reserve the roe for the sauce. The carcasses can be discarded or saved for stock. Place the lobster claws in the steamer, cover and steam for 2 minutes; add the tails and steam 7 minutes longer. Transfer the lobsters to a platter and chill in the refrigerator. When the lobsters are cool, pull the claw and tail meat from their shells and remove the intestines from the tails. Slice each tail into six medallions; leave the claw meat intact. Cover the lobster with a damp paper towel, wrap in plastic wrap and refrigerate.

3. *For the coral sauce:* Prepare an ice bath for the sauce. Blend the roe, lobster broth and tomato paste in a blender. Pour the mixture into a medium saucepan and, over very low heat, whisk until it turns bright orange. Return the mixture to the blender and add the oil and vinegar. Season with salt and pepper and blend until smooth. The sauce should be as thick as a milkshake; if necessary, thin the sauce with additional lobster broth. As soon as the sauce is blended, strain it into a container, then, to preserve its vibrant color, immediately place the container in the ice bath. When cool, cover and refrigerate until needed.

4. *For the beans:* Cook the bacon in a medium saucepan over medium heat until it renders its fat. Add the garlic, thyme, cranberry beans and chicken stock. (The stock should just cover the beans; if it doesn't, add more.) Bring the stock to a boil, lower the heat and cook at a simmer for about 30 minutes until the beans are nearly cooked through. Remove the pan from the heat and allow the beans to cool in the broth. When cool, cover the pan and refrigerate until needed. (Reserving the beans in the broth will keep them moist.) When you are ready to use the beans, remove and discard the bacon, garlic and thyme. Drain the beans.

5. *For the vegetables:* Bring a large pot of salted water to a boil. Prepare an ice bath. Cut the outer ¼ inch of zucchini, that is the green skin and ¼ inch of flesh, into matchsticks that are 1 inch long x ¼ inch thick. (Reserve the inner part of the zucchini for another use.) Cut the eggplant in the same fashion and set aside. Place the zucchini in the boiling water and cook just until tender. Using a slotted spoon or strainer, remove the zucchini—reserving the boiling water—immediately to the ice bath to cool and set its color. Repeat the cooking and cooling process with the celery. When cool, drain the vegetables and pat them dry. Warm the olive oil in a sauté pan over low heat. Add the onion, garlic and thyme; season with salt and black pepper and cook, stirring frequently, just until the onion and garlic are tender; they should not take on any color. Add the red pepper and fennel and cook for several minutes. Add the eggplant and cook until all the vegetables are tender. Remove and discard the thyme, then scrape the mixture onto a plate to cool.

6. *To finish:* Set out 4 chilled plates. Make a lemon vinaigrette by whisking 3 teaspoons of the olive oil with the lemon juice; season with salt and pepper and set aside. Toss the lobster with the remaining teaspoon of olive oil and season it well with salt and pepper. Toss the arugula with enough of the lemon vinaigrette to coat the leaves lightly; set aside for the moment. Place the drained cranberry beans in a large bowl with the cooled vegetables and the basil; toss with enough lemon vinaigrette to lightly coat the ingredients. Spoon a mound of the mixture in the center of each plate. Arrange 3 medallions of lobster and 1 claw on top of the vegetables. Drizzle a ring of the coral sauce and another of the basil oil around each plate. Top the lobster with a small handful of arugula and sprinkle each plate with a few pine nuts.

Serves 4 as an appetizer

Edward Brown

Bouillabaisse

Ed Brown grew up at the Jersey shore (I did too) where, as a teenager, he worked unloading fish-ing boats for a nearby restaurant. This began a lifelong relationship with fish and shellfish—a relationship that has become his passion. Ed had early training in Paris with Chef Alain Senderens at the Michelin three-star Lucas Carton. He also worked for Chef Senderens at Mau-rice in Manhattan. Later, as executive chef at New York's Judson Grill and Tropica, he further de-veloped his direct but exuberant style. As chef of the Sea Grill, in New York's Rockefeller Center, Ed is considered one of America's foremost seafood chefs. This recipe is adapted from his book, written with Arthur Boehm, The Modern Seafood Cook *(Clarkson Potter, 1995).*

Bouillabaisse, a traditional fish stew from Provence, especially associated with the city of Marseilles, has many so-called authentic versions. When a dish becomes as world-renowned as bouillabaisse, it naturally becomes subject to many variations, even in its place of origin. In Provence, I have eaten it made with only fish and with a mixture of fish and shellfish, but never with lobster. Most American versions feature lobster, a nice addition, I think. The toast (*croutes*) and *rouille* (or sometimes aioli) are classic, but the fish and shellfish vary. Ed Brown's version has the traditional flavors of saffron and fennel and a hint of orange. For seafood, he pairs briny clams with sweet scallops, monkfish and lobster. If any of these items are not available at market, substitute mussels for clams or scallops and bass, hake, wolffish, or hal-ibut for the monkfish. You may make the rich broth, the *croutes* and aioli well in advance, so all you have to do is cut up the lobsters and add the fish at dinner. Large soup plates work best for this dish. Put an extra bowl on the table for empty shells.

Equipment: You will need a large stockpot (10 to 12 quarts) preferably one that is at-tractive enough to set at the table, a medium Chinese cleaver or large chef's knife, a food processor, a slotted spoon and a ladle.

3 tablespoons extra-virgin olive oil

1 tablespoon unsalted butter

1 medium leek (3 ounces), cut in half lengthwise then across in ½-inch pieces, rinsed and drained

1 small fennel bulb (6 ounces), top dis-carded, bulb cut in quarters, cored and thinly sliced

1 rib celery (1½ ounces), cut into thin diagonal slices

1 large onion (5 ounces), peeled and thinly sliced

1 bay leaf

¼ teaspoon fennel seeds

½ teaspoon saffron threads

kosher or sea salt

3 cloves garlic, minced (about 1 table-spoon)

1 tablespoon tomato paste

½ cup dry white wine

1 can (14.5 ounces) Italian plum tomatoes, coarsely chopped, with their juice

2½ cups fish stock or Quick Lobster Stock (page 57)

¼ teaspoon cayenne pepper

1 tablespoon very finely sliced orange zest, white pith removed

freshly ground black pepper

2 live 1¼-pound lobsters

12 littleneck clams

¾ pound monkfish fillet, cut into 1½-inch pieces (about 8 pieces)

12 sea scallops (about 8 ounces)

Roasted Red Pepper Aioli (recipe follows)

½ French baguette for *croutes* (see Cook's Note)

1. In a large heavy soup pot (10 to 12 quarts), heat 1 tablespoon of the olive oil with the butter over medium heat. Add the leek, fennel, celery, onion, bay leaf, fennel seeds, saffron and about ½ teaspoon salt. Cover and cook for about 10 minutes, stirring occasionally, until the vegetables are soft.

2. Add the garlic and, stirring frequently, cook 2 minutes longer. Add the tomato paste and cook, stirring, for 1 minute. Add the wine, bring to a boil and cook for 3 minutes. Add the tomatoes with their juice, the fish stock and cayenne; bring back to a boil. Cover and simmer for 15 minutes. Stir in the orange zest and remove from the heat. Season to taste with salt if needed and pepper. Transfer the broth to a smaller container, as you will be using this large pot again, and keep refrigerated unless using within an hour. The broth can be made up to this point as much as a day ahead.

3. Warm the vegetable broth before you proceed with this recipe. Quarter the lobsters (page 34). You will get 12 pieces from the 2 lobsters. Scrub the clams and check the fish for bones. Check the scallops for shell fragments as you remove and discard the strap, the stringy little hard piece of flesh on the side of the scallop.

4. Place the large heavy pot over high heat. Add the remaining 2 tablespoons of olive oil and bring to the smoking point. Remove the 4 pieces of lobster tail and set aside. Add the remaining lobster pieces, along with the clams and cook, stirring often, for 2 to 3 minutes until the lobster shells turn red. Add the broth and bring to a boil. Cook for 3 minutes, then stir in the lobster tails. Cover and cook 1 minute. Add the monkfish and continue to cook, covered, for 1 minute. Add the scallops and cook for 1 minute more. Cover and remove from the heat. Serve this family style with a plate of toasted baguette and a bowl of Roasted Red Pepper Aioli on the side.

Serves 4 as a main course

COOK'S NOTE: *To make enough* croutes *(toasts) for 4 people, you will need at least half of a long baguette. Cut the baguette on a slight diagonal into ¼- to ⅓-inch-thick slices. Line the slices on a cookie sheet and bake at 350°F for about 20 minutes until golden brown and crunchy.*

Roasted Red Pepper Aioli

2 egg yolks

2 cloves garlic, peeled

2 red bell peppers, roasted, peeled and seeded

Juice of ½ lemon

1⅓ cups good-quality olive oil

Tabasco sauce

kosher or sea salt

freshly ground black pepper

1. Place the egg yolks, garlic, roasted red peppers and lemon juice in the bowl of a food processor. Puree for about 2 minutes until the mixture is smooth.

2. With the machine running, slowly pour the oil through the feed tube until a creamy emulsion has formed. Season with Tabasco sauce, salt and pepper, being generous with the pepper.

Makes about 2 cups

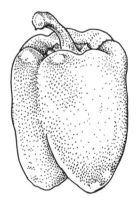

Gerald Clare

Lobster Pad Thai

Last autumn, I cooked a lobster dinner at the James Beard House in New York with three of Maine's most accomplished culinarians: Nancy Harmon Jenkins, Sam Hayward and Gerald Clare. There were six different lobster dishes, all top-notch, but Gerald Clare's Lobster Pad Thai was off the charts.

Jerry Clare is the chef and proprietor of The Belmont, an elegant Edwardian-style inn located in the scenic coastal village of Camden, Maine. The inn was fully renovated and restored in 1988 and has become a mecca for weary travelers and savvy diners. The Belmont's acclaimed cuisine is inspired by a wealth of superb local ingredients: garden vegetables, herbs, poultry, cheese, fish and shellfish, especially lobster. Jerry has studied cooking in Boston, New York, Italy and Thailand and infuses these influences into his version of New England cooking; his Lobster Pad Thai recipe is an extremely tasty example. Jerry has been featured in many national and international publications and on the PBS series "Great Chefs of the East."

You will need to visit a specialty Thai, Cambodian or Southeast Asian market in order to find several needed ingredients: lemongrass, Thai basil, shrimp paste, chili paste, fish sauce and medium rice sticks (noodles). As with all stir-fry dishes, it is imperative that you have all ingredients fully prepped and organized before you start the dish. If you do not have a wok, substitute a 12-inch sauté pan. As is the custom in Maine, the lobster portion is very generous. If you wish to use smaller lobsters, you may do so without making any changes to this recipe.

6 live 1½-pound hard-shell select lobsters

1 package rice stick noodles, medium width (14 ounces)

4 tablespoons peanut oil

3 tablespoons minced fresh ginger

3 tablespoons minced fresh lemongrass

1 tablespoon chili paste (more if brave, less if timid)

1 tablespoon shrimp paste

4 tablespoons sugar

2 tablespoons fish sauce

juice of 2 limes, plus 1 whole for garnish, cut into 6 wedges

juice of 1 lemon

1 bunch scallions, finely chopped

1 large egg, beaten with 2 tablespoons water

3 tablespoons chopped fresh cilantro

3 tablespoons chopped Thai basil, plus 6 sprigs for garnish

1 cup dry roasted unsalted peanuts, ground

1 package bean sprouts (12 ounces)

1. Fill a 10- or 12-quart pot with water about two-thirds full. Add enough salt to make it distinctly salty (¼ cup) and bring to a rolling boil. With your hand on the carapace of each lobster, place 3 in the pot and cook for exactly 4½ minutes. Using tongs, remove the lobsters and allow them to cool at room temperature. Bring the water back to a full boil and repeat the process with the remaining 3 lobsters. If you are using smaller lobsters (chickens or quarters), refer to the timing chart for partially cooked lobsters (page 30). When the lobsters are cool enough to handle, remove the claws with the knuckles attached. Remove the meat from the the knuckles and claws (also remove the cartilage from the claws). With one hand on the carapace and one on the tail, break the tail away from the carcass. Split the tail in half lengthwise; remove the intestine and cut each half into two pieces. Break the antennae off the lobster carcasses and save for garnish. Reserve the carcass, with the tomalley, for soup. Cover the lobster meat with plastic wrap and refrigerate until ready to use.

2. Soak the rice sticks in warm water until they have softened; this will take about 20 minutes. Drain well. Prepare and organize all the other ingredients.

3. Heat the oil in a wok or large sauté pan (12 inches) over high heat. Working quickly, add the lobster and stir-fry for 2 minutes. Then add the ginger and lemongrass and cook for 1 minute. Add the chili paste, shrimp paste and sugar and cook for 1 minute. Lower the heat slightly.

4. Add the noodles along with the fish sauce, lime juice and lemon juice. Add the scallions and egg and cook 1 to 2 minutes longer, being careful not to scramble the egg. Remove from the heat and allow to sit a minute before dishing up.

5. Divide the Pad Thai among 6 plates; try to distribute the lobster evenly: 2 claws, 2 knuckles and 4 pieces of tail meat each. Sprinkle each plate with cilantro, chopped basil, ground peanuts and sprouts. Garnish with a lime wedge and sprigs of Thai basil and crisscross the lobster antennae over the top.

Serves 6 as a main course

Larry Forgione

Lobster & Wild Rice Risotto

More than any other chef, Larry Forgione has articulated and defined the cooking that became known as New American in the early 1980s. His insistence on top-quality American ingredients cooked in an American style inspired a generation of other young American chefs, including me. I first tasted Larry's cooking in 1981 at the River Café in Brooklyn, New York. His bold American menu was a breath of fresh air. In 1983, Larry opened An American Place on Lexington Avenue in New York City. James Beard, the "Dean of American Cooking," assisted him and consulted on the desserts served at the new restaurant, which quickly became the talk of New York and of the food world nationwide. An American Place has long since moved to a larger space on Park Avenue and is still one of the greatest restaurants in New York. Larry also runs The Grill Room in Manhattan and The Beekman Tavern in Rhinebeck, New York. His book, Cooking from an American Place *(William Morrow), was released in the spring of 1996. It is a reminder of just how much Larry Forgione has contributed to contemporary American cooking.*

Larry's risotto is a wonderful combination of lobster, wild mushrooms, butternut squash and short-grain and wild rice. Although this risotto is made differently from traditional Italian risotto, the final cooking, the texture and the consistency are similar. The flavor is American all the way. The recipe calls for the wild rice, short-grain rice and diced squash to be precooked. The lobster is also precooked, and the meat is then diced. Once these steps are done, the final cooking of the dish takes less than ten minutes. Serve as a main course for lunch or a light dinner or in smaller portions for a seafood course.

2 live 1½- to 1¾-pound hard-shell select lobsters

4 tablespoons unsalted butter

1 tablespoon minced garlic

1 cup fresh chanterelles or other mushrooms, cut into 1-inch pieces

1 cup cooked wild rice (see Cook's Notes)

kosher or sea salt

freshly ground black pepper

½ cup cooked short-grain or Arborio rice, slightly underdone (see Cook's Notes)

1 cup hot Savory Lobster Broth (page 54), Quick Lobster Stock (page 57) or chicken stock

½ cup cooked finely diced butternut squash (see Cook's Notes)

3 tablespoons heavy cream

1 tablespoon sliced fresh chives

2 tablespoons grated aged Jack or Parmigiano-Reggiano cheese

1. Fully cook the lobsters by steaming (page 32) them. Using tongs, remove them from the steamer or pot and let cool at room temperature. Remove the meat from the claws, knuckles and tails; remove the cartilage from the claws and the intestine from the tail. Save the carcasses for soup or broth. Cut the meat into 1-inch dice; if there is any roe, finely chop it and add it to the meat. Remove the tomalley; place it in a small bowl and mash with 2 tablespoons of the butter. (This step is optional; the tomalley can be omitted, but it really does bring the dish to a higher level.) Cover both the tomalley butter and the lobster meat separately with plastic wrap and refrigerate.

2. Heat the remaining 2 tablespoons butter in a heavy 3- or 4-quart saucepan over medium heat until the butter begins to foam and turns light brown. Add the garlic, chanterelles and wild rice. Stir, season with a little salt and pepper and cook for 2 to 3 minutes. Add the short-grain rice and lobster broth. Simmer and stir for about 5 minutes as the rice absorbs the stock and thickens. Add the squash, cream, chives and lobster meat. Cook for about 2 minutes until the lobster is heated through.

3. Remove the risotto from the heat and stir in the tomalley butter and the cheese. Spoon into shallow bowls or soup plates and serve at once.

Serves 4

COOK'S NOTES: *For 1 cup cooked wild rice, combine ½ cup wild rice with 1½ cups chicken stock or water in a small saucepan (1 quart). Simmer, partially covered, over medium heat for about 40 minutes, stirring occasionally. When the rice is tender but not mushy, drain and let cool.*

For ½ cup short-grain rice, combine ¼ cup short-grain rice with about ½ cup lobster broth, lobster stock, chicken stock or water in a small saucepan (1 quart). Simmer, covered, over medium heat for 12 minutes. Remove from the heat and let cool in the remaining liquid. For arborio rice, first heat ½ cup lobster broth, lobster stock, chicken stock or water. In a small saucepan, stir ¼ cup rice with 1 tablespoon unsalted butter over medium heat until hot. Add the broth a little at a time, allowing it to be absorbed before adding more. When all the liquid has been absorbed and the rice is slightly underdone, remove it from the heat and let cool.

For the butternut squash, you will need a small piece of peeled squash weighing about 4 ounces. Cut the squash into ¼-inch dice and simmer for about 3 minutes in lightly salted water. The squash should still be firm. Drain.

Johanne Killeen and George Germon

Spicy Braised Lobster with Charred Parsley

"Lusty," "distinctive," "exuberant," "sensual" and "simple" are the words most often used to describe the cuisine that my good friends Johanne and George have created at Al Forno restaurant in Providence, Rhode Island. The purity of their food, their ability to bring the most flavor out of every ingredient and their tireless attention to detail caused Patricia Wells of the International Herald Tribune *to declare Al Forno one of the top ten casual restaurants in the world. For more than fifteen years, these talented chefs, both trained as artists at the Rhode Island School of Design, have practiced their unique style of cooking, which was first defined in their cookbook* Cucina Simpatica *(HarperCollins, 1991).*

This recipe for braised lobster is typical of Johanne and George: a few choice ingredients used in a way that appears very simple and yet is utterly innovative. The dish tastes purely of sweet, fragrant lobster with just the right amount of spice. Follow the directions carefully. Be sure the parsley is dry before you add it to the oil, or it will steam rather than fry. Look for a deep green color before you add the lobster. As soon as the lobster comes in contact with the heat, it will release liquid that will allow it to "braise." Don't worry—the parsley won't burn. The lobster is served whole, with the juices and oil as a dipping sauce.

Equipment: For cooking, you will need a Dutch oven or similar type of pot with a tight-fitting lid. For serving, you will need lobster crackers, small bowls for dipping and a large bowl for the empty shells.

¼ cup extra-virgin olive oil, plus more for serving

¼ to ½ teaspoon dried red pepper flakes

1 tablespoon finely minced garlic

1 cup loosely packed chopped Italian parsley

4 live 1½-pound hard-shell select lobsters

1. Heat the oil in a large Dutch oven (10 to 12 quarts) over high heat until it is very hot. Add the red pepper, garlic and parsley. The mixture should begin to sizzle immediately. Stir until the garlic is golden and the parsley darkens. Turn the heat down slightly.

2. Add the lobsters, cover and cook over medium-high heat for 12 to 14 minutes until the lobsters are cooked. Serve immediately with the juices on the side for dipping. Add a little extra olive oil to each serving if desired.

Serves 4 as a main course

Bob Kinkead

Salt Cod & Lobster Cakes

When I think of great seafood cooks, I think of my pal Bob Kinkead. Originally from Providence, Rhode Island, he was the chef at some of New England's best restaurants: Chillingsworth on Cape Cod, the Harvest in Cambridge and 21 Federal in Nantucket, before moving to Washington, D.C., in the mid-1980s. New England's loss was Washington's gain, and they know it! In 1992 Bob was voted Chef of the Year by Washingtonian *magazine, and in 1995 he was named Mid-Atlantic Chef of the Year by the James Beard Foundation. The* Washington Post *frequently sings his praises and says he "just keeps getting better," music to any chef's ear. And it's true. At Kinkead's, his big brasserie on Pennsylvania Avenue, he offers a menu that is distinctly American in style, yet eclectic in its inspiration. Bob cooks with great authority; his seafood is robust but always true to its natural flavors.*

Bob Kinkead's lobster dishes are sensational. Forget the Smithsonian; his Lobster with Savoy Cabbage, White Beans and Truffle Oil or his Lobster with Leeks, Potatoes and Corn Pudding are, alone, worth a special trip to D.C. But my favorite, Salt Cod and Lobster Cakes, a recipe Bob learned from his grandmother, is real Yankee soul food! This is a recipe to treasure; the cakes are easy to make and don't call for much lobster. You can shape this into small cakes for an hors d'oeuvre or appetizer or, for a traditional New England dinner, make larger ones and serve them with tartar sauce and baked beans. And, as Bob says, if you want to be really authentic, "fry 'em in bacon fat."

8 ounces boneless salt cod	3 shallots (2 ounces), minced
1 live 1¼-pound lobster, or 4 ounces fully cooked lobster meat	2 scallions, finely chopped
1 cup all-purpose flour	⅓ bunch chives (about 10 chives), finely chopped
2 teaspoons double-acting baking powder	¼ teaspoon freshly ground black pepper
2 large eggs, lightly beaten	1½ cups dried seasoned bread crumbs for coating
½ medium red bell pepper (3 ounces), finely chopped	¼ cup vegetable oil
	2 tablespoons unsalted butter

1. Soak the salt cod in a pot of cold water, covered and refrigerated, for 12 hours, changing the water every 2 hours. The water should be clear and almost fresh-tasting before you cook the cod.

2. If you are using live lobsters, fully cook them by steaming (page 32) or boiling (page 29). Let cool at room temperature. Remove the meat from the tail, claws and knuckles. Reserve the carcass for soup. Remove the cartilage from the claws and the intestine from the tail of the cooked meat. Chop coarsely. Cover and refrigerate until you are ready to use.

3. Drain the salt cod, place in a 10-inch sauté pan and cover with cold water. Place over medium heat, cover and simmer until the cod is cooked through, about 15 minutes. Drain and let cool. Chop the salt cod coarsely.

4. In a mixing bowl, combine the cod, lobster, flour, baking powder and eggs and mix well. Then add the bell pepper, shallots, scallions, chives and black pepper. Mix again and taste for seasoning. Shape into cakes: about 16 small ones for appetizers or 12 large ones for dinner. Dip the cakes into the bread crumbs, then place on a cookie sheet and chill in the refrigerator for 10 minutes. These can be made up to 6 hours in advance.

5. Heat the oil and butter in a 10- or 12-inch skillet over medium heat. Add the cakes without crowding the pan and cook for about 3 minutes on each side until both sides are browned. Serve at once, bringing out each batch as it cooks, with tartar sauce and baked beans.

Serves 6 as a main course

Emeril Lagasse

Emeril's Portuguese Lobster

Emeril Lagasse, host of "The Essence of Emeril" on the TV Food Network and proprietor of Emeril's and NOLA, both in New Orleans, and Emeril's in Las Vegas, is a chef with incredible energy. His cooking embraces Creole and Cajun cuisine but is distinctively marked by infusions of Asian, Mexican and especially Portuguese flavors. He calls it "New New Orleans Cooking," which is the name of his cookbook as well (William Morrow, 1993). Emeril grew up in Fall River, a small port city in southeastern Massachusetts, where he was weaned on the Portuguese cooking of his mother. An accomplished musician, he turned down a full scholarship to the New England Conservatory of Music at the age of eighteen to pursue his passion for cooking.

Emeril's Portuguese Lobster is cooked in a hearty broth with chorizo, peppers, olives, tomatoes and potatoes. The relatively short cooking time results in a stew that explodes with the individual flavors of the ingredients without losing the underlying fragrance of lobster. The substantial amounts of potatoes and vegetables make this a very satisfying dinner. Serve in a large pasta bowl or in individual bowls.

Equipment: You will need a 10-inch sauté pan or skillet with a lid. If you want to double the recipe, you will need a 12- or 14-inch pan. You will also need a small pot to cook the potatoes, a pair of tongs, a ladle and a medium Chinese cleaver or large chef's knife.

2 cups diced (¼ to ½ inch) potatoes (12 ounces)	2 tablespoons chopped parsley
1 live 2-pound hard-shell select lobster	½ cup chopped Spanish green olives
2 tablespoons olive oil	½ cup chopped ripe black olives
6 ounces chorizo, casing removed and finely diced	1½ cups chopped tomatoes
2 bay leaves	½ cup dry white wine
1 cup finely diced onions	1 cup Savory Lobster Broth (page 54), Quick Lobster Stock (page 57) or water
3 tablespoons finely diced red bell pepper	1 teaspoon kosher or sea salt
2 tablespoons minced shallots	½ teaspoon dried red pepper flakes
1 tablespoon minced garlic	¼ cup thinly sliced scallions (2 large or 3 small)

1. Simmer the potatoes in a small pot of lightly salted water for about 5 minutes until tender but still firm. Drain and rinse with cold water to stop the cooking. Organize and prepare all the ingredients before starting the lobster, because the cooking time is only 12 minutes.

2. Using a cleaver or chef's knife, split the lobster in half lengthwise (page 34). Remove the head sac and intestine. Crack the claws on both sides.

3. Heat a 10-inch sauté pan or skillet over medium-high heat. Add the oil and heat until hot. Add the chorizo and sauté for about 1 minute to release its delicious fat. Add the bay leaves, onions, bell pepper, shallots and garlic and sauté for about 2 minutes until the vegetables are softened. Add the potatoes, parsley, olives, tomatoes, wine and lobster broth. Season with salt and red pepper. Bring to a simmer.

4. Immediately add the lobster, shell side down, cover and simmer for 8 minutes. Use tongs to remove the lobster. Ladle the hearty broth into a warmed shallow bowl or platter. Place the lobster directly on top and sprinkle with the scallions. Serve at once.

Serves 2 as a main course

Wolfgang Puck

Roasted Lobster with Pickled Ginger & Crisp Spinach Leaves

It would take pages and pages to list the accomplishments of Wolfgang Puck. His first and most famous restaurant, Spago, in West Hollywood, sparked an entire genre of Mediterranean-inspired California cuisine that has been copied around the world. His second restaurant, Chinois on Main, in Santa Monica, was one of the first—and is still one of the best—examples of what East/West fusion cooking can be. One of the hardest-working and most creative chefs in America, Wolfgang has written three books and continues to open one successful restaurant after another: Granita in Malibu, Postrio in San Francisco, Spago in Las Vegas and several Wolfgang Puck Cafés at various locations across the country. His execution of techniques learned during formal European training in his native Austria and in Paris earned him respect and a great reputation early in his career. But it is his creativity, his tireless search for exciting flavors and his daring style (along with that of his wife, designer Barbara Lazaroff) that make him so brilliant.

This Thai-inspired recipe is from Postrio in San Francisco. It is based on a technique similar to the one used in Jasper's Pan-Roasted Lobster with Chervil and Chives (page 46). Wolfgang's recipe for one select lobster, to be shared by two people, is intended to be served on a large plate or small platter.

If your pantry is not stocked with Asian ingredients, you may need to shop at an Asian market. This recipe calls for rice pilaf to serve with the lobster, so make your favorite recipe and have it ready a couple of minutes before the lobster, which takes about 15 minutes to cook. You can prepare the sauce and pickled ginger in advance, but the spinach should be cooked at the last minute so that it is still hot when you serve it.

Equipment: You will need a 9- or 10-inch ovenproof skillet (or a 12-inch skillet if you double the recipe), a medium Chinese cleaver or large chef's knife, a medium saucepan (1 quart), a strainer, a whisk, a small skillet, a wok or deep saucepan for deep-frying the spinach, a deep-fat thermometer and a slotted spoon.

SAUCE

2 tablespoons peanut oil	½ cup port or plum wine
3 cloves garlic, chopped	¼ cup dry white wine
peels from 1 ounce fresh ginger (about ½ ounce), chopped	½ cup fish stock
2 scallions, chopped	1 cup heavy cream
1 tablespoon curry powder	2 tablespoons Chinese black vinegar
	½ teaspoon dried red pepper flakes

2 tablespoons unsalted butter

1 teaspoon chili oil

kosher or sea salt

freshly ground black pepper

OTHER INGREDIENTS

½ ounce fresh ginger, peeled and cut into very thin strips (julienne)

1 cup plum wine

¼ cup rice vinegar

1 heaping cup cooked rice pilaf

1 live 1½- to 1¾-pound hard-shell select lobster

2 tablespoons peanut oil

1 scallion (white part only), cut into very thin strips (julienne)

1 batch Crisp Spinach Leaves (page 215)

1. *For the sauce:* Heat the peanut oil in a medium saucepan (1 quart) over medium-high heat. Add the garlic, ginger peels and scallions and sauté for about 1 minute until wilted. Stir in the curry powder and cook for 2 minutes more. Add the wines to deglaze the pan and reduce by half (⅓ cup). Add the stock, cream, vinegar and red pepper and simmer over low heat for about 30 minutes until quite thick (about ½ cup). Strain and return to a clean pan. Whisk in the butter and chili oil and season to taste with salt and pepper.

2. *For the other ingredients*: Combine the ginger, wine and vinegar in a small skillet. Simmer over low heat for 10 minutes. Strain, reserving the ginger and liquid in separate bowls.

3. Start cooking the rice before proceeding with the lobster. Preheat the oven to 450°F.

4. Using a cleaver or chef's knife, split the lobster in half lengthwise (page 34). Remove the head sac and intestine. Crack the claws on one side. Heat the oil in a 9- or 10-inch skillet over high heat until sizzling hot. Place the lobster, meat side down, in the pan. As soon as it begins to sear, put the pan in the oven and roast for 8 to 10 minutes. Remove the lobster to a work surface and discard the oil from the skillet. Return the pan to medium heat and add the liquid that was reserved from cooking the ginger to deglaze the pan. Add the sauce and simmer for 4 to 5 minutes. Meanwhile, remove the meat from the claws, knuckles and tail of the lobster. Pull the lobster's carapace off the carcass. Discard the carcass. Use a cleaver to split the carapace in half lengthwise. Save the split lobster head for garnish. At the last minute, add the lobster meat to the sauce and reheat briefly.

5. Place a heaping cup of rice pilaf in the center of a medium platter and spoon the lobster meat with the sauce over the rice. Spoon any extra sauce around the platter. Sprinkle the scallion strips and reserved pickled ginger over the lobster. Garnish the platter with the lobster head and Crisp Spinach Leaves (page 215). Serve at once.

Serves 2

Crisp Spinach Leaves

peanut oil for frying (2 to 3 inches)   kosher or sea salt
spinach leaves (5 or 6 per person), stems
trimmed

1. Heat the oil in a wok or high-sided heavy saucepan (2 quarts or larger) to 375°F.

2. Rinse and dry the spinach thoroughly. At serving time, fry the spinach leaves for about 2 minutes until crisp and translucent. Drain well on paper towels. Season with salt and serve at once.

COOK'S NOTE: *Spinach for two can be fried in a single batch. If you double the recipe or make extra, you will need to do it in batches and keep it warm in a low oven. A wok is perfect for this job; otherwise, use a high-sided heavy saucepan (at least 2 quarts). A deep-fry thermometer is essential. Use a slotted spoon for removing the spinach from the hot oil.*

Stephan Pyles

Lobster-Papaya Quesadillas with Mango Cream

Stephan Pyles, one of the originators of modern southwestern cuisine, was part of a culinary movement in the early 1980s that redefined the cooking once known as Tex-Mex. Along with chefs Mark Miller, John Sedlar, Dean Fearing, Anne Greer and Robert Delgrande, he established modern southwestern cuisine as a dominant force on the American food scene. Stephan's vibrant and spicy flavors, refined without losing any of their boldness, reflect both his youth spent helping out at his family's Truck-Stop Café in West Texas and his training with the masterful three-star French chefs Alain Chapel, Michel Guerard and the Troisgros brothers. In 1983, Stephan opened the Routh Street Café in Dallas, which quickly became one of the most talked about restaurants in the country. He is now chef and proprietor of two Dallas restaurants, Star Canyon and Aquaknox. This recipe is adapted from Stephan Pyles's The New Texas Cuisine *(Doubleday, 1994).*

These elegant quesadillas are infused with the deep southwestern flavors of roasted poblanos and goat cheese and brightened with the addition of mango, papaya and lobster. They can be served as appetizers or as an hors d'oeuvre. Once you gather and prepare all the ingredients, the cooking is quick and easy. The recipe can easily be doubled.

Equipment: You will need a medium Chinese cleaver or large chef's knife, a 10-inch nonstick skillet and a food processor or blender.

5 ounces cooked lobster meat, or 1 live 1¼-pound hard-shell lobster

2 ounces fresh goat cheese, crumbled

2 ounces Monterey Jack or caciotta cheese, grated

1 teaspoon pureed roasted garlic (optional)

¼ cup chopped onion

½ poblano chile, roasted, peeled, seeded and diced

½ red bell pepper, roasted, peeled, seeded and diced

1 teaspoon minced fresh cilantro

1 teaspoon fresh lime juice

kosher or sea salt

1 medium papaya, peeled, seeded and chopped

4 flour tortillas (8 inches), at room temperature

2 tablespoons unsalted butter, melted

1 cup Mango Cream (recipe follows)

1. If using live lobster, boil or steam the lobster according to the timing charts on pages 29 and 32. Let cool at room temperature, then remove the meat following the instructions on page 36. Cut the tail into ¼- to ½-inch slices and combine with the claw and knuckle meat in a large mixing bowl. You will have about 5 ounces meat. Cover with plastic wrap and refrigerate.

2. Combine the cheeses in a large mixing bowl and stir in the garlic, onion, poblano chile, bell pepper, cilantro and lime juice. Season with salt (about ⅓ teaspoon). Carefully fold in the lobster meat and the papaya.

3. Spread the lobster mixture over half of each tortilla and fold over. Brush both sides of each tortilla with melted butter. Heat a large nonstick skillet (10 inches) over medium-high heat. Cook the quesadillas 2 at a time for 2 to 3 minutes on each side until golden brown. Cut each one into 3 triangles (or 4 triangles for hors d'oeuvre) and serve with the mango cream.

Serves 4 as an appetizer

Mango Cream

> 2 ripe medium mangoes
> ½ cup sour cream
> juice of ½ lemon

1. Peel the mangoes and cut the flesh from the seeds. With your hands, squeeze the juice from the flesh into a bowl, then puree the flesh in a food processor or blender until smooth. (Chill the juice and drink it later.) Add the sour cream and lemon juice and blend, scraping down the side with a spatula as necessary. Cover and refrigerate until needed.

Makes about 1½ cups

Joël Robuchon

Nage of Lobster with Ginger & Spring Vegetables

Chef Joël Robuchon is considered by many to be one of this century's great masters of French cuisine. At his Michelin three-star restaurant Jamin in Paris, Chef Robuchon built a reputation for exacting technique, sensitive use of excellent ingredients, intensely flavored food and beautifully conceived dishes. In 1991, Joël Robuchon closed Jamin and opened a new Paris restaurant called Robuchon. Chef Robuchon retired in 1996 and is spending his time writing and consulting for Regent Hotels in Asia.

As he demonstrated in his book *Simply French,* coauthored by Paris-based food writer Patricia Wells, Robuchon often relies on simplicity to achieve perfection. Although the following recipe could hardly be called simple, it is not overly complex. Most of the preparation can be done earlier in the day, making this dish fine for entertaining. In it you will find many of Robuchon's signatures: bursts of ginger, lemon zest, tiny vegetable balls and a flourish of fresh herbs. Choose a top-quality burgundy like Batard Montrachet for this very special dish.

Equipment: You will need a ¼-inch melon baller, a 10-quart pot, a medium pot, a strainer, tongs, scissors and a medium Chinese cleaver or large chef's knife.

2 quarts Ginger Shellfish Court Bouillon (page 220)	3 tablespoons unsalted butter, softened
4 live 1-pound chicken lobsters	6 tablespoons heavy cream
1 small carrot (2 ounces), peeled	3 tablespoons minced fresh ginger
½ small cucumber (2 ounces), peeled	2 teaspoons freshly squeezed lemon juice
6 mushroom caps, trimmed and cleaned	kosher or sea salt
1 shallot (1 ounce), sliced into thin rings	freshly ground black pepper
½ cup fresh peas	small bunch snipped fresh tarragon
2 tablespoons grated lemon zest	small bunch snipped fresh chives

1. In a large pot (8 to 10 quarts), bring the 2 quarts ginger court bouillon to a rolling boil over high heat. Turn the heat to medium and, with your hand on the carapace, plunge the lobsters headfirst into the court bouillon. Timing from when the lobsters hit the water, cook for 5 minutes. Remove the pot from the heat and let the lobsters sit, uncovered, in the hot court bouillon for 30 minutes. The lobsters will finish cooking and will stay moist.

2. Using a ¼-inch melon baller to prepare the vegetables, cut balls out of the flesh of the carrot, cucumber and mushrooms. (Or cut the carrot, cucumber and mushrooms into neat

¼-inch dice.) Combine the carrot, cucumber, mushrooms, shallot, peas and lemon zest in a bowl and toss with 1 tablespoon of the softened butter.

3. Near serving time, preheat the oven to 200°F.

4. Using tongs, remove the lobsters from the court bouillon. Drain thoroughly. Strain and reserve 2 cups court bouillon. Remove the claws with the knuckles attached. Remove the meat from the knuckles and claws (also remove the cartilage from the claws). With one hand on the carapace and one on the tail, break the tail away from the carcass. Break off the tail fins and, from the back end of the tail, push the tail meat out in one piece. Make a thin incision along the top of the tail and remove the intestine. Reserve the carcass for soup. Place the lobster meat on a warmed platter, covered, and keep warm in the oven.

5. Warm the court bouillon over low heat in a medium saucepan. Whisk in the cream, then add the ginger, lemon juice and remaining 2 tablespoons butter. Season with salt and pepper. Add the buttered vegetables and heat for about 1 minute until the vegetables have been warmed through and the broth is hot but not boiling.

6. Divide the meat evenly among 4 large soup plates with a whole lobster tail in the center and 2 claws and 2 knuckles around each. Ladle the hot broth over the lobster meat and garnish with snippings of tarragon and chives. Serve at once.

Serves 4 as a main course

Ginger Shellfish Court Bouillon

Chef Robuchon's court bouillon, a rich broth made with water, fresh ginger, vegetables, spices and aromatic herbs, is used first to cook the lobsters and then later as the base for the "nage" in the preceding recipe. It can also be used to cook lobsters for other preparations that combine ginger with lobster, like Vietnamese Cabbage Salad with Lobster on page 154 or Lobster Pad Thai on page 204; it is also excellent for poaching shrimp and other seafood. This court bouillon can be made several hours in advance and brought back to a boil at cooking time.

1 large carrot (5 ounces), thinly sliced

1 large onion (5 ounces), thinly sliced

1 rib celery (2 ounces), thinly sliced

2 plump fresh cloves garlic

1 ounce fresh ginger, peeled and trimmed

bouquet garni: several parsley sprigs, celery leaves and thyme sprigs wrapped in the green part of a leek and securely fastened with cotton twine

1 teaspoon fennel seeds

1 teaspoon white peppercorns

1 segment star anise

3 tablespoons kosher or sea salt

2 cups dry white wine, preferably Chardonnay

2 teaspoons white vinegar

grated zest of 1 orange

1. In an 8-quart stockpot, combine 4 quarts water with the carrot, onion, celery, garlic, ginger, bouquet garni, fennel seeds, peppercorns, star anise and salt. Cover and bring to a boil over high heat.

2. Reduce the heat and simmer gently for 20 minutes. Add the wine, vinegar and orange zest and simmer for 5 minutes.

3. If you are going to cook the lobsters right away, bring back to a boil. Otherwise, remove from the heat until ready to use. Strained, the court bouillon may be refrigerated for 2 days.

Makes 4 quarts

Douglas Rodriguez

Lobster Seviche with Hearts of Palm

Douglas Rodriguez is one of the most exciting chefs around. After gaining national attention at Yucca in Miami Beach, he moved to New York to open his restaurant Patria. His Nuevo Latino cuisine combines the native flavors of the Caribbean and all of Latin America in a lusty, contemporary style while maintaining the integrity of traditional Latino flavors. The excitement over Doug's food is contagious. When I ate at Patria recently, the customers and the staff alike seemed thrilled to be there. Doug's cookbook, Nuevo Latino *(Ten Speed Press, 1995), is filled with recipes which have the vibrant flavors and great ideas that are the heart of Patria.*

Doug has used the seviche, a traditional Latin dish of chilled cured seafood, as inspiration for a whole new category of dishes. He uses raw, partially cooked and fully cooked seafoods in his spectacular renditions of these refreshing dishes. Most of the ingredients in his lobster seviche are readily available, though you may have to shop around for hearts of palm. Latin and specialty-food markets are good choices for finding them. If you cannot locate hearts of palm, the seviche is excellent without them.

1 pound cooked lobster meat, or 4 pounds live hard-shell lobsters

1 pound fresh hearts of palm

1 large yellow tomato (5 ounces), pulp and seeds removed, cut into ½-inch dice

1 small red onion (3 ounces), halved and thinly sliced

¼ cup fresh cilantro leaves (6 sprigs)

¼ cup sliced scallions (2 large or 3 small)

½ cup freshly squeezed orange juice

½ cup freshly squeezed lime juice

3 tablespoons Dijon mustard

1 tablespoon brown mustard seeds

1 tablespoon grated fresh or prepared drained horseradish

1 tablespoon chopped onion

1 rib celery, peeled and chopped

½ cup Savory Lobster Broth (page 54) or Quick Lobster Stock (page 57)

1. If using live lobsters, boil or steam them according to the timing charts on pages 29 and 32. Let cool at room temperature. Remove the meat following the instructions on page 36. Cut the tails into ½-inch slices and combine with the claw and knuckle meat in a large mixing bowl. You will have about 1 pound meat. Cover with plastic wrap and refrigerate.

2. Set up a vegetable steamer and steam the hearts of palm for about 2 minutes until tender. Chill in ice water, then drain well. Cover with plastic wrap and refrigerate.

3. Add the tomato, red onion, cilantro and scallions to the cooked lobster. Cover with plastic wrap and keep chilled.

4. In a blender or food processor, combine the orange juice, lime juice, Dijon mustard, mustard seeds, horseradish, chopped onion, celery and lobster broth; blend well. Pour over the lobster mixture, toss lightly and chill thoroughly.

5. Divide the hearts of palm among 4 plates, which should be either well chilled or set on crushed ice, and spoon the lobster seviche over. Serve immediately.

Serves 4 as an appetizer

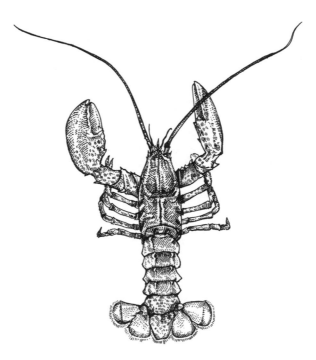

Lydia Shire

Lobster in Green Curry Broth

Lydia Shire, owner of Biba and Pignoli restaurants in Boston, has long been one of the most exciting chefs in America. Among the many honors bestowed on Lydia was 1993 Best Chef in New England by the James Beard Foundation. Her impeccable palate and sense of style, combined with her fearless approach toward blending flavors and textures, have earned her a reputation as an innovator who never rests. Her style, which is exotic and often esoteric, is the result of growing up with parents who were both professional artists. But unlike much of the so-called fusion cooking so popular these days, Lydia's food is both original and familiar at the same time. Her food is based on a lifetime of hard work, classical French training and extensive research through travel. Lydia and I first worked together nearly twenty years ago and were a team for five years. To this day, she remains one of my very best friends.

Lydia's food—whether inspired by Asia, North Africa, Latin America, Europe or New England—always bears her mark of bold flavors and contrasting textures. And she never ever skimps on the little bit of extra butter or oil that elevates and intensifies the ingredients in any of her dishes. In her recipe that follows, the lobster is partially cooked, then finished by gently sautéing it in butter. It is then placed in a soup plate and surrounded by a rich Thai-inspired green curry and lobster broth. Classic Lydia—instead of warming the lobster in the broth, she brightens its flavor by cooking it separately, allowing it to echo against the lobster-flavored broth. The lobster remains the featured ingredient of the main-course soup, not just a garnish.

This is a dish for those of you who are lucky enough to eat and cook lobster often. Because it is such a spicy and heavily seasoned dish, it would be lost on those who eat lobster infrequently. The recipe calls for several ingredients that will be easiest to find in a Thai or Cambodian market. If you cannot find green curry paste, Lydia says it is also delicious with yellow curry paste or powder. This recipe can be made well ahead of time (up to one day), and then the broth can be reheated shortly before serving. If you wish to serve only four, I still recommend you make the entire recipe. You can save the other two portions for the following day, and once you taste this fantastic concoction, you'll be glad you have extra.

6 live 1-pound chicken lobsters

1 medium fresh coconut

¼ cup peanut or vegetable oil

2 stalks lemongrass, outer leaf removed, finely chopped

2 large or 3 medium cloves garlic, peeled and smashed

one 1-ounce piece ginger, peeled and finely chopped

2 small Thai chiles, split open (optional; see Cook's Note)

12 scallions, 6 coarsely chopped, 6 thinly sliced on a diagonal

1 medium onion (8 ounces), coarsely chopped

2 ribs celery (4 ounces), coarsely chopped

1 pint ripe cherry tomatoes, halved

2 quarts chicken or fish stock

4 cups water

2 cups white wine (not too dry)

2 tablespoons kosher or sea salt

1 small bunch cilantro, leaves picked and stems saved for stock

3 tablespoons Thai green curry paste

freshly ground black pepper

2 tablespoons fresh lime juice

6 tablespoons unsalted butter

6 sprigs Thai basil

1. Preheat the oven to 375°F.

2. Fill a 10- or 12-quart pot with water about two-thirds full. Add enough salt to make the water distinctly salty (¼ cup) and bring to a rolling boil. With your hand on the carapace of the lobster, place three in the pot, one by one, and cook for exactly 3½ minutes from the time the last one goes in. Using tongs, remove the lobsters to a pan or platter and let cool at room temperature. When the water returns to a boil, repeat this process with the last three lobsters. Pour the hot water out of the pot and save the pot to make your stock. When the lobsters are cool enough to handle, remove the meat from the tails, knuckles and claws; try to leave the claw meat intact. Cut each tail in half lengthwise and remove the intestine. Cut into large (¾- to 1-inch) pieces and reserve. Split the carcass in half and discard the head sac. Remove the roe if present and chop it. Add to the lobster meat, cover and refrigerate. Leave the tomalley in the body to flavor the stock.

3. Bake the coconut in a small roasting pan for 15 to 20 minutes until the hard shell of the coconut cracks. Lower the heat to 300°F. Let the coconut cool for about 10 minutes. Poke a small hole through the coconut, drain the "water" into a cup and reserve. The coconut will be easy to remove from the shell; remove all the meat and discard the shell. Using a potato peeler, peel away the dark skin. Use the peeler to make shavings with a quarter of the coconut. Bake on a cookie sheet until lightly toasted, about 15 minutes. Let cool, then place in a small bowl and cover loosely. Grind the remaining coconut in a food processor until very finely shredded.

4. Heat the oil, lemongrass, garlic, ginger, Thai chiles, chopped scallions, onion and celery in the soup pot over medium-high heat. Stir-fry for 6 to 8 minutes until they begin to brown. Add the tomatoes, stock, water and wine. Bring to a boil. Add the salt, cilantro stems, ground coconut and curry paste. Stir well, then add the lobster carcasses. Bring to a boil, then reduce to a steady simmer. Cook for about 1 hour.

5. Using tongs, remove all the lobster carcasses. Puree the soup in small batches in a food processor or blender and, using a medium strainer, strain the broth into a large bowl or soup pot. Season with pepper and the lime juice and check the seasoning. If you are serving the soup right away, keep hot. If not, cool it quickly and refrigerate.

6. Reheat the soup about 15 minutes before you intend to serve it. Heat the oven to 200°F to warm the soup plates. Check the seasoning again; you may wish to add a little more salt or lime juice. In a large sauté pan (12 inches), melt the butter and gently cook the red side of the lobster tails as well as the claws and knuckles for 5 minutes. Turn the knuckles and claws over but leave the tails. Place one lobster in the middle of each soup plate (2 claws, 2 knuckles and 2 halves of the split tails). Add a little broth to the sauté pan and, using a wooden spoon, loosen any particles and add the liquid to the soup. Garnish the lobster meat with a few sprigs of Thai basil and the cilantro leaves. Ladle a heaping cup of the hot broth around the lobster and over the herbs. Sprinkle the toasted coconut and 1 tablespoon sliced scallions evenly over the 6 bowls. Serve at once. If you wish, you can serve small bowls of steamed jasmine rice on the side.

Serves 6 as a main-course soup

COOK'S NOTE: *Green curry paste is quite spicy and will make this soup mildly hot without the additional Thai chiles. However, if you would like your soup to be authentically fiery, add the chiles as instructed.*

Nina Simonds

Lobster Cantonese

At the age of nineteen, Nina Simonds traveled to Taipei, Taiwan, to study Chinese cuisine and culture under master chef Huang Su Huei. In the three years she lived there, she apprenticed in restaurant kitchens specializing in the cuisines of Chekiang-Kiangsu (eastern), Hunan and Canton, and became fluent in the Mandarin dialect. She rounded out her training by spending a year at La Varenne, École de Cuisine, in Paris. With her background in both Eastern and Western cuisines, she is uniquely qualified to teach Asian cooking to westerners. Nina has translated and edited three Chinese cookbooks—Chinese Cuisine No. 1, Chinese Cuisine No. 2 *and* Chinese Snacks—*and has authored five cookbooks, all of which have been nominated for awards. Her most recent cookbooks are* China Express *(William Morrow, 1992) and* Asian Noodles *(William Morrow, 1996). She is a regular contributor to* Gourmet, The New York Times *and many other publications. Nina and her husband, Don Rose, are dear friends of my wife, Nancy, and me. Our children are good friends too. Nothing makes the entire family happier than when she takes us out to eat in Chinatown.*

Nina's ability to translate complex Chinese dishes for the home kitchen is demonstrated here in her version of the famous Lobster Cantonese, also known as Lobster in Black Bean Sauce. The rich sauce, intended to balance the natural leanness of lobster, features ground pork and fermented black beans. It is simply called Lobster Sauce when served with shrimp or other seafood. In Nina's recipe, a 1¼- to 1½-pound lobster is ample for two people.

Equipment: You will need a medium Chinese cleaver or large chef's knife, a wok or large heavy skillet (12 to 14 inches), a slotted spoon and several small mixing bowls. Serve on a large warmed platter with steamed rice on the side.

SAUCE

1 cup chicken broth (see Cook's Notes)	1 tablespoon sugar
1½ tablespoons soy sauce	1 teaspoon dark sesame oil
2 tablespoons rice wine or sake	¼ teaspoon freshly ground black pepper

OTHER INGREDIENTS

3 live 1¼- to 1½-pound hard-shell lobsters	1 teaspoon dark sesame oil
8 ounces lean ground pork	2½ teaspoons cornstarch
1 tablespoon soy sauce	2 tablespoons water
3 tablespoons rice wine or sake	2 tablespoons safflower oil

2 tablespoons salted or fermented black beans, rinsed thoroughly, drained and coarsely chopped (see Cook's Notes)

1½ tablespoons minced garlic

2 scallions, white and green parts separated, then minced (about 2 tablespoons each)

1. *For the sauce:* Combine the sauce ingredients and set aside.

2. *For the other ingredients:* With a cleaver or chef's knife, split the lobster in half lengthwise (page 34). Remove and discard the head sac and intestine. Remove the claws and knuckles, cutting the knuckle close to where it meets the carcass. Break the knuckle away from the claw and cut it with your cleaver on one side so that the cooked lobster meat is easy to extract. With the back side of your knife, crack the center of each claw on both sides. Remove the tomalley and the roe if present and place in a small bowl. Break into pieces using a fork and cover with plastic wrap. Quarter each lobster by cutting down, in one swift motion, where the tail and carcass join. Cut each piece in half, keeping the cut in the same direction as when you quartered the lobster. From each lobster you will have 8 pieces from the tail and carcass, plus 2 claws and 2 knuckles—36 pieces in all. Place the pieces of lobster on a plate, shell side down, so that you can slide them into the hot pan.

3. Place the ground pork in a bowl. Add the soy sauce, 1 tablespoon of the rice wine and the sesame oil. Stir to blend. In a separate bowl, dissolve the cornstarch in the water.

4. Heat a wok or large heavy skillet over high heat. Add the safflower oil and heat until hot. Add the black beans, garlic and scallion whites. Stir-fry for about 10 seconds until fragrant. Add the ground pork mixture and stir-fry, mashing and breaking up any lumps of meat, until it loses its raw color. Add the lobster pieces and the remaining 2 tablespoons rice wine. Stir-fry over high heat for about 1 minute. Add the sauce mixture and bring to a boil. Cover and cook for 4 to 5 minutes, then stir in the tomalley and roe and cook for 1 minute more. Using a slotted spoon, transfer the lobster pieces to a warmed platter. Slowly add the cornstarch mixture to the sauce, stirring constantly to prevent lumps, and cook until thickened. Season to taste, adding more soy sauce if necessary. Spoon the sauce over the lobster, sprinkle the minced scallion greens on top and serve at once.

Serves 6

COOK'S NOTES: *To make a quick Chinese chicken broth, mix ½ cup good-quality chicken broth and ½ cup water in a pot. Add 3 slices smashed ginger and ⅓ cup rice wine or sake. Bring to a boil, then lower the heat and simmer, uncovered, for 10 minutes. Remove the ginger before using.*

Salted or fermented black beans can be bought in Asian markets.

Mail-Order Suppliers of Lobster and Other Seafood

FOR THOSE of you who want fresh live lobsters but live far from the North Atlantic, buying by mail is an alternative to consider. On pages 6 and 7, I have explained what you need to know about this type of purchase. There are hundreds of companies in New England and Northeastern Canada that will ship lobster and other seafood directly to your home. For your convenience, I have put together a short list of companies that I recommend. My list, however, is far from complete, and it is not intended to reflect negatively on the many companies that are not listed. Simply put, I have ordered from the following companies (for various reasons) and was quite pleased with the lobsters I received. For a complete list of Maine purveyors, write to, call or fax Maine Lobster Promotional Council, 382 Harlow Street, Bangor, Maine 04401; tel: (207) 947-2966; fax: (207) 947-3191.

Lobster prices can vary for a number of reasons. I recommend you do a bit of comparative shopping before you place your order. The companies listed below usually ship by UPS or Federal Express; some prices include shipping, while others do not. Ask! All companies accept prepayment by check; most accept MC/Visa, and a few accept American Express. (I do not list the terms of payment because they are subject to change.) Remember that many of these companies are also excellent sources for steamers, rock crabs and other New England seafood.

MASSACHUSETTS

Steve Connolly Lobster Co.
431 Main Street
Gloucester, Mass. 01930
(508) 283-4443

James Hook Lobster Co.
15 Northern Avenue
Boston, Mass. 02210
(617) 423-5508

Legal Sea Foods, Inc.
33 Everett Street
Allston, Mass. 02134
(800) 477-LEGAL

Captain Marden's Seafoods, Inc.
33 Linden Street
Wellesley, Mass. 02181
(617) 235-0860

RHODE ISLAND

Sakonnet Lobster Co.
26 California Road
Little Compton, R.I. 02837
(401) 635-4371

MAINE

Browne Trading Co.
260 Commercial Street
Portland, Maine 04101
(207) 766-2402

Mill Cove Lobster Pound
P.O. Box 280
Boothbay Harbor, Maine 04538
(207) 633-3340

Beals-Jonesport Co-op, Inc.
P.O. Box 195
Jonesport, Maine 04649
(800) 531-0125

Finestkind Fish Market
855 U.S. Route One
York, Maine 03909
(800) 288-8154 or (207) 363-5000

Leslie's Maine Lobsters
HC 62, Box 29
Pemaquid, Maine 04558
(800) 766-2966 or (207) 563-1541

Trenton Bridge Lobster Pound
Route Three
Trenton, Maine 04605
(207) 667-2977

OTHER RECOMMENDED MAIL-ORDER SUPPLIERS

The Vermont Country Store
P.O. Box 3000
Manchester Center, Vt. 05255
(802) 362-2400
common crackers and other regional specialties

The Harrington Ham Company
Main Street
Richmond, Vt. 05477
(802) 434-3441
cob-smoked bacon and ham, Vermont cheese and other specialties

Hudson Valley Foie Gras
80 Brooks Road
Ferndale, New York 12734
(914) 292-2500
moulard (duck) foie gras

Gaspar's Sausage Company
P.O. Box 436
N. Dartmouth, Mass. 02747
(508) 998-2012
Portuguese chorizo and linguica

Gray's Grist Mill
P.O. Box 422
Adamsville, R.I. 02801
(401) 636-6075
jonnycake meal and other freshly milled grains

Index

About the Author

Winner of the 1991 James Beard Best Chef in the Northeast Award, Jasper White is one of the country's leading chefs and authorities on contemporary American cooking. He rose to prominence in the early 1980s as the innovative chef de cuisine at Season's restaurant in Boston. In 1983, Jasper and his wife, Nancy, opened Jasper's, their own restaurant, on Boston's waterfront. Jasper was appointed to *Food and Wine*'s honor roll in 1983 and *Cook*'s Who's Who in 1984. His restaurant was named "Best Restaurant in Boston" by *Boston Magazine* for eleven out of twelve years. He sold Jasper's in 1995 and has used the hiatus from the restaurant business to work on this book. He is now a restaurant consultant. Jasper White lives in Lincoln, Massachusetts, with his wife and three children.